The Thoughtful Guide to Religion

The Thoughtful
Guide to Religion

IVOR MORRISH

BOOKS

Winchester, U.K.
New York, U.S.A.

First published by O Books, 2007
O Books is an imprint of John Hunt Publishing Ltd.,
The Bothy, Deershot Lodge, Park Lane, Ropley,
Hants, SO24 0BE, UK
office1@o-books.net
www.o-books.net

Distribution in:

UK and Europe
Orca Book Services
orders@orcabookservices.co.uk
Tel: 01202 665432
Fax: 01202 666219 Int. code (44)

USA and Canada
NBN
custserv@nbnbooks.com
Tel: 1 800 462 6420
Fax: 1 800 338 4550

Australia and New Zealand
Brumby Books
sales@brumbybooks.com
Tel: 61 3 9761 5535
Fax: 61 3 9761 7095

Far East (offices in Singapore, Thailand, Hong
Kong, Taiwan)
Pansing Distribution Pte Ltd
kemal@pansing.com
Tel: 65 6319 9939
Fax: 65 6462 5761

South Africa
Alternative Books
altbook@peterhyde.co.za
Tel: 021 447 5300
Fax: 021 447 1430

Text copyright Ivor Morrish 2007

Design: Jim Weaver

ISBN-13: 978 1 905047 69 7
ISBN-10: 1 905047 69 X

A CIP catalogue record for this book is available from the British
Library.

Printed in the US by Maple Vail

Contents

For Jean

Preface

The object of this book is to provide both the student of religion, and the general reader, with an outline of some approaches to religion, and with a brief account of the more important religions of the world as well as some of the interesting (though minor) sects, both historical and current.

Throughout I have tried to be as objective as possible and to allow each religion to speak for itself, but I cannot claim to have been completely unbiased in all my comments. Having taught and lectured on most aspects of religion for over thirty years, I am fully aware that prejudices are not easily eradicated. In this respect I have to thank all my former students and colleagues for their unrelenting challenge of any unfounded or dogmatic statements that I may have made in any discussions with them. I can only hope that this is a better book because of it.

The End Notes and Bibliographies are designed to assist the student who wishes to pursue any particular theme or religion in greater depth. The teacher of religious studies should find the material of special value in teaching in a multicultural society and in multiracial schools. Similarly, it should provide a useful text for teachers in training.

I believe that a proper and sympathetic study of religion can prove to be a uniting force among peoples of different culture and race. Prejudices arise, in the main, out of ignorance and half-truths, and so we can never know too much about other ethnic groups, their mores and their beliefs – nor, indeed, about our own. This present study does not claim to be more than just a starting point towards such knowledge and understanding.

Ivor Morrish

SECTION ONE:
INTRODUCTORY

1 The Study of Religion

There was a time when, if one referred to the study of religion, one would have meant in particular a study of theology, and more specifically of Judaeo-Christian theology. Even the study of Judaism might have been a very cursory one, limited almost entirely to the development of Jewish religion during the period covered by the Old Testament, with little or no reference to Jewish writing generally or to the more recent developments and departures of Judaism as a religion in its own right. Any study of 'Comparative Religion' as it was initially called, was usually regarded at both university and college level as something of an exotic extra, or perhaps as an optional paper or as specialist postgraduate study. It was certainly not regarded as an essential part of religious studies in most theological or divinity departments.

More recently, however, the chances are that, in many university and degree courses generally, Christian theology as such will take a minor place in Religious Studies courses, which will be involved in a great variety of disciplines from archaeology, history and anthropology to philosophy, psychology, sociology and comparative analytical study. This means that there has been, in many instances, a change from a more dogmatic and authoritarian approach to a more open and objective or scientific one. There are many reasons for this, not the least being the fact that during the last forty years or so we have seen in our Western societies the development of a large number of minority groups who possess their own customs, moral standards and religious ideas and commitments. In addition, through increasing mobility and travel globally, we are all coming into closer contact with other racial groups and their behavioural systems.

We are all now beginning to accept that, if we are to know and understand other racial groups and cultures, we must at least make the effort to get some sort of insight into their religions and cultures. This alone would be a sufficient reason for anyone to read through, for example, a well-informed book on the religions of the world. But information by itself is not enough; and the selection or pre-selection of such information, as well as its presentation, might be sufficient to convince the reader that his own religion was the only adequate one, not only for himself but also for all others, whatever their race or origin. Religion, indeed all religions, sectarian beliefs and cults, need to be presented with a great deal of personal understanding and sympathy. Of course, this does not mean an uncritical approach either, but criticism needs to be of a constructive kind.

The Hindus have a concept of religion which, in its essential Vedantic philosophy, is both inclusive and tolerant and is worth considering. The symbols of the mandala and of the mountain are relevant here. In the mandala image, mankind begins on the circumference of the circle and makes his way towards the centre. There are an infinite number of radii which link the centre to the circumference, and these may be seen as individual approaches to truth, reality or God at the centre, where all paths meet. The mandala also represents the total Self, and as the individual approaches the very centre of his own being so, inevitably it would seem, he must find all the others.

The mountain symbol is similar but, whereas the mandala is an inward-looking view, that of the mountain is outward and upward-looking. We all begin life somewhere at the foot of the mountain, according to the accident of birth in a particular location, at a particular time, and with particular parents – although, of course, on some views it would not be an 'accident' of birth but a deliberate and personal choice. The path we choose, then, to climb the mountain is initially a path selected for us because of the country or the immediate surroundings in which we are born. As we make our approach towards the top we may view other paths which seem preferable for a variety of reasons: the south col may present a safer or easier aspect than the north face, or the struggle on one path may seem too intolerable and we, therefore, seek the apparent tranquillity of another, ostensibly less arduous, path. But all the paths, when pursued to the end, lead eventually to the top where truth, reality or God may be found in perfection.

Of course, not everyone reaches the top, nor does everyone strive to climb, but the opportunity is there; some may be content even just to run around the mountainside, moving from one path to another, gathering crumbs of wisdom or new techniques for self-realization, and perhaps ever remaining unfulfilled. Some may pursue one path quite oblivious of the other paths or of the other side of the mountain, concentrating entirely upon the difficulties of their own path to God; whilst others may adhere to the path that seems to suit them, always pressing on towards the top, but at the same time making every endeavour possible to get to know the nature, problems and difficulties of other paths through those who are treading them – and thereby getting to know both their brothers and the mountain better.

The point being made here is one that has been made by poets, seers and philosophers throughout the ages, and Kenneth Walker[1] stated the position well when he wrote:

> There are not many truths, but one truth, although the language in which it is formulated will differ according to a man's type, his education, and his level of understanding. There is only one religion, although the expression of it differs with the culture, temperament, education, and understanding of its exponent. Differences of creed, differences in ritual, varieties of ceremonial are necessary in a world in which men differ so profoundly, and the greater the number of sects, the better the chance that any individual man will find that which is best suited to his own particular needs.

There is a richness in the variety of religions, sects, denominations and philosophies which may eventually find a response for most people, provided that there exists perpetually a tolerance among all religions. There are religions which are, by their very nature, isolationist and authoritarian, brooking of no variation or alternative. This is very sad and, of course, makes for disunity as well as antagonism. One is reminded that, according to St John's Gospel[2], Jesus once said, 'Other sheep have I which are not of this fold'; and that, according to St Matthew[3], at the Last Judgement it would not be those who apparently adhered consciously to a specific creed who were found worthy and acceptable, but rather people who were quite unconscious of the fact that what they did with love and compassion for the sick and the needy among their brethren they did for the Lord himself. There are people on the upward path to God who travel in a most unselfconscious manner, but they are known not by their words but by their deeds.

Today one is not merely impressed by the different modes of study of religion, one is almost embarrassed by their variety, complexity and total coverage. The sacred and the secular have for so long been separated in our society, and in many other societies, that it has seemed quite natural to some to regard 'religious' people as odd or effete, and religion as a philosophy of life quite outmoded and unsuitable to modern 'scientific' existence. But the facts do not in any way support this attitude. Whilst it may be true that in some societies an increasing number of people are divorcing themselves from the more formal and orthodox religious sects, it is also true that in some societies an increasing number of people are finding new ways and novel approaches to spiritual experience arising from contact with other societies and from the publication, in more popular form, of the history, aims and aspirations of other religions. It is perfectly true that such popularization often misrepresents the original truth of a particular religion or philosophy – Yoga in particular has often suffered in this respect – but at least the Western world has been introduced to some forms of Eastern beliefs in a way that Christianity, for example, has never been presented to the East, until more recent years. Christianity has always been burdened by Christendom and its accompanying commercialism, industrialization and 'civilizing' appurtenances, Eastern religions offer nothing but their philosophy and doctrine, and perhaps a simplicity and humility in their attitude towards life, which might lead one to suppose that they are presenting mainly a *via negativa*. As we shall see later *there are* life-affirming aspects of almost every religion even though virtually all of them may present possibilities of self-denial, celibacy, withdrawal from society, and a contemplative life.

Disciplines of Study

There are certain subjects of study – education is one of them, and religion another – which lean heavily upon already well-founded disciplines. Education as an academic study, for example, makes considerable use of the disciplines of philosophy, psychology, sociology, history and comparative analysis[4]. Without some knowledge and understanding of such disciplines it is very difficult, if not impossible, to make a serious study of education. Similarly, in any study of religion it is necessary to have regard to the many different approaches to the subject and to the disciplines which contribute to it.

So, before we look at some of the more general themes in religion, such as myth, ritual and magic, we shall discuss briefly some of the possible approaches to religion which have themselves, in turn, become specialisms demanding expert training in each particular field. Whilst one cannot today be an expert in every branch of religion, any more than in every aspect (say) of physics, at the same time one cannot even evaluate one's own specialism without some general knowledge and understanding of the whole field. The parameters of any particular study become more and more extended if one is to make a worthwhile judgement upon anything. Events, people, experiences and data cannot, without a great deal of dangerous misrepresentation, be viewed in isolation. They must all be seen in perspective, in context and in relation to other people and their experiences.

The *history* of man obviously involves not merely his own physical and environmental evolution, but also the development of his thought, beliefs and culture. So vast is the general study of history that it has a great variety of subdivisions involving every aspect of man's interest and concern – political history, social history, economic history, ecclesiastical (or church) history, military history; the history of education, of philosophy, of medicine – and so on. Thus it is impossible to regard religion as one element in man's culture and to pursue its growth, its change and its social effects in a merely historical way. The data of history, however gathered, will record man's struggles, and even crusades and wars, to preserve his ideals and beliefs. Many of these struggles have been muddied by secondary aims and aspirations, such as the destruction of any who might disagree with the religion considered to be the only right one, or the sacking of cities and gaining of booty. Many such secondary aims in the past became prime considerations.

The study of historical institutions has also formed an important part of the history of religion; whilst the history of the Jewish people at one time formed a disproportionate element in the history of religion as studied in university departments of theology, and certainly in the various theological colleges run by Christian denominations. All such histories have been reconstructed in part, at least, from the religious and pseudo-religious literature of the people concerned. From time to time the history of religion – like any other history – has to be modified, however slightly, by the discovery of new documents (such as the Dead Sea Scrolls), or of new artefacts which, when dated and generally evaluated, have revealed new insights or have thrown fresh light upon previously puzzling and unsolved problems.

Linked closely with the historical approach is, quite naturally, the *archaeological* one from which historians obtain so much of their supporting materials for their ultimate data and conclusions. In his discussion of 'The Historian at Work', A Marwick[5] has stated that

The historian has learned to use the materials and, therefore, the tools of the archaeologist. Surviving factory installations, old brick-work, old machinery, are a valuable source of industrial history ... J R Green called the landscape a basic document; Michelet and Bloch tramped the French countryside in their search for primary evidence; historians now supplement the inadequate gleanings of their own eyes with the revelations about land forms and earlier patterns of cultivation revealed by aerial photography.

Archaeology has that very wide interest in man's past that, in itself, demands a very rigorous training and discipline, in order to distinguish carefully between considered judgement and wild speculation, which might be based upon heavily instilled preconceptions. The archaeologist is not only committed to knowing the history already formulated and generally accepted, he is also committed to 'making' history, and he is often responsible for changing or modifying the 'long-established facts' of history. In terms of the study of religion, his discoveries in the area of temples, sacred objects and inscriptions are, of course, always interesting; but perhaps what may prove to be even more vital for interpretation are the general methods and orientations of burial, and the sort of artefacts that are buried with or near human bodies, presumably for their continued use after death.

The sciences of physics and chemistry have gone hand-in-hand with archaeology to establish dating-systems. Thus, radiocarbon, thermoluminescence, potassium-argon (K-A), and other processes for dating have all helped considerably in setting limits for the dates of materials, manuscripts and objects, and at least in demonstrating whether certain important events or elements are contemporaneous or not. Such methods as these, as well as obsidian dating and dendrochronology, may not ultimately prove to be infallible but they are at least supportive, and are independent of any purely subjective archaeological methods. The techniques of archaeology have become increasingly scientific, technological and exact over the years; and much that we know today about the religions and cultures of past civilizations has depended to a large extent upon the archaeological discoveries of and the judgements made by professional archaeologists upon the usages of the past.

It is not our purpose to examine in any detail the nature of every discipline which contributes something to the study of religion. For example, both *social anthropology* and *sociology* have a considerable contribution to make to the examination of cultures and their religions. As a discipline, social anthropology has tended in the past to be applied almost exclusively to those societies and groups which could be examined, by direct observation, as small units. Because of this it concentrated, for many years, on the investigation of so-called 'primitive' societies, and upon the data of tribal existence as viewed in the totality of social experience and interaction. Gradually, however, the techniques of social anthropology have been applied to all forms of group and society, both developing and developed. Sociology, in its more general sense, is a synoptic study of society. From the data assembled by sociologists an attempt is made to analyze social structure, social institutions and composition, the culture of a particular society and its lifestyle, and the development and testing of both quantitative and qualitative methods[6]. In a study of religion, one is involved with the impact that religion makes upon society and the effect that any particular society or change in society has upon religion.

In Durkheim's work[7] on the study of religion, for example, he argued that a distinction was made in every society between 'sacred' and 'profane' things; and he emphasized the collective aspects of society to such an extent that ultimately society and God were virtually identified, and he was more concerned with religious ritual than with religious behaviour. Later sociological study of religion centred more upon ethical and moral teachings, as for example L T Hobhouse in his *Morals in Evolution*[8], where his chief concern was with the moral doctrine of Christianity in particular. Max Weber[9] was more concerned with the influence which religious beliefs and ideas had upon economic behaviour; he also examined the relationship between varieties of religious belief and the position of social and other groups in the economic system.

In contemporary social studies there is a great interest in the sociology of knowledge, and the development of the concept of the 'social construction of reality'[10]. There is the important view that religion is a 'social construct', and that social anthropology and sociology are therefore involved in a study of the 'realities' of religion from this point of view[11]. One must beware, however, of any theory of religion and its origins that bases itself upon a *nothing but concept*. One can claim that any particular *form* of religion is a social construct without necessarily saying anything particularly enlightening about the origins and evolution of religious sensibility as such. The danger of studying so vast a subject as religion by means of any one discipline in isolation is that one can lose view of the great insights and analyses of other disciplines. Truth ultimately is one, and its coherence at any particular stage in history depends upon an overview which takes into account every single datum of any importance and relevance that we may have. That there are different approaches we have already accepted, but they must not be hermetically sealed off from one another if even our own social construction of reality is to have meaning any more in a world which is becoming smaller in every sphere of thought and behaviour.

Psychology is, literally, a study of the *psyche*, that is, the mind or soul. It is concerned with the nature and working of the mind and its aberrations, and with behaviour generally. Psychology, in fact, began as a speculative branch of philosophy and was primarily concerned with ways of talking about mental facts; it was abstract and theoretical, and initially not much concerned with any practical application of its theories, or with any experimentation to establish a scientific basis for them. The chief source of information was introspection, or the process of 'looking inwards', in order to observe our own mental operations. The second main method in the earlier days was the anecdotal one. There are some fields (such as animal psychology) where introspection is impossible; but, as R H Thouless[12] points out, anecdotalism becomes a vice when it is mistaken for scientific method.

Towards the end of the Nineteenth Century psychologists began to approach the subject in a more critical and experimental way.

Through experimentation it became clear that behaviour could become an objective study, and that it could to some extent be measured under controlled conditions. Various schools of psychology began to arise, such as the Gestalt ('form' or 'pattern') psychology of Germany, which developed the theory of configuration, or organized wholes, as a revolt against the experimental methods of W Wundt. Later, the hormic theory of W McDougall made conation and purpose its central features, and it was asserted that these could not be the effects of purely physiological causes. Hormic psychology emphasized feeling and conative urge, and also the importance of instinctive impulses and *purposive* striving.

It was the use of hypnotism which first revealed mental processes below the level of consciousness. Hypnotism is a technique for inducing the state of hypnosis or trance, which is characterized by considerably heightened suggestibility, and by the reduction of censorship, or the repressing force which prevents memories and ideas from entering into consciousness. Through Sigmund Freud, and those associated with his work, a new world was opened up – the subcontinent of the Unconscious Mind, which Carl Jung took a stage further into the realms of the Collective Unconscious. The development of the theme of the Unconscious, and its effect upon religious ideas and beliefs, is of course much older than Freud's or Jung's application of it. Von Hartmann, writing on the *Philosophy of the Unconscious* in 1868, referred to the Unconscious as 'the creative activity of the Divine'. Freud's essay on *The Future of an Illusion*[13], embodied

> a very general criticism of the validity of religious beliefs which cannot be ignored. At least we can be sure that the result of applying psychoanalysis to their understanding is likely to be some profound modifications in religious thought and practice[14].

God, for Freud, appeared to be a sort of Father-substitute projected by the individual unconscious into the Blue Inane. Similarly, the Church was a projected Mother-figure. Man, according to Freud, had a psychological need for the Father-figure who offered a considerable sense of security and protection against the buffetings, the hardships, the disappointments and the sufferings which we experience in the world. Freud considered that, irrespective of any factual proof or demonstration of God's existence, psychology and psychoanalysis showed that there was in man a psychological necessity for this belief – at least until he learned to be self-reliant and mature. God was the result of a wish-fulfilment and, therefore, as far as Freud was concerned, he was in psychological terms an 'illusion'. Carl Jung[15] had a rather different view which saw in religion 'the fruit and culmination of the completeness of life'. The collective unconscious of man contained psychical dispositions; these were primordial images, symbols or archetypes which were non-personal, archaic and common to all races and all times. All men inherited the mental structures for the possibilities of certain ideas about God, man, the universe and all their interrelationships.

In his *Psychology and Alchemy*, Jung stated that

> When I say, as a psychologist, that God is an archetype, I mean by that the *type* in the psyche. The word 'type' is, as we know, derived from *tupos*, 'blow' or 'imprint': thus an archetype presupposes a printer....The religious point of view puts the accent on the imprinter, whereas scientific psychology emphasizes the *types*, the imprint, the only thing it can understand[16].

The psychological approach cannot prove or disprove the existence of God, any more than any other discipline can when applied to the study of religion. What it does is something similar to sociological investigation, which is increasingly interested in social phenomena and their meaning for the group in constructing some sort of reality. Psychology, and perhaps more especially psychoanalysis, are both able to investigate the phenomena of the individual psyche, and to say in relation to religious matters in particular what are man's psychic needs, what are the contents of his unconscious mind, and – at least in Jungian terms – what elements may enter into his individuation.

Psychology has revealed a close link between religious behaviour and the sex drive. R H Thouless[17] points out that in many primitive rites there are frequently expressed phallic and other sexual symbols, and that this fact is often adduced as evidence that religion is solely based upon sexuality. But such symbols are more likely to be connected with the object of securing some magical control of animal fertility. Thouless goes on to add that E D Starbuck's observation[18] of the connection between puberty and conversion is of greater importance, and suggests that many of the phenomena of mystical experience appear to be sexually conditioned or preceded by sexual deprivation. The further importance of understanding the psychological development of the child, from early childhood to adolescence, before attempting a programme of religious education has been fully emphasized by the work of Dr R Goldman[19] and others. Goldman's concept of 'readiness for religion', based very much upon Piaget's more general concept of readiness for learning at various stages in development, at least bears some relation to the further and more philosophical concept of initiation into different ways of thinking, as well as to the socio-anthropological concept of initiation into society. This initiation usually takes the form, amongst other things, of being taught the 'secrets' of that society.

There certainly was a time, before the advent of the logical positivists and the existentialists, when *philosophy* was regarded as a universal discipline which attempted to analyze, organize and evaluate all human experience in the light of some final or absolute principles. Philosophy, or metaphysics, sought to give an overview of the whole of human learning, knowledge and experience. This inevitably resulted in the development not merely of 'schools' of philosophy (such as, idealism, realism, naturalism and pragmatism), but also of different branches of philosophy itself. These branches include the philosophy of history, or metahistory, of science, of art, of education and of religion. Religion is a fact, a datum – and an important datum – of man's history and experience, and so philosophy seeks to interpret the volume of sociological facts which are being amassed in our current society.

Once more we see the dependence of one discipline upon another. Any philosophy of religion must study the data and materials provided by the history of religions, and by the comparative study of religions which, as we shall briefly see, provides both knowledge and understanding of the differences between, as well as the common features of religions. Here again, the philosopher has to lean heavily upon not merely the facts provided but also upon the generally agreed interpretations of those facts; and human activity, whether social or individual, whether political or religious, cannot be fully understood without the assistance of *psychology*. The psychical nature of man is the principle of unification which underlies the great variety of religious experience; and the philosophy of religion is concerned with the problem of the ultimate validity of that experience, and with the ultimate truth of religion as expressed in some final ground, called God, Allah, Brahman, the All-Father, the Mother-Father, Spirit or just It. But the variety of religious experience seems almost unlimited and unamenable to either generalization or statistical analysis. Because of this virtually limitless expression of experience it would seem impossible to develop a final philosophy of religion, except in very simple and very general terms[20]; or perhaps, alternatively, in an unassimilable, complex and very detailed manner.

Theology is concerned more with the realm of dogmatics, and must usually be related to a particular religion with specific beliefs and doctrines. Theology is, in fact, an organized and articulated system of religious dogmas and creeds; it naturally presupposes the existence of God or gods, who are worshipped with precise rituals in any particular cultus. Because a theology is evolved largely for the purposes of teaching, and of proselytizing, it tends to harden into specific forms sanctified by synods, councils and by age itself; and it will be modified only with difficulty and usually with considerable opposition.

> Theology is and must remain the exposition of the doctrines
> of a definite and historic religion. The principle of authority
> to which it appeals must not be external, but the enduring

spiritual experience of which the religion is the practical and institutional expression[21].

Thus, the theology of any particular religion can add to our store of knowledge and understanding of that religion. But there is nothing final about it even within the context of that particular religion, and it may indeed be further modified by synods, or changed by pressure groups within the rank and file of the religion. Moreover, points of doctrine may well cause individuals to form splinter groups, schisms, deniers of particular elements of ritual, and even sects with entirely new theologies and doctrines. Theology is based very much upon what individuals and groups may regard as revelational or inspirational, and much will depend, in turn, upon their collective and individual charisma as to whether some new dogma is developed.

Lastly, in recent years the *comparative approach* to the study of religion has been one of the most popular. This is again a discipline which has developed considerably over the years. It began as a somewhat self-conscious attempt to demonstrate, in a subjective way and by rather general and loose (if highly selective) comparisons, that one religion was better, more comprehensive and more final than all the others. Today, however, the comparative study of religions (sometimes still referred to as 'comparative religion') is an objective account of the history and development of the phenomena of religion in general, and of the great world religions in particular. Sometimes it examines each major religion in turn; sometimes its approach is via certain specific topics, such as sacrifice, worship or ritual, which are common to most religions; and sometimes it analyzes religions by means of structures and paradigms. In this comparative approach some attempt is made to discuss similarities and differences in religions – not with just Christianity as a reference point – and to evaluate each religion in terms of its society or societies, as well as in terms of any individual insights it has produced.

The comparative method is used in an increasing number of universes of discourse, as for example in sociology, in education, and in linguistics. Aristotle himself employed the method in his consideration of political systems. In the use of such a discipline one is not concerned merely with a description of similarities and differences, but also with the way in which these occur, and with how far any religion and its cultus in one society is transferable to another. In the area of social anthropology, the comparative method has developed into cross-cultural comparison, with a formulation of broad generalizations derived from many societies and tested statistically. Such techniques are applied also in the area of religion; and in the testing of certain hypotheses it has proved to be of considerable value.

Thus, all of these disciplines mentioned, and others, may assist the student in her study of religion as a central and persistent phenomenon of social reality. One may not, in fact, seek to be 'religious'- whatever connotation may be given to that word – nor may one seek to pursue one particular religion, sect or cult, but the intelligent member of society certainly cannot afford to ignore what others believe and the ways in which their beliefs affect their behaviour. There can be no denying that disciplines involve one another. One cannot fully appreciate what religion means today without some knowledge of the developments of science and the ways in which these have modified our models of the universe from the particle of the atom to the space of the Universe itself. Whilst there was perhaps not much that was really outrageous, or even novel, about J A T Robinson's *Honest to God*[22] – except that a prominent clergyman was trying to be really honest about his intellectual problems – at least the book made the general public realize that scientific discoveries and philosophical movements could not possibly leave either orthodox religion or conventional theology untouched.

That no one can become master of all the disciplines is freely acknowledged; but anyone seeking to write seriously about religion must bear all such disciplines in mind, with their analyses, findings and judgements. An overview cannot possibly do all this in depth, but it can at least provide a broad canvas for the reader to dwell upon further and to explore. Without anticipating the end before the beginning, it may well be that we shall discover that most (if not all) religions have certain common features, and that all have something to contribute to the rich variety of life and to a deeper understanding both of man's eternal search for truth and reality, and to his longing to discover the secrets of life and the Universe. Of the function of religion E O James[23] has said:

> At every crisis, personal or collective, it is called in aid to prevent disintegration, strengthen the bonds of human cohesion and cooperation, and sanctify human life and conduct.

In consequence, when the supernatural sanctions were removed, disintegration almost inevitably followed.

Of course, 'disintegration' is not necessarily just a political or social malaise, but it concerns essentially man's very psyche. However, it is certainly true that – as James goes on to comment – in the past, at least, religion has been the expression of forces whereby societies and groups have 'maintained their solidarity and ensure thereby their continuity as well as their unity'[24]. In more sociological terms, it does seem true that man realizes himself through specific projects worked out in his society. It is this which provides for him a sense of futurity and purpose. In the words of P L Berger[25]:

> Human existence is always orientated toward the future. Man exists by constantly extending his being into the future, both in his consciousness and in his activity. Put differently, man realizes himself in projects. An essential dimension of this 'futurity' of man is hope.

Without this hope in his futurity, it may well be that man and his society would disintegrate completely, for without some hope there is not much else left to man. But hope in his futurity does not necessarily imply something religious; he may see his hope in education, in communism, in fascism, in world domination, or in business success. At the same time, as Berger goes on to point out, most theodices have hope as a key ingredient, and will therefore appeal to one group of people or another. Such hope is grounded usually in some form of after-life, and however blasé man becomes, it is often this, with a correlate hope of self-vindication or compensation, that keeps man struggling towards his goal or particularized project.

* * *

That there are special difficulties with regard to the study of religion no one would deny. In any such study we are concerned with the individual personality and with personal values; we are seeking to enquire into and analyze the beliefs, hopes, fears and standards of private individuals as well as those of corporate groups and societies. These are very sensitive areas, and we should perhaps remember the admonition of W B Yeats[26]:

> But I, being poor, have only my dreams;
> I have spread my dreams under your feet;
> Tread softly because you tread on my dreams.

People's personal constructs of reality are important and meaningful to them; they epitomize their own personal sense of security; they are able to find their way about, as it were, in *their* world. It is true that time, technology and circumstance may modify their world considerably, but very often they discover their own modes of adaptation and accommodation. What we are pleased to call other people's *heresies* are, in fact, their personal choices (Greek *hairesis* means 'choice'). And people should be allowed to make their own religious choices freely and without any form of deliberate external pressure.

2   Myth: Its Nature and Function

1   The Meaning of Myth

We are, unfortunately, used to employing the word 'myth' in a very general and popular sense of something that does not exist, something that is imaginary and absurd, and strictly for children. 'All that's quite mythical', or 'It's only a myth, an old wives' tale', we say. And so, we imagine, we take away the sting of the story and its fanciful manufacture. This can only be regarded as a depreciation of the whole concept and significance of myth in the history of man, and it has some rather sad consequences when we come later to speak about 'demythologizing' the accounts of the life and work of any of the great religious leaders.

What then is a myth? The word is derived from the Greek *muthos*, which meant anything delivered by word of mouth, a word or speech. The Greek verb *mutheomai* meant to speak, tell or name, and what was spoken was *muthos*, a word. There seems also to be a connection with the Greek verb *muein*, meaning to initiate into the mysteries, to instruct, to open (the hidden secrets). This was done by means of *muthoi*, or words. Thus, a myth acquired the sense of a story which was told to explain or to open up the divine mysteries. So that myths were always essential elements in the Mysteries or Mystery-cults, and rituals were very much a part of this mythical element whereby there occurred a dramatic reconstruction of the fundamental meanings of the divine mysteries. These mysteries were invariably concerned with such basic and elemental concepts as Creation, Birth, Initiation, Death, Resurrection or Rebirth, Flood, Fate, Saviour-gods, and the swallowing-up of the men or hero-gods, such as Jason, Jonah and Hiawatha by a great fish or dragon, or by the devouring Earth Mother.

It must be emphasized here that a myth is not the same as a 'tall story', or a fairy tale, or even a legend; nor can it be dismissed lightly in the same way as we might dismiss a story that has clearly been invented to impress. Myths have a deep religious and psychological function we shall examine as we proceed in this chapter. G Stephens Spinks[1] makes the point when he says that

> Mythology is not a series of elaborate fairy tales, it is the psychologically created medium whereby transcendental reality (using these words in a theological sense) is given a 'this-worldly' objectivity. This *muthos* is the only way by which the Christian belief that Jesus is at one and the same time both fully God and fully man, can be satisfactorily presented.

2   The Permanence of Myth

There is a permanent element in the myth, as distinct from the mere story, which provides an essential model for future belief or behaviour in the society in which the myth is promulgated. Myths may, in fact, be referred to in general terms as 'paradigms for posterity'[2]. They do not belong to any particular, assignable period of time; they are timeless and, unlike the fairy story of 'once upon a time', they claim no place in any particular phase of human history. The myth presents an 'opening', as it were, or an initiation into the Great Time, the Dreamtime which is 'out of time' altogether, and before the existence of the moon whereby men measured events. It is a happening or series of occurrences, a level of consciousness, an awareness which belongs to 'Everywhen'.

Myths are attempts made at *metaphorical* descriptions of certain factual levels, within consciousness if not within history or pre-history, for which there is no longer any apparent evidence of a purely scientific nature. Whether we are referring to the universal concept of Man's Fall from innocence and goodness, or his loss of Paradise itself in the primeval past, or the consciousness of sexuality, or the necessity for work, or the inevitability of death, we invariably resort to language of a metaphorical or analogical nature. In the production of the myth, the storyteller finds himself forced to resort to symbolic and dramatized language. T S Eliot[3] was right when he said, through the mouth of Thomas Becket, that 'Human kind cannot bear very much reality'; it has to be wrapped up in symbolic form and produced as a drama so that its essential, and often dreadful, meaning may be temporarily disguised until we have gradually absorbed the chameleon-like facets of its truth.

A symbol (Greek *sumbolon*, a mark or token) is something that brings two sides together. It is thrown across, as it were, from one party to another, and it stands for the reality which has to be absorbed. It is stylized, however, in such a way that we can endure it and become accustomed to it – and so it becomes a token of the reality. Sometimes its awesomeness is so successfully removed that, as a result, we can no longer recognize the original and terrifying reality, the *mysterium tremendum*, but merely see the symbol as a 'thing-in-itself'; and this reification of spiritual experience may lead eventually to sterility. In fact, it reduces the living myth to just another story which can be infused with life once more only through the intuitive awareness, and the sense of the spiritual or the divine, by whoever is mediating the myth.

3   Some Archaic and Mythical Realities

Most prevalent amongst all peoples of the world is the myth of Paradise. M Eliade[4] has commented that 'from the Phoenicians to the Portuguese, all the memorable geographical discoveries were the result of this myth of the land of Eden'. In recent years, in keeping with the popularization of psychological terminology, the myth has been referred to as the 'Paradise syndrome'. There was a time – a primeval time, a Dreamtime – when man dwelt in a state of perfection and purity, unalloyed by suffering, pain, sorrow, sin or death. But, in some inexplicable way, sin entered his Paradise through his succumbing to subtle temptation; he became self-conscious or self-aware and laden with a sense of guilt.

Linked with the Paradise story there is usually some account of the creation and role of woman, who either proceeds from some part of man or is the result of some adaptation of man. Thus, among the Munkan, an aboriginal people living on a portion of Cape York Peninsula, fronting the Gulf of Carpentaria, there is a story of two brothers[5]. The younger brother, Min Tuktaiyan, submitted completely to the needs of his older brother, Min U:ka, and became subservient and obedient to him as a woman is towards her mate. Eventually Min Tuktaiyan was created in the form of a woman by castration and other physical adaptations, and became the wife of Min U:ka. The sense of sin and guilt subsequently arises through the breaking by young men of tabus, which have been imposed during initiation, by eating flying fox and sharing their food with young girls[6]. Eventually, then, with man's sense of personal sin and guilt, whether in the Genesis story of Adam in the Garden of Eden or in the Munkan myths of tabu breaking, there enters an awareness of sex, of suffering and of death. So, by his Fall, man lost his Paradise and his innocent state; now he is for ever looking back to his origins, to the utopian moonless Everywhen before all Time began.

Bound up with this concept of the retrieval of his utopian past there are two possible journeys through life, one leading to Heaven and the other to Hell. Both possibilities seem to have been realities for man as long as history has recorded his thoughts, his aspirations and his fears. The journey to Heaven is seen as a semi-physical approach to God via some sacred mountain, tree, ladder or liana; and in the hero-myths of many ancient religions we can discover the flight or fugue to Heaven accomplished at some point where Heaven and earth meet. For the Indian Hindu, Mount Meru has always been a sacred meeting point; Mount Sinai (whatever its original location) was one of the several numinous places where God and man met among the ancient Israelites, and where Moses spoke face-to-face with Yahweh and received the Ten Commandments. The Oracle at Delphi was the very navel (*omphalos*) of the Universe, where communication took place between the human and the divine; and where enigmatic utterances were heard which, if correctly interpreted, would assist man in his personal struggle in life. Among the Norsemen the tree Yggdrasil was the sacred ladder between earth and Heaven which was used by Odin himself. In the Akan-Ashanti mythology[7], the trickster god Ananse used a web by which he descended to earth to trick and confuse mankind, as well as the rest of the animal kingdom, and by which he ascended to Heaven again to account for his activities to the great sky-god Nyankonpon. It is particularly interesting to note that the activities of Ananse (or Anancy) and his son Ntikuma (Tacooma) are still retailed in the island of Jamaica[8] and in the West Indies generally, as well as in Surinam (formerly Dutch Guiana) and in parts of North America.

The mythology of any respectable religion incorporated the concept of Hell, which was usually situated below the ground. The journey to Hell was a ritual death, as if the individual were being swallowed up by some devouring monster; it was a return to chaos, to the pre-parturitive embryonic state. Such a return was regarded as essential before there could be any new creation, and it is reflected in the Faustian longings (in Goethe's *Faust*) when Faust seeks the Eternal Realm of the Mothers[9]. He is aided in the fulfilment of this longing and search by Mephistopheles who generously, if not disinterestedly, offers him the means to achieve it:

Here, take this key ...
Follow it down, it leads you to the Mothers.

One of all the greatest recurrent myths is that of the god who submits to the human and natural cycle of birth, life, death or sacrifice, and rebirth or resurrection. Arnold Toynbee has somewhere said that in this recurrent cycle there are many epiphanies but only one passion. In the mythology of the religions of the world, God in the whole of man's experience is seen in a sequence of avatars or incarnations, such as Vishnu, Zarathushtra, Odin, or Christ; and eventually he has sacrificed himself upon a cross, a stake, a gibbet or a World-Tree. The Tree is the Axis Mundi, and in the case of Dumuzi or Tammuz it was the tamarisk or the willow tree. The nature of the tree varies with the geography of the location, and sometimes – as in the case of the Buddha under the bo or bodhi tree – the sacrifice is a spiritual rather than a physical one. But the sacrifice is there for all these saviour-gods, rejecting earthly life or its material benefits, in order that others may have eternal life or be shown the way. Nietzsche[10] said:

> O Zarathustra ...
> Now
> Alone with thyself,
> Split in thine own knowledge,
> Amidst a hundred mirrors ...
> Strangled in thine own snares,
> Self knower! Self-hangman!

The god-man offers himself up as a sacrifice once he fully knows the nature of his own purpose. This is further expressed by Odin in the following words after he has learned the wisdom of the runes:

> I know that I hung
> Upon wind-torn tree
> Nights full nine,
> With a spear transfixed,
> And to Odin I offered
> Myself – myself unto myself[11].

The archaic, but permanent, myth is also seen in the struggle of Good and Evil, between hero and anti-hero. This takes innumerable forms in the history of religion[12]; there is Yahweh opposed to Lucifer, Christ opposed to Satan, the Buddha to Mara, Ormuzd to Ahriman, Muhammad to Iblis or Shaitan, and so on. In all of man's mythology this struggle of the hero against the forces of evil is one of the most commonplace. As T S Eliot writes in *Choruses from 'The Rock'*:

> The world turns and the world changes,
> But one thing does not change.
> In all of my years, one thing does not change:.
> However you disguise it, this thing does not change:
> The perpetual struggle of Good and Evil[13].

In this perpetual struggle, man considers from time to time that the resolution of all his existing problems will come only from above, and so he pursues the 'Millennium', which (as its name implies) originally signified a period of a thousand years of peace and prosperity. In current religious terms it means any sort of utopia projected into the future, and making its descent from the realms of Heaven above. The present time is regarded as a period of unpleasantness in which problems remain intractable and insoluble; the past was a golden era of Paradise; man must, therefore, seek somehow to escape from the present in the myth time-scale, and he must look to the future millennial dispensation when the faithful will be redeemed[14].

One can see the development of this particular mythology in sects such as Jehovah's Witnesses, and the politico-religious sects of the Ras Tafarians in Jamaica (and today in certain cities of England), as well as those who pursue the various Cargo Cults in Melanesia and the Pacific Islands generally. In the teaching of the Jehovah's Witnesses, Jehovah will establish his millennium upon earth and will call in the faithful. Among the Ras Tafarians[15] there was, and is, a firm belief in the redemption of God's children in captivity in Babylon (that is, Jamaica or any society to which they have emigrated), and their return to an African theocratic paradise in Ethiopia. The Melanesian Cargo cultists[16] have now for many years looked for redemption by their god through the arrival of a ship laden with cargo to supply all their needs. Representation of a ship, or just as often a plane, are displayed as symbols of the coming millennium. There will be a more detailed treatment of this theme in Chapter 15.

4   The Four Cycles in the Evolution of the Hero Myth

In his classical work on *Hero Cycles of the Winnebago*, Paul Radin[17] distinguished four separate cycles in the efforts of social groups among North American Indians to deal with the problem of growing up. They were: (a) the Trickster Cycle, (b) the Transformer Cycle, (c) the Superhuman Power Cycle, and (d) The Twins Cycle. These cycles in their representations of human development and consciousness are highly symbolic, and man's behaviour is represented largely by that of animals. Such cycles are not peculiar to the North American Indians whom Radin studied, but they may be paralleled in the mythologies throughout the world; only the symbols are different.

(a) The Trickster Cycle is usually represented by the activities of such animals as Brer Rabbit, Reynard the Fox and Ananse the Spider. W A Lessa[18] has traced such Trickster figures throughout the islands of the Pacific; as for example, Iolofath or Olofat in the Caroline Islands, and Qat, Ambat and Tagaro among the Melanesians. All these possess the universal Trickster traits – that is, they are almost invariably high-born and have experienced some strange forms of birth; they are very precocious and involved in strong sibling rivalry. This is a cycle in which the physical propensities, appetites and aspirations of the individual have dominance over other forms of behaviour, and in which there can be discerned an infantile mentality that exists at the level of seeking to trick and overreach others. There is complete lack of feeling in the action performed, which seems to be quite unrelated to any sense of morality or to what is socially becoming. The only sensation felt would appear to be one of selfish satisfaction in any cruelty enacted, and a childish but cynical delight in tricking everyone available. Thus, when some inexplicable mischief has been performed to the discomfort of a Jamaican, the latter will frequently dismiss the matter by saying, 'Oh, Ananse – he do it'. The trickery, in this context, is not always evil, or with mischievous intent; sometimes it is performed to assist the individual, and to do things for him that he is unable to do for himself. At other times, however, the Trickster is regarded almost as a somewhat juvenile Satan, working hand-in-hand with the great Sky-god and acting as his messenger and medium for dispensing wrath and punishment. There is one myth in the Ananse cycle of the Akan-Ashanti[19] which relates how Nyankonpon, the Sky-god, caused Ananse to bring such diseases as 'syphilis, stomach-ache, headache, leprosy, guinea-worm, smallpox, yaws, fits, diabetes, and madness' among the tribe.

There is, however, a somewhat unusual story[20] in this cycle which runs contrary to the overweening hubris of the Trickster. Ananse had swept up all knowledge, gathered it together and placed it in a gourd pot. He then decided to climb a tree and hang the gourd upon it, so that 'all wisdom on earth would be finished'. Despite many attempts, he failed to climb the tree because he had hung the gourd around his neck in front of him, and it perpetually got in the way. His very young son, Ntikuma, suggested to him that it might be better if he turned the gourd round and put it on his back. Ananse was very reluctant to take this advice, which he referred to as 'old-fashioned', but after many further attempts he decided to give it a trial. He swiftly reached near the top, and then said to himself:

I, Kwaku Ananse, by the lesser god, Afio, I might as well
be dead, my child who is so small, so small – there was I, I
collected all wisdom (so I thought) in one place, yet some
remained which even I did not perceive, and lo! my child, this
still-sucking infant, has shown it to me.

Out of the mouths of babes and sucklings! Ananse then seized the gourd and smashed it to the ground. In this way it became possible for everyone to obtain wisdom; a somewhat uncharacteristic action of the Trickster, and with an unusual pose of humility.

(b) The Transformer Cycle of hero mythology, according to Radin's account, is represented by the Hare or the Coyote. The Hare in particular is regarded as the founder of human culture despite the fact that he is animal in form; and it is claimed that it was he who gave the great Medicine Rite to the Winnebago tribe. Thus, the Hare was their culture hero, supported with his powerful medicine, peyote; and he was in consequence regarded as their saviour. When Christianity was able finally to make inroads upon the tribe, it was with considerable reluctance that its members agreed to modify either their quite peaceful peyote ritual or their devotion to Hare. Indeed, as we shall see later, peyote still plays an important part among various American Indian cults. Hare himself was regarded as either a forerunner of Christ or Christ himself in an earlier cult-hero form. This particular cycle is an advance on the Trickster cycle in that the infantile and malicious activities of the Trickster are corrected, and man is 'transformed' into a socially responsible being, with a developing code of morals, law and general social behaviour.

(c) The Superhuman Power Cycle was led by Red Horn, the youngest of ten brothers. He is the archetypal hero who wins races, destroys his enemies in battle, and with considerable superhuman power overcomes giants. Sometimes his strength is mingled with not a little guile, indicating that the trickster element is still there, though transformed into a non-mischievous ability. Red Horn has a very powerful friend in the Thunderbird (or 'Storm-as-he-walks'), whose incomparable strength is always able to compensate for any latent weakness that Red Horn might display. In this cycle we have a clear demonstration of the primeval or archaic world in which the aid of extra-human powers and gods is sought in order to ensure man's victory over all the forces of evil that beset him.

(d) The Twins Cycle is concerned with twins (or sons of the Sun) who are human, and who in reality represent two aspects of one person forced into two in the process of parturition. They clearly always *belong* together, although they are very often represented as opposites, particularly in complementary aspects of man's own dual nature. One is mild and acquiescent, altogether introvert, and lacking in drive and initiative; the other is rebellious, dynamic, inventive and extravert. One represents the light and good side of man's nature, the other his dark and evil side. Sometimes, however, they jointly abuse their combined powers. It then becomes necessary for one or both to die as a result of their pride or hubris. Sometimes, one betrays the other and the world is saved by the death of the light twin. At other times, both twins are spared insofar as they show regret for their ungovernable pride, and finally a level of equilibrium is reached. At the more psychological level there is a recognition, by such psychoanalysts as Carl Jung, that the twin mythology belongs not merely to an archaic or archetypal *stage* in human history, but that it is, in fact, part and parcel of the archetype paradigmata of the individual and collective unconscious present in the human race.

5   The Christ Myth

Any discussion of religious mythology and hero myths is faced with the eternal enigma of the figure of Christ. Bultmann[21] , for example, argued that the life and activities of Christ as recorded in the New Testament belonged to a cosmology which posited a three-storied structure of the world: a heaven above, an earth upon which man dwelt, and a hell beneath. The earth was the stage on which was set the supernatural activity of God and his disciples, supported by angels, and their complete opposition to Satan, followers of witchcraft, and demons. Bultmann considered that this mythological view of the Universe with its miracles and its evil spirits was being rejected by modern man. There were myths – such as the virgin birth, the supernatural aura, the various signs and wonders which accompanied the first Christmas, the miracle stories, Christ's vicarious atonement, his descent into hell and his physical resurrection, his ascension and future second coming – which were all dispensable.

Bultmann argued that the life of Christ needed 'demythologizing'; that is, the myths should be taken out of the historical accounts. But in all this demythologizing activity one has to be very careful not to throw out the baby with the dirty bath water. Mythology, as we have already seen, is a means of expressing man's belief concerning the transcendent and the ineffable. There are matters, experiences, realities which cannot be expressed in logical form and which are irreducible in terms of mathematics or science. The only language left to us is the language of imagination, of poetry, of metaphor, of anagoge (that is, spiritual or allegorical interpretation of myth). And if we completely excise the 'mythological' elements of religion, we may find that there is very little left in the way of a common means of communication between God and man; or, indeed, of meaning itself. Paul Tillich[22] has rightly said that 'myth is more than a primitive world view...it is the necessary and adequate expression of revelation'.

New myths tend to replace old ones; *de*mythologizing tends to be supplanted by *re*mythologizing. This is very clear in the way in which the 'myths' of the old psychology are being gradually replaced by novel ones in the new forms of psychology; or in the way in which old paradigms and models of physics have been supplanted by the new models of current physical science[23]. These things, which are little more than guessed at or imagined (such as anti-up quasars and anti-down charm), proceed to be reified and sanctified by models in the new mythology. Physicists are positing the existence of forces or particles today through mathematical analysis and logic in much the same way as the Curies determined the presence of polonium, radium and curium even before they were actually discovered.

A fully demythologized Christ may turn out to be no more than a man with extraordinary charm, powers of persuasion and suggestibility and charisma. But in religious and spiritual terms we may still have to ask ourselves whether that is really enough; and, indeed, new myths in relation to Christ may arise, as they are, for example, in the pronouncements of the Aetherius Society.

6   The Myth of 'As If'

In his somewhat underrated *The Philosophy of 'As If'*, Hans Vaihinger[24] has emphasized very clearly man's need to create 'mental fictions' or levels of mythology based upon common conceptions and interpretations. Our fictions arise from our common apperceptions; that is, we seem to perceive the same things and, therefore, we act 'as if' they were so. For example, most of us feel that we have freedom; and if we don't have it, or don't *feel* that we have it, we demand it not only as a right but also as something really within the realms of possibility. And yet freedom is not something that can easily be demonstrated or proved; indeed, there is a lot of evidence to the contrary and in favour of some form of determinism. But our society is based upon the generally accepted view that we *are* free, and that we are able to consider and premeditate what to do. This is, in fact, a current 'myth' or fiction. We act 'as if' we are free.

To take another example, the world of human aspiration is largely fictitious. We look for a purpose, some sense of teleology, both in the world and in our private lives, but we may well fail to find any. As Merleau-Ponty[25] has remarked, 'Life makes no sense, but it is ours to make sense of'. We have to *create* purposes for ourselves in order to make life really worthwhile. They are our personal myths – myths of purpose in an apparently purposeless world. They are what makes life really worth living, and when people tread upon our dreams and destroy the very basis of our purpose, they destroy for us the myth of life itself. We are henceforth, as T S Eliot says in 'Burnt Norton',

> Caught in the form of limitation
> Between un-being and being.

We can never *just* demythologize; we need our myths and our dreams, and they are the very dynamic whereby we live. We live 'as if' they were true. They may not always be myths of a high religious or moral nature, but they are, in essence, the means whereby each individual manages to survive life's pettiness and its awful puerilities.

That there are 'cults of unreason' we are all perfectly aware, and we shall discuss some of them in Chapter 16; but there is no denying that their mythology fills an empty void often created by religionists themselves. We should, therefore, perhaps be somewhat less critical of those who desire

> To communicate with Mars, converse with spirits,
> To report the behaviour of sea-monsters[26].

Or to investigate the mysteries of the pyramids, the Bermuda Triangle, the Loch Ness Monster, or Unidentified Flying Objects. Our mythology is, after all, an attempt at *remythologizing* much of the material already demythologized by the theologians. These myths and mysteries may or may not, in themselves, be important, but they do provide a new mythology upon which people may expend their energies and interests, and even begin to establish some new millennial faith and hope, 'as if' life had meaning and purpose.

Such fictions have a cyclic history. The future is all uncertain, unknown, and unpredictable, and so we seek to stabilize it, to make it 'as if' it were certain, by repeating the past. We accept that, despite our astrologers, our seers and our clairvoyants,

> We do not know very much of the future
> Except that from generation to generation
> The same thing happens again and again[27].

And because the human spirit yearns for some form of redemption beyond itself, it begins to reify the myth that it has created, and to act 'as if' it were a fact, a reality. This is not to make any judgement upon the validity of what people believe; it is merely to assert that most people find it imperative to believe in something which is beyond the narrow limits of immediate and more commonplace human experience. The reification of such beliefs depends very much upon the sort of age in which we live, and the extent to which the archaic myths have been demythologized. Yesterday's myth may be today's absurdity or superstition; today's myth may be tomorrow's factual history or risible naivety; tomorrow's myth may well be the propagandist construction of some Big Brother[28].

7 Ideas, Archetypes and Paradigms

The myths of the past have sometimes been formulated into some sort of philosophical or psychological theory. Under the tutelage of Socrates, Plato[29] was one of the first in the philosophical field to develop the theme that, behind the fleeting phantasmagoria of activities and the fading visions of everyday life, there existed a realm of universals, or 'ideas' and 'forms' which were the only true realities. Whilst these appeared as 'absolutes', and as abstract essences of material modes of expression, they nevertheless had a concretion all their own. Only the philosopher or abstract thinker was able to recognize them by the very process of abstracting the underlying essences of the existences perceived around him. These 'ideas' had a mythology of their own which was so often represented in the less abstract figures, personalities or actors in the theogonies of a great variety of religions. Such personalities – gods and goddesses – gave a somewhat gross concretion to the ideas of Beauty, Truth, Justice, Law, Love and Order.

At the psychological level, Carl Jung[30] saw the archetypes of the unconscious as factors which did not participate in the historical time of the individual life but in the time of the species, even of organic life itself. Such archetypes belonged to the levels of the collective, racial or even cosmic consciousness (which Jung called the Collective Unconscious). Such levels were more uniform than history or historical representations. Jung argued that in order to bring *reality* from the unconscious levels to the level of consciousness man needed certain archetypal forms or myths. In his development of the theme of man's unconscious, he finds such universal 'myths' or paradigms as the persona, the shadow, the anima/animus, the

Wise Old Man, the Chthonic Mother, and so on. He regarded these 'mythological' elements, or archetypes, as vitally important to the health and well-being of the individual, to such an extent that, in his analysis, it became essential for individuals actually to 'meet' their shadow or their anima, to identify within themselves the Wise Old Man[31], and to come to terms with the persona or the ego. The reification of these mythological elements, and the recognition of their freedom and function within the Self, were essential features in self-discovery and self-fulfilment, that is, in individuation.

In his *Diagnosis of Our Time*, Karl Mannheim[32] pursued Jung's theme and suggested that we must become increasingly aware of the archaic potentialities of the mind, with its archetypes, heroes, myths and paradigms. He further argued that there was a despiritualization of modern life through the evaporation of the primordial images or archetypes which have directed the life-experience of mankind through the ages. In particular, Mannheim named such myths or archetypes as those of the Hero, Sage, Virgo, Agape and Sacrament. The changing media of expression in our society, he thought, had left little room for the continuance of such mythologies at the spiritual level.

8   The Corruption of Myths and Their Return at Lower Levels

But the myth or paradigm is not quite so easily disposed of, for its function is essentially to tell us something, to open our eyes to basic truths and to give *meaning* to life. Such meanings are passed on from one generation to another where there is close familial unity and purpose (Cf Confucius, Chapter 10). Mircea Eliade[33] points out that myths have a tendency to degenerate into epic legends, into romances and ballads, some lofty and some very pedestrian; or they may survive only in the attenuated form of superstitions, of vestigial customs, and of vague, unidentifiable but yearning nostalgias.

Interestingly enough there is a tendency always to recreate myth at lower levels through children's stories, or more generally and more popularly through newspaper and TV cartoons. We have had in the past Jane, and the daughter of Jane, as archetypes of the Virgo; there was Mekon, the strange, magnetic and amoral visitor from Outer Space; and the giants and supermen, sons of the gods, have frequently made their appearance in various media, and they include such personalities as Garth, the Miracle Man and Superman. In the stories of Batman and Robin we can find most of the levels of mythological development, from the Trickster cycle (the Joker, Penguin etc) to the Transformer and Superhuman cycles (Batman and Robin themselves); although the fourth cycle of the Twins is hardly achieved, unless once more Batman and Robin are seen in this guise with their incredible proclivity to hubris and frequently resulting discomfiture. Certainly many of the other cartoons, such as Bugs Bunny and the Road Runner, are very much at the Trickster level.

The use of myth may also be seen in the advertising of the various media. There is an esoteric magic about words and names, and a miraculous element associated with the activities and properties of certain commodities. It is a form of myth which most people may *consciously* reject, but which may still affect many at subliminal levels. 'Have you heard the word? – Kentucky Fried Chicken' 'Schh! you know who.' 'X washes whiter than white!' And there is the ethereal and entrancing music which sometimes accompanies such products as wines and spirits, and which seeks by association to force the myth upon us.

It is also interesting to note that in some branches of sport a type of surrogate mythology arises. In freestyle and all-in wrestling[34] we have all the symbolic elements and rituals in the drama of the struggle of hero and anti-hero, the fight of good against evil. The masked wrestler may (though not invariably) epitomize the anti-hero and all the evil and dirty tricks that may be associated with him. Throughout the bout there may be detected a sequence of compensation or paying of karmic debts, and the crowd responds wholeheartedly to the general situation of 'an eye for an eye and a tooth for a tooth'. The total participation of the spectators in the myth is seen in the reaction of little old ladies who try to hit the anti-hero with their umbrellas or handbags. There is a stylization about the whole routine, redolent almost of a religious ceremony, through gestures, expressions, responses, and even the individual rituals of specific wrestlers. The combatants pass through a sequence of suffering, defeat, humiliation, justice, virtue rewarded and evil punished. But, like life itself, it has its reversals and the hero is by no means the eventual winner. And inevitably there arises from time to time a Trickster or Jester figure who livens up the whole proceedings by his exaggerated but amusing antics. It is perhaps not too much to say that wrestling, or some other form of spectacular sport, such as soccer, provides for a vast number of people a substitute for religious ceremonial and mythology.

Thus, many cartoon myths, TV commercials, sports etc reveal the fact that, though we may demythologize one set of events or beliefs, they have an uncanny knack of returning in some other form. The cycle of futurity has for many been broken, and perhaps we no longer overtly believe in an afterlife, or indeed in any certainty as such. But we still have a yearning to share models and beliefs about society, and to create new fictions or beliefs. The integration and stylization in forms of stability of any society depend very much upon the increasing identification of archetypes, paradigms, symbols, myths and rituals. This has been the chief mode in the past in establishing consensus in society. Indeed, there is a social construction of reality which is going on the whole time, and which is being internalized by the members of society[35]. Just as the oldest universe-maintaining conceptualizations are in mythical form, so too are the latest, even though quasars and 'charm' may have replaced the gods in our cosmologies.

The world as we know it is being interpenetrated by forces which, ultimately, are indescribable. The best that we can do is to provide names and symbols for them. But the socialization of the individual in any society is effected through the internalization of Reality, however it may be constructed, conceived or finally delineated.

9   The Impact of Science

Increasingly we are coming to realize that science (perhaps physics and astro-physics in particular) is a modern mythology. The older terminology and symbols are fast disappearing, and new symbols, descriptions and scientific rituals are taking their place. Sir Arthur Eddington once said of the electron that 'something unknown is doing we know not what', whilst Albert Einstein said of our descriptions of the Universe that they resembled a man's attempts to describe the inside of a watch which he had in fact never seen, and there was no way of opening the case. At best the descriptions might be termed the inspired guesses of induction. They are metaphorical expressions to describe the ineffable. Models, paradigms or myths are being currently developed to produce a picture in the mind of the reader not of what the 'thing' looks like, but rather of the way in which it behaves[36]. The actual terms used to classify the intangible are themselves of a metaphorical or poetic nature, such as: quark, anti-quark, up quark, down quark, anti-up quark, anti-down quark, strange quark, charm, anti-charm, naked charm, pion, muon, meson, neutrino, proton, gipsy (J/psi), matter, anti-matter, Starbreaker, Starcrusher, and so forth. Many scientific descriptions and categories are really no more than the expression of statistical averages in order to produce a changing but coherent view or paradigm of the Universe. Some are the reification of immense and intricate mathematical calculations produced by phenomenal scientific minds.

Nigel Calder[37] describes how Geoffrey Chew was led from 1959 onwards to propound what was called the 'bootstrap theory' or 'nuclear democracy'. This involved the 'conscious rejection of the traditional objectives of physics, to explain events in terms of forces acting between clearly defined particles'. Chew maintained that no particles were more fundamental than any others, and that one should not therefore enquire too closely into details of their behaviour, either in place or time. Particles were to be regarded no longer as objects for analysis, but rather as 'conjectured connections between events'.

Fritjof Capra, a disciple of Chew, revelled in some of the philosophical implications of all this in his *The Tao of Physics* (1975). In that work he saw a convergence between bootstrap scientists and Eastern mystics. In their dance, the particles of the Universe became the Dance of Shiva of the Hindu. We were being led out of science into the world of *acintya*, into the unthinkable.

But it was not long before Chew's theory became eclipsed, and the 'undemocratic' behaviour of particles was restored. As Professor Abdus Salam wryly remarked, 'All particles are elementary but some are more elementary than others'[38]

Nevertheless, if the whole business does not resemble the Dance of Shiva, it is still somewhat redolent of the Hindu myth of the Dark House, which a number of people entered. In one room there was an elephant that no one could see. When they all came out of the Dark House, there was complete and baffling disagreement among them concerning the nature and shape of the elephant. One said it was like a huge fan – he had felt its ear; another claimed that it was solid and tubular, like a pillar – he had felt its leg; a third argued that it was broad and hard like a throne – he had sat on its back; whilst a fourth said that they must all be mistaken, for it was long, mobile and apparently hollow like a water-pipe – he had felt its trunk. None in fact was a true description of the elephant, or of its nature and function; and the consequent 'elephant mythology' was confused and inconsistent. Something similar may be said about our constructions of the realities of the Universe itself, despite all our sophisticated equipment and techniques. Each scientist, however much he shares his observations and findings, may provide a different reification of ultimate reality, and of cosmological and astrophysical theory. Some, because they differ widely from others in their mythology, may be referred to in almost religious terms as 'heretical'.[39]

In less than fifty years' time our current descriptions of the Universe will in all probability be regarded as the somewhat naive and outworn myths of a people, though strangely immature, who were on the verge of quite staggering and awe-inspiring discoveries. For myths they are, however useful and indispensable in operation they may be. They are not unlike the 'myth' of the 'operator i', used particularly in radio-physics where the dimension of Time is such an important factor. This operator, the square root of minus one, is an irrational number or surd – an inexplicable myth, however vital in operation.

10 The Master Myth of the Self

The Master Myth, for centuries in the East and increasingly today in the West, is the myth of the Self (already touched upon in section 7 of this Chapter). Life is here regarded as a search for and discovery of the Self, variously expressed as the Overself[40],the Overmind, the Superego, and the Total Self. In theological terms, some would regard this as the inner spirit (*pneuma*) as opposed to the soul or mind (*psyche*) and the body (*soma*). In some psychological models it would be seen as the Superego as opposed to the Ego and the Id; in others it would be the Higher Self as opposed to the Lower Self. Radhakrishnan[41] has said that, 'Religion is essentially the art and theory of the remaking of man. It assumes man's ability to change himself'. Thus, there is a need for man to examine his own make-up, to review his 'divided self' and to discover how he may find ultimate integration by 'changing' himself through some reorganization of his essential elements.

The need for hero symbols and myths begins to arise when man finds that his ego requires strengthening, when the conscious mind needs assistance in some task that it cannot accomplish unaided or without drawing upon the sources of strength that lie in the unconscious mind. It is then that there is recourse to the religious or semi-religious mythology of which we have been speaking.

There are also developing in the West (often through what is termed 'transpersonal psychology') various techniques which seem always to have existed among certain peoples at varying levels in the East – namely, the techniques of meditation, introspection, self-analysis, hetero-analysis, and yoga. Sometimes the Total Self is sought through some form of sacrifice or ego-denial – 'Self-realization through self-sacrifice'. Self-sacrifice is seen here not only as a virtue in itself but, through the sacrifice of the lower self, as a means of discovering or reorientating the Higher Self. The Japanese kamikaze pilots committed suicide not merely for their country and their Emperor-god, but also that they themselves might immediately become gods (*kami*). The myth of the *kami* represented to them the attainment of the Total Self. In a similar way, many Christians have regarded Christ, the Word or Logos, as a symbol of the complete Self, and have sought to practise his presence, so that 'I live; yet not I, but Christ lives in me'[42].

11   The Re-creation of Myths in Our Own Time

We have already mentioned the way in which, as a result of the demythologizing process, myths have a habit of reappearing at somewhat lower levels – as in cartoons etc. There is, however, an ever-recurrent attempt to recreate myths and rituals in regenerated forms, which are essentially their original forms adapted for modern times. This occurs particularly in the realms of the occult, magic, witchcraft and divining. Later we shall consider in greater detail some of the current developments in these areas (see Chapter 16); it is perhaps sufficient here to say that certain developments of occult groups and mystic cults connected with the Great White Brotherhood are, in effect, attempts to recreate the mythology of the past. There is also a renewed and sustained interest in Arthurian myths connected with the search for the Holy Grail; in myths associated with stones and their mystical mana, such as Stonehenge, the Pyramids, cromlechs, menhirs and all ancient stone monuments with mystical orientation or meaning. The millennial myths are supported by the many sightings of Unidentified Flying Objects (UFOs), by societies such as the Aetherius Society, and by such declarations as 'Jesus is alive and well and living on Venus'[43]. Carl Jung[44] himself made an acute analysis of the UFO cult, in which he saw the circular object as a celestial, but visionary, representation of the mandala symbol of the Total Self.

The popular and almost compulsive interest in the scaling of mountains, peaks and heights – 'climb every mountain' – linked with yogic meditation in the Himalayas, is a further development of the concept of getting closer to God through the external ascent of the mountainside (Cf Moses), and through the pursuit of the Self by means of introspection and meditation[45]. As a part of the realization of the mythology, the final effects would appear to be the same: for at the top of the mountain we all have the same view and meet the same Lord of the Mountain. And when we have entered into the very centre of the Self, we find that we have arrived at the cosmic awareness or consciousness in which all men are one.

The interest in and development of the paranormal in our own times is not in reality something new, however differently we may be approaching it. Whatever terms we may have used in the past, there have always been interest in and attachment to extrasensory perception, telepathy, telekinesis, levitation, dowsing and so forth. All this is but a recreation of the myth of the miraculous, which more people than would perhaps like to admit it have believed in and have accepted as a part of the spiritual and psychic norm. Turgenev once remarked that all prayers could be reduced to one paradigm: 'Great God, grant that twice two be not four'.

The ancient myths concerning the Aquarian Age and also the submerged archaic civilizations on the continents of Atlantis, Lemuria and Mu have always fascinated mankind; but in our time, with the onset of disasters, floods, diseases, famines, volcanic eruptions, and earthquakes, man has looked again to their cyclic reappearance or resurgence. We are told, with not a little equanimity and certainty, that the Age of Aquarius is upon us, and the consequent devastations will be followed by the rising again of Atlantis[46].

Interesting too is the reintroduction of the mythology of the Lord of the Dance as, at least, a joyous and celebratory element in the Christian religion, if not also as a representation of a primitive form of fertility ritual. Sydney Carter's hymn, 'Lord of the Dance', gives lie to the common belief that religion is a miserable and over-serious business without any sort of joyousness or relaxation.

In some meditation exercises there is quite an emphasis upon mantra yoga, in which names and statements, such as 'Hare Krishna!' and 'Om mani padme hum!' are repeated ad nauseam; whilst in Transcendental Meditation (TM), introduced by the Maharishi Mahesh Yogi, there is an esoteric *word* suitable for each individual which is given to him, and to him alone. The meditation upon this word, and its mental if not vocal repetition, will (so it is said) eventually bring completion or wholeness to the devotee within the realm of cosmic consciousness.

There are today other myths associated with the ambrosia or soma drug of the gods. Currently such 'heavenly' drugs are *amanita muscaria* (fly agaric), mescalin, lysergic acid (LSD) and peyote – the hallucinogens of the Mexicans, Incas and north American Indians. They have become cultic among certain elements in a great number of societies, each possessing their own rituals and mythologies. The new dimensions of experience, the colours, the sensations, the quickly varying perceptions of place and time, the sense of awareness of entirely novel psychological and spiritual levels, the feeling of disembodiment, the trance states and the belief in the ability to predict and to diagnose – all these are essential 'prophetic' elements to be found in a new mythology of drug addiction. By 'prophetic' here we mean that ecstatic element[47] in religious experience, represented by trance and possession, which results in the prophecy and apparent precognition of shamans and seers[48]. Amongst the millenarian cults (see Chapter 15) there is also a tendency to exist on the levels of hope and expectancy, as among the Ras Tafari sects in Jamaica, with their ganja weed. Many religious groups perform rituals in order to induce trance or ecstasy so that the nature of present time may be altered – indeed, to conquer time itself[49]: There is produced, through these various means of ecstasy, soul-washing, rhythmic dancing, hand-clapping, singing, intoning and shouting, a period of concentrated, dissociated time in which the individual seeks identity 'out of time' in the total and archaic Everywhen. Our sophisticated age has seen the great possibilities of the use of dissociation, for a variety of purposes from mind-therapy to religious or political conversion; and as a result there is an increasing use of electrical, electronic and radionic equipment in order to alter people's levels of consciousness and experience of time. With the aid of those media a new psychic, or psychodynamic, mythology is being developed.

Among many, particularly the disaffected, disillusioned and anomic, there is a self-conscious attempt, or rather a variety of such attempts, to create a new mythology or even an alternative form of society. The development of the 'antiestablishment' group is one of the leading social phenomena of our time. The fashions and styles of dress and hair, with accompanying esoteric language and accents, are all symptoms of group participation in a counter-culture, with the 'gang-bang' used as a symbolic rejection of generally accepted norms. This belongs partly to the myth of adolescence itself, although it certainly does not stop there.

Other myths involve such elemental matters as race, and the general exploitation of the emotionally and intellectually inadequate who are served up a confection of interplanetary brotherhoods and pseudo-psychological myths. At the same time there has been a prodigious outburst of mythical themes and primordial images from the unconscious expressed in a great variety of surrealist art forms.

All that we have said indicates that man has an interior mythical vision which is not simply a reflection of an ancient mythical tradition, but which unveils a new form of the cosmos and of history. There are, and always have been, the myth-makers such as Tolkien and his *Lord of the Rings*[50]; but in the main the modern literary myth-makers are more concerned with the realm of science fiction. That their myths are basic, and reducible to a small and limited number of models, becomes clear as one analyzes their output. But such basic paradigms are fundamental to man's need to escape from his humdrum and routine existence to the more promising and exciting world of the hopefully not-too-distant future. We are developing technologies that exceed the scope of most people's comprehension and imagination, and the need to preserve social identity and consensus has to be fulfilled at a simpler, even more naive, level.

The myth is an essential element in our social and personal survival in the face of destructive and unintelligible forces. Myth is a sort of speech that we can all understand, and in which we can all participate. As Wittgenstein[51] pointed out, '*The limits of my language* mean the limits of my world'. By a rigorous process of demythologizing, people begin to limit the multivariate possibilities of their world, which begins to become dry, factual in a data-processing way, and unimaginative. Myth as a system of signs and symbols, of metaphorical and anagogical language, provides meaning for people when they feel that their life has lost its meaning. In fact, myth is a language, or metalanguage; and it affords the paradigmata for the meanings which it has elicited from life. In the words of P Maranda[52]:

> Myths display the structured, predominantly culture-specific, and shared, semantic systems which enable the members of a culture area to understand each other and to cope with the unknown. *More strictly, myths are stylistically definable discourses that express the strong components of semantic systems.*

It is through such 'semantic systems' that society becomes consolidated and stabilized, and the role of myth generally may be seen as a means of developing a 'mass psychology', as in George Orwell's myth of the Big Brother whom everyone loves, or at least *believes* that he loves. In fact, the use, function and value of myth in modern developed society vary little from the way myth is employed in so-called 'primitive' communities[53]. We all have to create our own realities, and we feel much safer as well as saner if there is at least some identity distinguishable in the realities that we have severally constructed. Only in this way can our meanings, whether religious, social or political, be conveyed from one person to another.

We have all met people with different sets of meanings and different semantic systems, and we have been fully aware that there is practically no way of translating our meanings into theirs. They have an entirely different universe of discourse from ours, and words alone will not adequately represent nor even indicate the real points of contact. We have, in some empathic way, to get inside their skins and they inside ours. They have to begin to think with our categories and we have to visualize with their models and paradigms. To this extent, at least, Bultmann was right: we need to get behind the myths themselves in order to penetrate the *experience* out of which the myths arose. Such a process takes time, effort and understanding, and not a little humility and compassion. The only way is to live with one another until we reach the situation described so admirably by Ursula McConnell[54] in her analysis of the Munkan mythology:

> We may briefly describe the function of the 'myth' in this society as a means by which the individual objectifies his personal experience in terms of a social world outside himself in which he participates and finds his 'place', and towards which he develops a 'social self' in accordance with its patterns. In the 'myth' he sees himself in perspective as in a mirror. In this mirror all gazing see themselves and each other reflected in an ordered relationship, recognize the familiar landmarks directing them towards common goals, and experience those warm emotions which bind them together as one people with a common destiny.

3   Ritual and Initiation

Myths are concerned with words and their inner meanings: rituals are concerned with activity and with specific actions performed with a specific purpose. Rituals always tend to harden into precision; that is, the acts that are performed are not of a voluntary or inventive nature – at least, not the essential actions involved in the rites. Ritual actions are almost invariably prescribed and repetitive, and any latitude permitted is within a generally accepted and limited range of alternatives. The reason for this is that magico-religious acts imply a certain causal relationship; the act is performed for a purpose, and in order to obtain the requisite result the act must be seen to conform to the tried and tested formula for that particular end. The relation between the means and the end of such actions is not something that has a rational, scientific basis in current terms, but rather something that has evolved from observation. It is more in the nature of reasoning along the lines of *post hoc ergo propter hoc* (after the event, therefore because of the event); or in Jungian terms it is concerned more with *synchronicity*[1] – that is, there is no logical or demonstrably scientific connection between two events, but they appear always to happen together. Thus, after certain rain ceremonies and rituals there always seems to be a downpour of rain. The timing may be related to known seasonal occurrences, such as the period of the monsoon, or to observed oncoming rain-clouds; but in the event the worshipper believes in a causal relationship between the ritual practice and the end achieved (or perceived).

In this causal relationship, however, there is little or no conception of *material* cause and effect. The worshippers are involved in symbolic acts which relate to spiritual values and spiritual entities, and the rites performed react in a spiritual way to produce the required effect. In. other words, there are powers, spirits or deities who are concerned with the cycle of life, and ultimately it is they who are responsible for flood, famine, drought or abundance. Nor is this just a case of pleasing or placating these supernatural or spiritual powers: the ritual performed is of *positive assistance* to the deities concerned – it helps them to develop the necessary spiritual atmosphere and *mana* (that is, supernatural energy or power) either to change, or just to continue in a normal and orderly fashion, the course of nature.

1   The Life Cycle: *Rites de Passage*

The peoples of most societies are involved in a concern for what is termed the Life Cycle, that is, Birth, Adolescence and its Initiation, Marriage, Death and Reincarnation (or some other form of Afterlife); and there are rites and ceremonies concerned with each aspect or stage of the cycle. Some rituals are specifically concerned with the individual and higher progress through life; others are more involved with the social and terrestrial aspects of the cycle, although there is always a close relationship between the good of the individual and that of society at large. In some simpler societies, for example, there is the practice of the couvade in relation to birth. In this ritual there is a 'lying-in' of the father upon a specially prepared bed at the time of the birth, and frequently for several days after. Whilst the mother may have a relatively painless experience by giving birth quietly in some secluded spot, the father may ritually give expression to the agonies of childbirth on his bed. His imitation of the travail is not so much for the purpose of bearing the pangs suffered by the wife, as for attracting the evil spirits and influences which might otherwise attend the real place of birth, waiting for a chance to seize the newborn spirit as it arrives in the babe, and to control it.

The *rites of passage*[2] are particularly interesting at the stage of puberty or adolescence, when the individual is about to become an adult and fully-fledged member of society. There are many societies, even among primitive peoples, which have no such ritual for the nubile females, although most of them will go through some form of instruction, if only to prepare them for the rite of marriage. The majority of the initiation rites for males follow a particular pattern, although of course details will vary from group to group, and from tribe to tribe. A van Gennep speaks of three distinct elements in the concept of the rites of passage: (a) a separation from the old order of things, and the previous social condition, which he refers to as *preliminary* rites; (b) a marginal or transitional stage, which he calls the *liminal* stage involving *liminary* rites; and (c) the incorporation or aggregation into a new condition or social situation, referred to as *post-liminary* rites.

Maya Deren[4] has described in some detail the various stages, in the Haitian society, of the birth of a man. Before the youth goes through the ceremony he is referred to as *bossale*, that is, wild, untamed and uninitiated. After his initiation he is called *hounsi canzo*, meaning one who has passed through the fire ordeal. Firstly, he must be purified both physically and spiritually. In order that this may be accomplished he makes a full confession of his sins to the *houngan* or *voudoun* (voodoo) priest. *Houngan* means literally the 'chief of the spirits'. After the confession the initiate withdraws, or segregates himself from the world for several days, and there is an intensification of the purification process. The initiate spends his time in meditation and bathes almost continuously, until at last it is considered that he has reached the state of innocence once more. He is, in fact, returning to the beginning of his life, and he here comes under the patronage of the female *loa*, Ayizan, who exorcises all evil and finally purifies the initiate. The whole of his past has been annihilated as if it had never been, and lying on a bed of stripped palms he is conceived all over again.

For a period of four days he goes through the process of having his body anointed at noon, when the sun is at its highest. After a sacrifice of chicken, and a mixture in a pot-de-tête has been made of elements of both the sacrifice and the neophyte (usually samples of his hair and nails), a *gros bon ange*, soul or metaphysical double, of the individual has been created[5]:

> It is a mixture of the cosmic loa and the immediate life essence of the person, defined as a singular amalgam contained in this pot-de-tête.

After this ritual, the initiate is baptized by two children and given a new name. This naming ceremony is worldwide and is represented in a variety of communities from the most primitive to the most developed – as, for example, among many Christian convent and monastery communities in which neophyte sister nuns and brother monks take on new names to represent their rejection of their old personality and allegiances, and their adoption of new ones.

Finally, in the Haitian initiation the youth goes through the ceremony of *bruler-zin*. This is basically the boiling of the sacred cooking vessels used in the rites, and the pouring of rum upon the ground and setting fire to it so that the *loa* or spirit may be heated up. This is regarded as a recharging of the life spirit, and during the ceremony the initiate 'breathes fire'. The next day he emerges as a new person, a newborn soul. Then, dressed in white and wearing a large straw hat, he is led under a white sheet which is carried over his head to form a canopy. Then he is introduced to the *loa* or god.

We have not included here all the absolutely essential minutiae of ritual in this initiation ceremony, although for its successful completion nothing may be omitted. For us the important elements are the initial separation of the individual from the rest of society, and his death to the old life, the old self and the world, as a preliminary ritual. Then the swallowing-up of the individual initiate in the earth, after a proper confession of all his sins, is accompanied by lustrations, meditation, and fire ritual as a series of liminary rites. After this transitional stage there is a gradual rebirth into a new life and a new personality, with a new name, and an introduction to the god. This represents the initiate's incorporation into the new social situation, and involves post-liminary rites.

In the Maki ritual of initiation in Malekula[6] on the small island of Vao in the New Hebrides, there is the taking of a new name, the lighting of a new fire, on which the food of the reborn must be cooked, and the becoming of a child for a period of thirty days, during which he may not cook his own food nor leave the holy place where he has taken up his abode. He has had a ritual rebirth, and one is reminded of the saying of Jesus, 'Except ye become as little children ye shall in no wise enter the kingdom of heaven'[7].

In many initiation ceremonies throughout the world there are flagellations and a variety of tests of courage and endurance; operations of circumcision, subincision and cicatrization; a series of hoaxes; and in some instances, physical burial and later resuscitation as a very realistic and usually frightening symbolism of death and resurrection. Among the Fijians[8], the initiate is suddenly faced with rows of 'dead' men, covered with pigs' entrails and blood. Without warning the 'dead' men arise with a bloodcurdling yell, and rush down to the river to cleanse, themselves, thus becoming 'alive' once more. Among the Yabim youths of New Guinea[9], initiation rites include circumcision followed by living in seclusion for some months. When eventually they return to their village they have to keep their eyes closed, and they appear to be unable to talk or even to understand what is said to them. They are virtually babes in behaviour and understanding, and they are ready to begin life once more, in a humble and spiritualized way.

2   Death Cults

Among the ancients, the cults associated with death were vitally important as we know from the monumental tombs and pyramids of the Egyptians[10]. The details involved in mortuary ritual were concerned not only with the preservation of the body through mummification, but also with the 'Opening of the Mouth' ceremony performed in a specific way by a priest in order to revivify the mummy and to ensure the retention of all the mental faculties. In this way, the recreated *ba*, or living soul, was afforded the strength and ability to confront those beyond the grave who were his spiritual adversaries. Even the dead man's entrails were preserved separately in four canopic jars in an initiatory ritual to represent what had been done to restore to life Osiris, Lord God of the Dead and of Vegetation. In the main these cults of preservation and recreation were restricted to pharaohs and other important personages from the First to the Seventeenth Dynasties, that is, from about 3000 BC to 1600 BC. During the Eighteenth Dynasty, however, the ritual became extended to local dignitaries, until eventually it became almost a universal practice in Egypt. A portrait statue was made of the dead person, or perhaps just a death mask, and the sculptor was paid good money for performing what was not merely an artistic role, but also – and more importantly – a religious and ritualistic one. Those who cared for their dead brought the statue to life periodically by means of libations of Nile water, by touching the ears, nostrils and eyes with a chisel, and by the plentiful use of censings.

The Ashanti[11] had elaborate funeral ceremonies spread over a period of eight days, during which the ritual involved a great deal of eating and drinking, general licence, the throwing of insults at one another, and a final laudatory speech concerning the dead person. It is of great interest to note that when the Ashanti, as well as other tribes of the Gold Coast area, were made slaves and were transported to the West Indies, they took their rituals with them. Some of these ceremonies, not least being the funeral rites, still exist in countries such as Jamaica[12]. Here death is a great occasion when fear, sorrow, adulation, rejoicing, confession, recrimination, story-telling, obscenity, singing, dancing, eating and drinking are all mingled in a long and virtually uninterrupted repetition of elemental rituals. Obeah (a form of magic), duppy or spirit catching, esoteric rites, ceremonies and formulas all have their place in the seemingly endless wakes which are the inevitable concomitant of a burial in such areas as Ocho Rios, and generally among the rural peasantry. For hygienic reasons, such wakes begin within twenty-four hours after the death in this tropical area. They are occasions for a general kinship reunion which welcomes at the same time any passing or homeless tramp, or interested visitor, who might be looking for entertainment or a free meal.

The Nine Days wake, however, must not be constructed as a sort of glorified self-indulgence without order or purpose. In fact, though it may be simple in form, the Jamaican wake is a carefully ordered and dramatized ritual. Not only does the kin group adjust to the fact that it has lost a loved one, it also ensures that the dead person's spirit cannot return, unless deliberately summoned by a special ritual such as the Cumina. This precaution is achieved, more specifically, by sweeping behind the coffin as it is conveyed to the family or group graveyard, which is usually situated in the kin-group yard which contains a washing area, a water tap and a communal latrine as well as a general hut for meetings, games, services and entertainments. The body is finally buried with an eastern orientation, and then the wake really gets under way.

This ritual continues for nine days and nights. Everything leads into the celebration of the Ninth Night when games, food and African stories eventually give way to a ritual of rhythmic music and dancing, the singing of 'sankeys' (that is, hymns from the Moody and Sankey collection), Bible readings and conscienceless flattery of the dear departed one.

At first blush, one element appears to be entirely out of character with the rest of the ritual, namely, the singing of obscene songs, the general mouthing of obscenities and the recounting of bawdy jokes. Fernando Henriques[13] argues that these activities can be considered as 'an outlet for the fear implicit in any situation concerned with the spirits'. It is certainly not easy to explain obscenity here in teleological terms; and anything so alien to the general tenor of the ritual, at least in terms of the Bible reading and hymn singing, clearly has no theological or philosophical rationale. An explanation of a psychological nature seems to be called for. The utterance of obscenity may be an expression of sheer bravado in the face of the ultimate terror of death. It may be a defiant demonstration that death has at least no power to claim *them* in the final hours of the Ninth Night, and their obscenities are an expression of their superiority over the dead man who has at last succumbed to the realm of the duppies.

The wake is an integral expression, in intensive microform, of the totality of the life of the participants. In a period of nine days they manage to cover all their normal activities and functionings, and the multiplexity of all levels of life. The obscene is no exception to this and it is a level which, for the most of the time perhaps, may be kept under control and will remain in the regions of the unconscious. In the wake, however, the individual and the group pass through the whole gamut of human emotions which are released in a ritualistic and stylized manner. The extended family and the kinship group are here demonstrated to be at the level of the racial. unconscious which holds the memories of their African past.

The whole of the Nine Nights or Nine Days ceremony is a period during which the spirit of the dead person seeks to wander back to its home to be entertained by its kinfolk, and to listen to the final flatteries, before eventually joining the world of the ancestral duppies, or Lomas Land – the Land of the Dead. But during this period the very presence of the friends and kinsmen of the departed will ensure his speedy and final return to the grave. In all this the Ninth Night is critical, and those involved in the ceremony have to be particularly vigilant. The exaggerated stories told about the dead person on this last night of the wake are calculated to provide his spirit with as great a send-off as possible; in consequence, a 'nine-night Lie' has come to mean a tall story.

It is inevitable, with the progress of time, the extension of compulsory education, and the increasing sophistication of life generally, that both the nature and the extent of the practice of the wake in Jamaica should be changing. It is universal neither in terms of geography nor in terms of social position. Its practice is far more common in the country areas and remote villages than in the towns; and it is observed more frequently by peasants working on the land than by any other groups in society. There is also a tendency for the more intelligent of the younger generation to despise the whole business, as well as any magical or pseudo-magical practices. They regard these occasions as the entertainment and superstitious beliefs of the older generation.

3   Fertility Cults

Many of the rites of primitive man, both archaic and current, have been concerned with the production and maintenance of fertility. Here again one needs to emphasize the view of causation held in respect both of fertility and of the many other blessings in life. This is expressed by Maya Deren[14] in the following terms:

> If one were to ask, 'Does his ritual cause things to happen?' the answer would be in the affirmative. But causation, in religious terms, is not causation as defined in scientific terms. The world of a religious man is governed by moral reason, not by material reason. The Haitian does not mean, for example, that health will *result* from certain ritual action; he means that health will be a *reward* for his performance of it.

This applies to the rites concerned with fertility and the mystery of birth generally. There is a great deal of symbolic representation by the members of a cult, in order to obtain the fecundity that they desire. For example, the cultus of the Mother Goddess in Crete, in the Aegean and in Western Asia generally, was represented symbolically by Venus figures, by figurines with large and pendulous breasts, by small and often squat representations of women in the last stages of pregnancy, and by Diana of the Ephesians covered by supernumerary breasts. It was also represented by the phallus and its generative power. Sexual intercourse was often a specifically ritual activity in which the male (the priest) represented the god in his fecundatory power, and the female was a chosen vessel, a temple prostitute, to ensure the fertility of the soil and of the people. This activity was certainly not regarded as promiscuity, but as a necessary, symbolic and ritualistic act.

Formerly, amongst the Hopi Indians[15] of North Arizona, there was a snake-dance ritual held every year during the month of August. This was a purely religious ceremony in which the Indians made a very elaborate series of prayers to their gods, particularly the Plumed Serpent. The object of the whole ceremony was to produce life-giving rain to save their crops of peaches, squashes, beans and corn. To this end they performed a dance with rattlesnakes, bullsnakes and garter snakes. These carried the prayers of this desert tribe to the gods who lived in the underworld, and requested them to send rain. The underworld is the Hopi heaven, and they believe that they themselves originated from Mother Earth through an opening in the ground. As August is the rainy season in this part of the world, their prayers and rituals were almost invariably rewarded. This peaceful people (the very meaning of 'Hopi') became the object that they held in their mouths – the symbol of the Feathered Serpent; they were themselves serpents engaging in a ritual dance. As E O James[16] comments when referring in general terms to ritual:

> Ritual thus becomes a vent of pent-up emotions and activity, the desire to act discharging itself on the efficacious symbol with which the performers identify themselves. To complete this identification they disguise themselves as the thing represented and behave as though they were actually that which they impersonate, or else they wear objects charged with potency, and frequently partake sacramentally of some part of the sacred species in the case of totemic rites.

Interestingly enough, the fertility and re-creative rituals of some of the aboriginal tribes of the Northern Territory of Australia are directed at the Feathered Serpent[17]. Eingana, the great Fertility Mother, is represented by a feathered serpent; she is the inexhaustible source of life and of the spirit, manifesting itself in a continuous cycle of birth, death and rebirth. She is involved in the resuscitation, fertility and resurrection of all things – man, animals and crops. The snake, Eingana, swallows up the initiates and worshippers, and spews them forth again into newness of life. Among the aborigines of Arnhem Land there is a renewal and fertility cult named the Kunapipi. This is open only to young men who have already undergone their tribal rites of initiation at puberty. The aim of the ritual is to ensure that all the energies involved in cosmic life and universal fertility are renewed.

In the ritual of this cult there is a general symbolism of return to the womb, and the complete regeneration of the initiate through gestation within the Great Mother, and rebirth. Mircea Eliade[18] has outlined a variety of vegetation, agriculture and fertility cults with their rites and symbols of regeneration.

4 The Dying and Rising God

Many rituals are concerned with the concept of the dying and rising god. In Egypt the god was Osiris, in Syria he was Adonis, and in Anatolia the god was Attis. These all represented different and local versions of what was basically the same fundamental theme. That theme was the dying-off of crops in the autumn of the vegetation year, and their coming to life again in the spring. The god, therefore, was generally represented as dying every year, and he immediately went down into the chthonic land of death and darkness, from which there was strictly no return without the assistance of the ritual performed.

The god himself was usually followed down by the Mother-goddess who sought to rescue him, whilst on the earth human mourners bewailed his fate and sought through their magical rites to ensure his resurrection and return. In the book of the prophet Ezekiel[19], for example, we read of the leaders or sheikhs of Israel participating in foreign totem worship in the temple of Yahweh; and in particular there were women wailing for the Babylonian sun and vegetation god, Tammuz or Dumu-zi (that is, 'son of life' or 'true son'). They had made an effigy of the dead god which they then proceeded to anoint, with their own tears as well as with balms and flowers. And after the period of mourning and the performance of the necessary rituals, the god was restored from the land of the dead, set free in the case of Tammuz by Ishtar, but in general terms by the Earth Goddess under whatever local name she might have. His resurrection gave new life to the parched earth in the spring, and the ground once more became productive of crops, fruits, trees and flowers.

In ancient societies, the king was himself involved in the ritual, and in Peru at the Spring Festival the Inca himself 'died' every year, remaining hidden from the populace and his own chiefs the while. A slave was chosen to take his place, and for a whole day he could do exactly as he pleased; but at the end of the day he was ritually sacrificed, and then the Inca himself would walk out as if he had 'risen' from the dead.

In Sumer and Akkad, under King Hammurabi, certain rites and celebrations were instituted to represent once more the decay of the crops and their final restoration to life and fertility. The god here involved was Marduk, and for eleven days a whole drama was enacted in which was portrayed the struggle of Marduk with the primeval water-goddess of chaos, Tiamat, whose equivalent in the Hebrew Old Testament was Tehom[20]. The Creation Epic was repeated as the festival proceeded, and precise forms of ritual had to be performed to link up with the recital of the myth. After his death in the struggle with Tiamat, Marduk was restored to life, thus promoting and ensuring the growth of the spring vegetation. On the fifth of the eleven days, the king himself was led to the temple of Marduk, in the company of the priests, and was there left alone in front of Marduk's effigy. The high priest next entered the sanctuary and began to divest the king of all his royal robes and insignia. Then he struck the king upon his cheek, pulled his ears and pushed him down before Marduk. There the king made a negative confession in which he claimed that he had not sinned nor been negligent regarding Marduk's divinity, nor had he been responsible for the destruction of Marduk's special realm of Babylon.

When this charade was over, the king was afforded complete absolution by the high priest, who has acted throughout as the earthly representative or intermediary of Marduk. He gave Marduk's blessing to the king, with promises of future signs of success in all his endeavours and prosperity throughout the land. Then his dress and insignia were restored to the king, and he was once more struck hard upon the cheek in order to produce tears. Once the tears were freely flowing, it was a sign of favourable regard by Marduk himself and everything would be propitious. On the eighth day, the king was reinstated to full powers over the land and his people; and between then and the eleventh day there was a ritual dramatization of Marduk's resurrection and the renewal of fertility to both the soil and the subjects.

5 New Year and Spring Festivals

Linked with the purpose of the rites of the dying and rising gods are similar ceremonies and festivals concerned with the New Year, with Spring, and with the magical control of the weather. Something of this may be seen in the voodoo rites in Haiti[21], in which it is the function of the gods, or loa, to direct the great mass of primal matter in the universe 'into patterns of intelligence and benevolence'. In order that this functional process might be ensured, it is man's constant duty to feed the loa, and as a result a constant flow of energy, or mana, will be elicited, and the weather will be helpful and the land productive:

> The kind of food, its preparation, the manner of serving it, and the selection and quantity of the portions, depend upon which loa is being fed, and vary according to the particular occasion, the local traditions, and factors of immediate expediency[22].

In ancient Egypt, rituals and festivals were related largely to the rise and fall of the River Nile, and both the calendar events and national occasions were based upon this and were regulated by it. Thus the new year began in June and July with the rise of the river, and the occasion was known as the onset of the Season of Inundation. At the end of the inundation, some four months later, there was the season of Coming Forth; crops were sown and quickly began to sprout. After the grain had been cut and harvested, there was a decline of the life-producing waters, and there now occurred the Season of Deficiency, during which the parched ground was bare of all life, and awaited the return of the Nile waters. The beginning of each of these seasons was regarded as a new year's day because it was an occasion of great fear as well as of expectation lest Nature should in some way fail to perform according to custom.

Rituals, therefore, had to be enacted to ensure that the god of the Nile was enabled to do his work properly. The Season of Inundation was of special importance, and so was considered to be the official new year. It was then that the dead god was resuscitated, and stalks of wheat were shown growing from his mummy which was kept in the temple of Isis at Philae. These stalks were ritually watered by a priest who held the *crux ansata* in front of the bier. During this spring festival beds of barley were made and watered for Osiris in order to ensure bountiful crops. They were then placed in tombs to bring life to those who were dead. Other festivals, such as that of ploughing and the Sed Festival, were concerned with the rejuvenation of the crops or of the sovereign through maintained, or improved, relationships between the heavenly deities and their earthly representatives and worshippers. All the rituals were geared to ensure this continuity of communion between heaven and earth, the past and the present, and the whole life cycle.

6   Eating the God

The ritual of the eating of the god[23] is one of the most universal ceremonies both in terms of time and of place, and it is to be found in the grossest as well as in the most sophisticated forms. This is often referred to as the sacrament of the first-fruits. The corn spirit has frequently been represented and eaten in human shape, whilst among the Aztecs the eating of bread sacramentally as the body of a god was practised long before the arrival of Cortez and the Spaniards. During May they made images of their god, Huitzilopochtli, in dough, which was cooked and then broken in pieces and eaten by his worshippers. At the festival of the winter solstice held in December, Huitzilopochtli was again represented in effigy form, usually of dough, ritually killed, broken into small pieces, and then eaten by the assembled throng. The development of the Christian Eucharist, Sacrament, Breaking of Bread or Mass – whatever term is used – is a symbolic representation of the 'eating of the god'. Among earlier civilizations and among primitive peoples, the main objects of the ritual have been to receive an identity with the god and to share in his spiritual and magical powers – to obtain his mana. The transubstantiation thesis of the Roman Catholic Church implies a real transmutation of the elements of bread and wine into the body and blood of Christ; and in this way the worshippers are quite literally eating their god, and feel spiritually (if not physically) strengthened by their sacramental experience.

The element of blood in offerings and in sacrifice always seems to have been of some importance, from Abel's sacrifice of sheep (as over against Cain's 'produce of the ground'[24]), the blood sacrifices graphically described in the Book of Leviticus, to the human sacrifices offered throughout the ages in many parts of the world as atonement for sins, or as food for the gods, or both. Among the Aztecs, child sacrifice was common when rain was required[25]; slaves were flayed and priests wore their skins whilst dancing to their gods; slave girls impersonated the Goddess of Young Corn and were later sacrificed; thousands of sacrificial victims had their hearts torn out and these were piled in a canoe with a boy and a girl, and the canoe was sunk; and after any tribal war the victims were ritually killed and then eaten. In this way, the essential energy and power of the enemy became absorbed and the individual was rejuvenated. Thus the gods and their worshippers shared in a common life-giving meal.

Sometimes, as in the Mithraic ritual of *Taurobolium*, the initiate or worshipper would drink a cup of a sacrificed bull's blood, and then would be thoroughly baptized in its blood as it flowed upon him from above. Such rituals identified the worshipper with the animals that were slaughtered, and these in turn were the physical representations of the god who was worshipped – thus Mithras himself was represented by the bull.

7 Ritual Language

Ritual and religious ceremonies generally have changed considerably over the years. At one time, not only the precise words in terms of meaning were requisite for a successful outcome to the ritual, but the *original language*, however archaic, in which the original words were first framed, was absolutely essential. Thus Maya Deren[26] says of the rites of voodoo in Haiti:

> One of the elements of ritual is langage, a kind of sacred language, which is understood to be the means of direct communication with the loa and more persuasive to them than address in Creole. Langage seems to be the vestige of African speech, and if this is so, then it was originally used to address the loa in words understood by everyone as being such an address.

The problem of 'langage' has been experienced in more recent years in the language used by the priests in the celebration of the Christian Mass. Until a few decades ago only the original Latin words, with their esoteric meaning, might be used. Today, however, not only must the vernacular or indigenous language of each group celebrating the Mass be used, but also the ancient Latin rites are forbidden. This is a complete reversal of the usual trend in ritualistic language in which the original language itself is regarded as essential for the efficacy of the rite. The uninitiated might regard it all as 'hocus-pocus', but the adepts know how essential are precise words and sounds, as well as actions and their timing. And there are many Catholics who today feel that the old Tridentine Mass, said in Latin, is the only valid and efficacious one; and a rite which is not efficacious cannot strictly be ritual, and is therefore void.

In his discussion of Malinowski and Radcliffe-Brown with regard to anxiety and ritual, G C Homans[27] concluded that there were seven elements involved in the development of ritual. We are not here concerned with the theories of Malinowski and Brown as such, but Homans' conclusions are of interest in any analysis of ritual. The individual has (i) a primary anxiety through his lack of means or techniques to secure certain desired results. In a simple society, dependent upon the forces of nature in terms of the weather, the seasons and the earth, this primary anxiety tends very much to be a collective one. This leads to (ii) a primary form of ritual in which the individual or the group will tend to perform actions which have no practical result. The group or society as a whole will usually determine the form that the ritual will take, and will expect individual members to perform the ritual on the appropriate occasions. Sometimes ritual tradition will be very weak in any society, and it is then that men will invent ritual when they feel anxiety.

The rites give them a sense of confidence and a feeling of inevitable success; indeed (iii) they will experience a secondary anxiety only when the rites themselves are not properly performed. Thus, there are many people in our Western society at the present moment who suffer from this secondary anxiety because the format of religious rites and ceremonies is changing. The very language and sometimes the accompanying dramatic expressions and performances are being deliberately altered. There are those who feel that their rites no longer possess any validity. Homans suggested that the feeling of secondary anxiety led to (iv) secondary ritual, which took the form of a ritual of purification and expiation which has the function of dispelling secondary anxiety. Its form and performance, like those of primary ritual, may or may not be socially determined.

There is, in all the performance of ritual activity (v) a process of rationalization going on. For example, it is argued that, from repeated experience, the performing of certain magico-religious rites does in fact produce rain. When it has failed there must have been some sin, crime or lack of belief amongst the worshippers that required purification or expiation before the ritual could work. Sometimes the ritual has not worked because the wrong person performed some essential element of it, or some part of the elaborate drama had been neglected or had been insufficiently expressed. If, for example, a layman were to celebrate the Mass of the Catholic Church, it would not be efficacious, and transubstantiation would not occur. Or if the Host were not properly elevated and the wrong words were spoken, the ritual would be void.

In all of this an important element is (vi) symbolization. The practical result which it is hoped will be accomplished does not determine the ritual action, although the element of imitation may sometimes occur. Thus, if rain is desired, water may sometimes be poured on the ground. But the ritual may be determined by other factors; it is symbolic, and each society develops its own symbolism. Some of this symbolism is in the form of sympathies or antipathies; some is highly complex and related to the fundamental mythology of the society. And this is so whether we are referring to the symbolic rites of the aborigines of Cape York or those of the Christian Church. Finally, Homans argues that (vii) ritual actions do not in themselves produce a practical result in the external world. The function of ritual is not related to the world that is external to the society, but rather to the internal constitution of the society itself. It, in fact, 'gives the members of the society confidence; it dispels their anxieties; it disciplines the social organization'[28].

This is, of course, a very neat analysis of the development of ritual, and it provides a useful paradigm whereby to understand it. It must be pointed out, however, that whereas rituals have arisen from giving voluntary attention to any particular problem or anxiety, the institution of rituals has often occurred quite spontaneously without any *deliberate* thought or design upon the part of the individual or group. Rituals have existed as a means of manipulating the world around us and of making it more easily understood and absorbed. Religious rites, with religious feelings and dogmas, are taken over from the social environment, but they are not *merely* social products. The group and the individual react to and reflect upon their experiences; and whilst Homans is right in suggesting that rationalization does take place, it is not always or inevitably so as he seems to suggest. Both the individual and the group will reason about their beliefs and ritual symbolization, and they will need to justify them intellectually before they finally discover a satisfactory adjustment to their problem. But intellectual criticism as distinct from rationalization does occur, and a rational element or dimension is added to the experiential one. As a result of the rational criticism, as opposed to rationalization, rituals and ritualistic symbolization have been adapted and modified in order to effect greater confidence in the religious system; and in this way, as Homans says, the social organization receives its discipline.

8   Ritual Today

There is perhaps a certain sadness in some contemporary views expressed concerning 'primitive' rituals, as if in a civilized modern society we had all outgrown such juvenile beliefs and practices. Mircea Eliade[29] has said that, 'For the primitive to *live* is to share in the sacrality of the cosmos'. For him all things are sacred, and when he constructs his long-house or his canoes he accompanies the actual building and craftsmanship with certain essential rituals to ensure the perfection and functional adequacy of his work. Today it is still sometimes regarded as essential (or at least beneficial, or the 'done thing') to bless a ship, or a church or some other building, although the actual process of construction may have been regarded as anything but sacred. Moreover, the only rituals involved may have been clocking-on and clocking-off, with the regular shop-floor meeting to discuss working conditions, industrial relations, or possibly potential industrial strike action.

It would seem that, whenever the techniques of modern industry are introduced into a 'primitive' or simple society, their ritualistic practices decline and disappear. Maya Deren[30] comments that:

> It has therefore been deduced that the purpose of ritual is the magical control of environmental forces, a function more effectively fulfilled by modern techniques, which it is argued, have therefore come to replace the rituals. However, only a small percentage of religious ritual (as distinct from magic rites) is concerned with such material phenomena. On the other hand, machines have not so much given man control over natural disasters such as drought, flood and epidemic disease, as made possible compensatory, remedial and rescue measures.

Deren goes on to emphasize the fact that the machine and its consequent culture have in their turn produced a whole gamut of disasters and disorders among primitive societies. In consequence, ritualistic appeal against catastrophe has not been eliminated since it is not clear that modern industrial man is any more secure than his 'primitive' brother.

It is also true, of course, that even modern industrial man cannot do without his rituals, even though he may have desacralized the earth, and even the universe itself. Man has a need for symbolization and for ritualistic acts and words, even though he may no longer associate them with God, gods, religion or magic. As Bocock[31] has pointed out, ritual has always been used as an effective way of socializing people and of assisting them to conform to values and ways of life which they have not selected for themselves.

We may have eliminated all our older forms of initiation into society, but even such an institution as the school has its rituals and formularies, and its means of initiating children into some of life's roles, however unsuccessfully. And when we come to the adult worker, the Trades Union Congress, with all its unions, branches, members and general ramifications, has provided industrial man with a whole range of mystique and mythology, with accompanying typical and symbolic expressions. In fact, it has a 'langage' which trips off the tongue of both the intellectuals and the illiterate with equal ease. We have all become familiar with 'comrades', 'brothers and sisters', 'negotiation', 'free collective bargaining', 'mediation', 'sitting around the table', 'putting on the table', 'lock out', 'sit-in', 'strike', 'walk-out', 'peaceful picketing', 'demonstration protest march', 'production schemes', 'incentive bonuses', 'rationalization', 'blacklegs', 'confrontation', 'differentials', and so on. The rituals of election, card-voting, branch meetings, delegation and debate are part and parcel of industrial man's life, and without these he would feel insecure and without purpose. The language he uses, with prescribed and agreed meanings, is the sole means of communication between himself, his comrades and his employers. There is a whole 'Us and Them' mythology in which antipathies appear to predominate, but in which at least social and employment roles are clearly delineated. It is part and parcel of the new age in which every form of work, including that of doctors, nurses and teachers, has ceased to be related to cosmic powers, processes and energies, and has become desacralized. It has, nevertheless, a mythology which, with its highly organized rituals, has become an essential part of the life of the average worker in our society. Like his more primitive cousins, he lives by myths and rituals – it is only his gods and his goals that are different.

4   Origins and Development of Religion

There have been many attempts to answer the question, 'How did religion arise among mankind?' It is still very much an open question. Many writers, in their discussions and speculations, have looked for one single cause for religion and have argued, with great conviction, on the basis of evidence elicited in favour of their particular thesis. In his search for the answer, man has used a great variety of approaches and disciplines, some of which have already been mentioned in Chapter One.

Before considering in any detail the more recent and more acceptable arguments concerning origins, it might be interesting simply to categorize some of the more general answers that have been supplied to the question. For example, Petronius and Lucretius among the ancients, and in more recent times Westermarck, traced the origin of religion to fear, that is, man's fear of the elements and of nature around him. Hobbes also inclined to this view, emphasizing in particular man's ignorance and, in consequence, his fear of the unknown. R R Marett underlined, amongst other things, man's awe of natural phenomena, whilst J G Frazer saw in magic man's answer to the problems involved in the control of the elements. Durkheim argued that in totemism man attempted to link himself with the animal and the plant kingdoms, as well as to his ancestry, back to some tribal originator or god. The philosopher, Immanuel Kant, thought that religion was based primarily upon such tribal sanctions as the Ten Commandments, which bore the *imprimatur* of 'Thus saith the Lord'. Man's moral behaviour, then, was guided, controlled and even dictated by divine authority – by Yahweh himself as far as the Israelites were concerned.

Schleiermacher traced man's religious sentiments to a feeling of absolute dependence upon some external spiritual source, whilst Sigmund Freud argued that man felt insufficient and as a result, in order to avoid becoming neurotic about it, he projected his need upon some Father-figure or substitute whom he referred to as God. Some, like Carl Jung, have suggested that religion derives from a whole catena of paradigms or archetypes existing in man's unconscious – in fact, in his racial or collective unconscious. Others have argued that man could not conceive of a life without some ultimate purpose, or without some sort of afterlife in which he could go on developing himself towards completion, or in which he was suddenly transformed into the likeness of God. The concept that death is the end of everything is more than perhaps most people can bear, and they look for some compensatory and continuing element after what may well have been a most unsatisfactory earthly life. Finally, some (like St Augustine) have even suggested that man by nature is a religious being, or (as R Otto proposed) that man has a special factor within his make-up that is related simply to the awesomeness of the holy, to the numinous. In the words of St Augustine himself, it may well be that man is religious because there is a God and 'God has made us for himself, and our souls are restless till they find rest in him'. But, perhaps as always, 'nothing but' theories tend to end up by being indefensible, and we may well find after some enquiry that man's religion arises from a variety of complex causes and occasions.

There is sufficient historical and archaeological evidence today concerning Palaeolithic man to indicate that he had some belief of a religious nature. Neanderthal man was first discovered in a cave in the Neander Valley near Dusseldorf in the year 1856. Since that date many examples of early *homo sapiens* have been uncovered, such as, for example, a youth buried at Le Moustier in Dordogne with flints, an oval hand-axe and a scraper. Not far away were the charred remains of the bones of an ancient ox. At La Chapelle-aux-Saints in

Correze, a human skeleton was unearthed which had been carefully buried in a trench, and with a number of implements placed close at hand. At Spy, in Belgium, two skeletons were dug up, and they were obviously buried in a pit in front of a cave in a manner similar to that of the skeleton discovered at La Chapelle-aux-Saints. Neanderthal man had clearly buried his dead with some considerable care, and apparently with some belief in a life after death in which the dead person would require his hunting materials. Indeed, the careful burial of dead Neanderthalers, often with funerary offerings, probably provides some of the oldest surviving evidence for religious beliefs.

In S W France and in the Pyrenees, at Altamira, Font-de-Gaume and Lascaux, there are some fine examples of early cave art in the form of wall paintings. The general theory is that the paintings and etchings represent the figures of animals that were suitable for food and therefore had to be hunted. The Sorcerer's Dance, in which the sorcerer dressed up to look like an animal, was an attempt to get *en rapport* with the animals being hunted. Many of the figures etched into the cave walls were daubed with red ochre, which represented the life-giving power of blood, and it is suggested that primitive man evolved rituals whereby he 'killed' the wall symbol of the animal that he wished to hunt before embarking on his food-collecting expeditions. There are also signs in some areas that he performed sacred dances for the purpose of ensuring the multiplication of the animal species. Thus, fertility rituals were enacted in order to maintain a steady food supply. In this way there developed a sacramental relationship between man and his environment, between himself and whatever inexplicable and mysterious forces might be responsible for the propagation of life.

Generally, during the Old Stone Age, the dead were buried ceremonially in earth that was stained red, and frequently the skulls of the dead were also painted with the life-giving red ochre. Even human blood was sometimes shed over the bones to promote the possibility of continuing life, or regeneration. The body was usually placed in a flexed or crouching position, which might indicate the hope of rebirth, or it may have been the flexing of the body prior to rigor mortis setting in so that the ghost of the dead man could not afterwards walk and molest those who were alive[1]. The burial of flint instruments with the dead man seems to indicate, however, that he would be expected to use them in some form of afterlife.

Gradually, primitive man would seek to constrain the whole of his environment to support his need for food, for fertility, for rain and sun, and for protection against the adverse elements. And so, little by little, his rituals and his religious concepts would be developed to support his particular needs at specific times in his personal development, and at special seasons of the year. The great personal events of birth, puberty, sexual relationships and death would be accompanied by rites of preservation; whilst the social, geographical, and economic conditions would be supported by ritual dancing, the development of tabus and the elaboration of the sacred. R R Marett[2] stated in his introduction to *The Threshold of Religion* that

> savage religion is something not so much thought out as
> danced out, that, in other words, it develops under conditions,
> psychological and sociological, which favour emotional
> or motor processes, whereas ideation remains relatively in
> abeyance,

Certainly primitive man makes no clear statement of his theology, and there may be many mutually conflicting ideas in his various rituals, but one thing he is sure of and that is that all of his rites, ceremonies and dances are essential for the production of particular desired effects. He may have had no means of writing these things down but, as J Layard[3] has amply shown, some of the oldest and most primitive groups possess an amazing racial memory, in which the smallest ritualistic detail is recalled, and in which the heroes and ancestors of the tribe are always remembered and their activities and exploits on behalf of their people celebrated.

In his work on primitive culture, E B Tylor[4] suggested that primitive man attributed the existence of a spirit or soul not only to people but also to plants and animals, and even to a variety of natural objects such as rivers, trees and stones. Tylor thought that early man had a felt need to give some sort of rational explanation for such occurrences as dreams in which he found himself in different places, and with other people many of whom had long since been dead. He felt that he conversed with them, and inevitably this led to a belief in the existence of some sort of indwelling personality or *anima* that survived death itself. This concept of religious origins was referred to as *animism*, and it was supported by Herbert Spencer as a primal element in the evolutionary development of man's religion. Spencer also made the attempt to find the root of all religions in some form of ancestor worship. Once one had accepted animism as a sort of minimum definition of religion, there resulted the concept of ancestors, with whom one might converse in sleep, as being ghosts or gods who became worthy of worship and propitiation. Spencer went on to suggest that there was, in the history of religion, a gradual development from animism, through polytheism and pantheism, to monotheism.

This theory was rejected by A Lang[5] writing in 1898. He suggested that there was no such evolution of the deities from ghosts to gods or to one God; that is, from animism to monotheism. In fact, he suggested, there were High Gods amongst some of the 'low' races. An examination of the beliefs of virtually all tribes of Australian aborigines has revealed the fact that they have always believed in Supreme Beings, or in a Supreme Being, who could not rightly be described as a spirit, or a ghost, or even as an ancestor. They were better characterized as a sort of tribal All-Father who was responsible for giving laws, establishing mores and ethics, and for the institution of the ceremonies and initiation rites. Their view seems to have been that the Supreme Being or All-Father lived on earth long before even death entered into the world, and that he walked about the face of the earth going anywhere he wished, eventually returning to his real home in the sky. There he continued to live as the All-Father of his tribal people, in remote seclusion from them. In 1931, Wilhelm Schmidt[6] argued that there is strong evidence to indicate that primitive man was from the beginning a monotheist, that other developments, such as pantheism and polytheism, represent not so much the earlier stages in man's religious evolution as later stages in its decay. There has, however, not been a great deal of support for this view, despite Australian aboriginal Supreme Beings and African Sky-gods.

In 1914 R R Marett[7] spoke of primitive man's sense of wonder at the unusual and unexpected behaviour of the objects of nature around him, from waterfalls and violent storms to volcanic eruptions. Marett argued that primitive man attributed these events to an 'impersonal force or power'. He said that there was 'a mystic impersonal force connected with mysterious persons, objects and situations'[8]. In his study of the Melanesians, R H Codrington[9] had noted the use of a particular word, *mana*, which was employed among the peoples of Oceania to describe this mystical force. It was a unique force, entirely distinct from what may be regarded as physical power; moreover, it acted in a variety of ways both for good and evil. Its possession enhanced the very nature of any natural process, or the particular qualities of objects and beings, from crops to human adults, from animal herds to children. This concept of mana, which Marett epitomized as a belief in animatism, was certainly not peculiar to Oceanic peoples. Among the North American Iroquois the word *orenda* has a similar connotation, including the same sort of mysterious and wonder-working element in nature, which is ambivalent in its power, being both creative and destructive. *Orenda* has some analogy with the will or the intelligence, and it provides both power and greatness to the shaman (or witch-doctor), as well as a specially successful skill to the hunter. Indeed, all things partake of *orenda* in some degree, even the animals that are being hunted, as well as the stones, the rivers and the trees.

In the form of *wakonda*, among the Sioux Indians, it means specifically 'the power that moves'; whilst among the Algongquians the term *manitu* appears to be moving directly towards the concept of a god or higher being. The sacred objects of the Algongquians – such as ceremonial pots, hunting spears, arrows and knives – all possessed something of the *manitu*. Other similar terms among North American Indians are *wakan*, the power which brings events to pass; *wakai* and *oki* (among the Hurons); whilst among the West Indians *zemi* implies something similar, as also does *manngur* among the Kabi aborigines of Queensland. Among the Moroccans, *baraka* indicates sacredness, or an indwelling supernatural principle; it was regarded originally as the power which the sultan inherited from God himself as the viceregent upon earth.

The ambivalence of this power may further be illustrated from the words used in a variety of religions and languages when seeking to convey the awesomeness of things, of people, or of events. Among the Romans the word *sacer* meant both sacred, or holy, and accursed; among the Greeks *hagios* indicated both what was pure and what was polluted. The Hebrews used the word *cherem* to indicate people, places and objects that were sacred, tabu, devoted or 'accursed'. The Polynesian word *tapu* (taboo) referred to things that may be helpful or harmful according to the way in which one approaches or uses them. In ancient Israel, the Ark of the Covenant was sacred and had to be carried in a certain manner by means of poles. But if one touched the Ark itself, even though by accident when seeking to prevent damage being done to it, the individual (so it was claimed) would be immediately destroyed. Objects that were sacred to Yahweh were tabu, and the general injunction was, 'Touch not the devoted thing'. In a similar way in Malagasy, *fady* or *faly* refers to the sacred, the tabooed or the ill-omened.

In 1912 Emile Durkheim[10] suggested that the entire concept of sacredness or holiness derived from the experience of the individual member of the group of the social norms. Durkheim had a collectivist view of religion, arguing that the function of religious rituals was to affirm the moral superiority of the society over its individual members. In this way the solidarity of the society was maintained, and what men called God was simply society itself; and so the latter had all the characteristics which one would normally attribute, in a developed society, to God himself. Durkheim sought to support his argument by what was already known concerning totemism amongst Australian tribes, whose totems were sacred, and were a symbol of the tribe itself.

What Durkheim purports to show... is that on important
social occasions among primitive people when the whole clan
or tribe has gathered, an atmosphere is generated which is
attributed to supernatural origins, but which, in fact, is simply
due to the collective excitement of the crowd. This atmosphere
carries over into the ordinary 'profane' life of the people. So
that all the symbols of society's presence take on a sort of
supernatural quality[11].

A totem was a species of plant or animal, or even natural object or
phenomenon, or it might be a symbol of any of these, signifying
the distinguishing features of one human clan, group or tribe as
against other such groups, similarly represented in the same society.
Associated with the practice of totemism was the rule of exogamy,
that is, a member of the clan could marry only a member of another
totemic group, not of the same group. There was also a tabu on the
killing or eating of one's own group totem – other clans could be
left free to kill it and so control it. J Wach[12] suggests that Durkheim
impaired the validity of his analysis of totemism and other primitive
religious institutions by his 'unwarranted assumption of an identity
of the worshipping subject with the object of religion'.

A R Radcliffe-Brown[13] argued that, in the folk-tales of primitive
peoples, the world in animal life was represented in terms of
social relations similar to those of human society. From these two
different universes of discourse – the animal and the human – there
developed a belief in relationships between animals and human
groups. There was obviously an interdependence between animals
and humans. Lévy-Bruhl[14] argued that in Australia there was a
supernatural and economic system organized on a totemic basis.
Each tribe was divided into small social groups or clans, descended
from and in some mystical alliance with an animal or vegetable
species or inanimate object, regarded as its sacred ally. There was a
'blood relationship' between the group and its totem: they all shared
a common life-principle. Occasionally the clan could partake of its
totem in a sacramental manner on specified ceremonial observances;

and each group was intent upon promoting its totem on behalf of the whole of society and for the benefit of its neighbours who could kill and eat it freely.

But one thing is clear and that is that the totem has never been regarded as a god and has never been worshipped among Australian aborigines. According to E O James[15] the institution of totemism establishes an intimate relationship with the sacred, which is regarded as a providential source of food supply. He adds that,

> Like ritual in general, it is a particular and specialized technique for controlling the forces of destiny which transcend his natural unaided powers, and call for reverential regard, coupled with a sense of kinship and affinity.

James further argues that totemism is primarily a system of economics among simpler societies, which has a religious sanction and is rooted firmly in a desire to secure an adequate means of sustenance for the community at large. Again it is clear that totemism is not a universal phenomenon even among some of the most simple cultures as, for example, the Pygmies of Central Africa. C Lévi-Strauss[16] concluded that as an integrate reality totemism in the classical sense is an illusion.

In *The Idea of the Holy*[17], Rudolph Otto spoke of the element of the *numinous* in man. The ancient Latin farmers believed in the *numina* or powers which were associated with particular places and functions. Otto used the word 'numinous', derived from this, to indicate a category in religion which was unique, similar to the uniqueness of the categories of beauty, truth and goodness. It was a unique and original feeling-response which could, in itself, be ethically neutral and which demanded consideration in its own right. There was an awesomeness, an overpowering mystery, a fascination related to this religious sense of the *mysterium tremendum et fascinosum*; it was an attachment to the *fas* (Latin word for 'right') which made it *fascinans* (that is, 'attractive'). Otto suggested that the daemonic divine object appeared to the mind as both an object of dread and horror and, at the same time something that possessed both allurement and charm. The worshipper was both attracted to it and repelled from it.

There seems, however, no way of demonstrating conclusively that the religious sense is something *sui generis,* or that it is in any way an underivative feeling. Religion would seem to grow out of the sheer necessities of human experience, and our deepest religious convictions would appear to be synchronous with our greatest need to solve specific problems. The needs of primitive man may, in this respect, be different from ours; and there is, as William James[19] has amply demonstrated, a great variety of religious experience. But such experiences are not 'wholly other' than our normal day-to-day experiences. They are rather an intensification of our realization of what has occurred within our own being. When Jacob said at Bethel, 'How dreadful is this place; this is none other than the house of God!'[20], he was saying something about his own personal experience in time rather than about the nature of the particular place itself. According to E O James[21]:

> Feelings and movements may predominate over thought and produce a realization of unification with an object or unseen force, together with the sense of power that comes from the union, without any violation of logical processes common to human mentality as a whole.

Lévy-Bruhl[22], for example, had suggested that there was something unformed about primitive mentality, in that primitive man was guilty of prelogical thinking – that is, that when he saw one thing follow another (such as the performance of magic followed by rain) he attributed this to a direct causality in the events: B followed A, therefore A was the cause of B. Now, whilst this may be fallacious reasoning, it is no more fallacious than a good deal of current argument in pretty well every universe of discourse. That primitive man is frequently guilty of arguing in a *post hoc ergo propter hoc* sort of way is due more to insufficient knowledge than to any fundamental lack of logical thought as such. He may not have our scientific approach to cause and effect, but at least he is fully conscious of the fact that every effect must have a cause of some sort. Indeed, he is a rational being, even though to a more advanced age or society he may appear to act irrationally. Future ages may, in fact, come to think the same about much of our own activities and ideas.

Religion, it would seem, cannot be confined to one aspect of man's being or to one area of his human activity. There have, of course, always been periods in man's history in which religion has been, or has seemed to be divorced from secular life; but man has eventually, and inevitably, found that life cannot be lived in hermetically sealed containers. Religion arises from man's whole psychological constitution. In this he differs from the rest of the animal kingdom, for it is his superior intellection, and his development of an involved and detailed language, that have led to his unfolding of religious awareness. Man is ever conscious of his own insufficiency. Even when he makes some earth-shattering invention or discovery, he finds that he is quite unable to control his own creations. Then he begins to look for some more cosmic and universal principles to solve the very problem he himself has created. He longs for fellowship with a Reality beyond himself, or possibly in a dimension deep within himself, through which religion may be realized.

Quite apart from man's individual needs, religion has a general social function which may be discerned in a variety of ways, amongst both primitive peoples and more developed societies. In this respect there is always something ambivalent about religion. It can act as a positive and cohesive force in society, linking and integrating all its separate elements. Or it can be a decisively negative and disintegrating influence. The history of man could be written on the basis of the effects of changes and developments of his religious beliefs, doctrines and practices. Virtually continuous wars, crusades and civil strife have been waged as the outcome of man's desire for uniformity in religious matters, and his inability to accept the possibility of different ways to God. He has so often reduced the mystery of religion to an argument about a Greek iota, a Hebrew tittle, or the precise location of Hell. And when he has felt sufficiently strongly about his principles he has nailed his 'theses' to doors, suffered cruel tortures, and even been burnt at the stake.

A primitive community is virtually unaware, and certainly uncritical, of its religion and culture. There are things that have always been done and always must be done; and the tribe or group is unconscious of the conditions, both geographical and social, that originally gave rise to their forms of behaviour. So much a part of their life have these forms of behaviour become that, even after conversion to some new faith, such as Christianity, they have sought to maintain their original ceremonies, or have incorporated them in some modified form in their new religion. Sadly, in some instances where there has been demand for them to reject completely the old paths, their society has become disintegrated because they are lost in the new culture. At the more secular level, one might draw a parallel with the more developed society, which is faced with sudden and rapid changes, through the introduction of new forms of technology. There may be a breakup of the old mores and standards of behaviour, and a change of attitude generally to the State or society which many may feel has betrayed them.

MAGIC

Some anthropologists have suggested that religion derives from magic, some that magic derives from religion, others that the two have developed together, and still others again that magic and religion are not directly related. Any cursory reading of the literature of the Hebrew Old Testament will reveal that magic and religion seem to have been contemporary phenomena, however related or unrelated. In her *Purity and Danger*[23], Mary Douglas remarks that

> a primitive world view looks out on a universe which is
> personal in several different senses. Physical forces are thought
> of as interwoven with the lives of persons. Things are not
> completely distinguished from persons, and persons are not

completely distinguished from their external environment. The universe responds to speech and mime. It discerns the social order and intervenes to uphold it.

This interweaving of the physical forces of the universe with the lives of individuals and society was referred to by Lévy-Bruhl[24] as a sort of *participation mystique*. And it was through this mystical participation with his surroundings that primitive man found the sanction for the social cohesion he deeply desired. Magic was related to man and to man's agency[25], and it had no transcendental reference to powers both supramundane and superior to man, and controlling the forces of nature. Magic was, so B Malinowski[26] insisted, an essentially human possession; it was a power enshrined in man himself, and it was transferred from one man to another 'according to very strict rules of magic filiation, initiation and instruction'. The real secrets of magic were, and still are, the specific spells, rites and mystical formulae that are calculated to bring about the desired effects. A 'magician' could use his powers for good or evil, to help or to harm others. In his work among the Azande, E E Evans-Pritchard[27] found that the evildoers were 'smelt out' by the medicine man by means of oracles and forms of divination. Moreover, in specific forms of sorcery he might use evil magic to harm others whom he disliked or who, in some way, opposed him.

Religion is clearly not the same as magic, although there are frequently those elements in religion, particularly within its ritual, which come close to magic as, for example, some forms of sacrifice. In his study of Nuer religion, Evans-Pritchard[28] emphasized that *sacrifice* had to be understood in terms of the relationship between man and something which lay outside the society itself. Sacrificial acts were not, according to him, a form of magic. When a man sacrificed to obtain rain it was not expected that the act would in itself magically produce a cloudburst. What was, in fact, implied by the *failure* of the rains was that the relationship between the people and their god(s) had been disturbed. This was manifested in the disruption of the natural order of man's relationship to man and to nature. The purpose of the sacrifice was to restore the lost mystical relationship; and the life of the animal was offered as a substitute for the group or the individual.

In practice, however, religion and magic tend to have a great deal in common. It has been said that religion is personal and supplicatory whilst magic is coercive. But the prayers of primitive man to his god are often coercive in expression, frequently in the form of a statement such as, 'Give me what I want or I will throw you to the dogs'. In his simplicity he feels that, if his gods will not grant his request, then he will outlaw them from his society, so that they no longer have any attachment to human beings. And if we examine closely the scriptures of the Old Testament, we shall find many examples of actions which are 'magical' in operation, however much they may be linked with the powerful figure of the God, Yahweh. Moses' use of a rod to divide waters, or to produce water from a rock, and his employment of homeopathic magic when he erected a brazen serpent in the wilderness in order to cure those suffering from snake bites, are but examples of the way in which 'magic' was employed amongst the ancient Israelites within the context of their religion. Such magic was generally concerned with preservation, food and water supply, as well as healing.

In a similar way, the aboriginal tribes of Australia[29] perform rituals to produce a plentiful supply of witchetty grubs; whilst the main ritual of the *intichiuma* ceremony is a food-producing one. Nevertheless, their ceremonies are not mere magic divorced from a religious belief. Their supreme gods may have different names, and may require differing rituals – whether it be Daramulun of the S E Australian tribe of the Yuin; or Twanyirika of the Arunta; or Nambakulla of the Central Australian tribes – but they are all associated in some way with man's needs for fertility and sustenance. E O James[30] notes that

> as far back as the archaeological evidence takes us, magic and religion appear to have been very closely related, and there is nothing to suggest that originally one discipline had priority over the other either in time or in importance.

The aboriginal Arunta word *churinga*[31] is a term applied to all sacred stones or sticks and to certain objects associated with the totems, such as bull-roarers. The bull-roarers are endowed with *arungquiltha*, or mana, which emanates from the Supreme Being or High God with whom it is associated. The Arunta have a sacred pole, or *nurtunga*, upon which are hung all the important *churinga*. In this way the whole group maintain their identity with one another, with their ancestors, and with the tribal All-Fathers. All their power, all their souls, may reside in the *churinga*. In the rites of the Arunta, called the *kauaua*, the sacred pole is completely smeared with human blood, and then ornamented with various *churinga*, such as eagle-hawk feathers, head-bands, nose-bones and tail-tips. Throughout all their ceremonies and initiation rites, it is felt that their High God is always there in the background, and the roaring and whistling noises produced by the frightening bull-roarers are none other than the voice of their God himself.

The life, history and religion of the Nuer people, a Nilotic group in East Africa, have been documented by Evans-Pritchard and others[32]. Among such people, God is regarded as a being of *pure spirit* and, like the air, he pervades everything, creating and sustaining all things. He is both transcendent and immanent; though invisible himself, he can see and hear all things. He is angry with those who deliberately do wrong, and he punishes them. Suffering is his will, and it must be accepted without complaint and with complete resignation. But he is also a merciful God; and if the evildoer is contrite, will pray to his God for mercy, and offer the appropriate sacrifices, God will forgive him and halt the consequences of his wrongdoing. In the words of Evans-Pritchard[33]:

> They may say of rain or lightning or pestilence '*e kwoth*', 'it is God', and in storm they pray to God to come to earth gently and not in fury – to come gently, it will be noted, not to make the rain come gently.... Rain and pestilence come from God and are therefore manifestations of him, and in this sense rain and pestilence are God, in the sense that he reveals himself in their falling.

This is a sort of panontism in which God is not simply the author of all things, he is the very *beingness* of all things, the very media through which he expresses himself to mankind at large. There is also here a marriage of magic and religion; to affect the elements or sickness or pestilence, one must in some way affect their inner beingness, which is God himself.

SECTION TWO:
RELIGIONS OF THE WORLD

5   Zoroastrianism

1   Ancient Iranian Religion

The very word 'Iran', the name of Persia, has the same origin as the word 'Aryan' and behind the ancient religion of Persia is much of the religion of the Indian *Rig Veda*, with its gods and demons. There are close parallels in the words used in the two religions; thus the *Rig Veda*'s deva, soma, Mitra, Yama and Vayu have become the Iranian daeva, haoma, Mithra, Yima and Vata. Much of the early Iranian religion was animistic, and nature was worshipped; the earth, water and fire were held sacred, and there was considerable development of fertility cult and ancestor worship. Remains of some totemism were there in which, in particular, the cow and the dog were regarded as tabu and were worshipped; it was, in fact, a capital crime to kill them. Because of the sacred nature of the earth, the dead could not be buried; nor could they be burnt, and so they were exposed in trees or upon slabs of stone. Coupled with the animistic forms of belief and worship there existed a polytheism, much of which derived as already suggested from the Aryan cult. One of the early members of the Iranian pantheon was the sun-god of continuing importance, namely Mithra (Mithras), who was the equivalent of the Egyptian Amun (Amen) and Aton, and the Babylonian Shamash. Mithra has always figured somewhere in Zoroastrian beliefs.

2   Zoroaster (Zarathushtra)

As with most religious leaders of the past, the very existence of Zarathushtra (Greek 'Zoroastres') has been questioned; and a great variety of dates has been given, by those who accept his historicity, for the period in which he flourished. It seems most likely that he was born not earlier than 650 BC, and R C Zaehner has offered the dates 628 BC to 551 BC as those having the greatest probability for the span of Zarathushtra's life. His early life is recounted with what must clearly be a considerable amount of legend, including birth stories which are variants of the virgin theme. His birth, so it is said, was attended by seven midwives, and as he entered the world he laughed outright. His own village was filled with a supernatural light and with fire; moreover, the immediate dangers that seem to have attended all such unusual births attended his, and demons sought by every means possible to destroy him forthwith. This demon attack continued throughout much of his life, but guardian spirits were always present to help him and to rescue him. As a very young child he had visions, in one of which he saw very clearly good people ascending into heaven and evil people going down into hell. This was accompanied by a strong sense of mission and an awareness of a new gospel which had to be promulgated throughout the earth.

At about the age of thirty he received his call, in dreams by night, to become a prophet. In one such dream he felt that he was meeting God face-to-face, and that he underwent a spiritual test conducted by one of God's great spirits, Vohu Manah. On being questioned about righteousness and truth, Zarathushtra replied that there were three perfections: the first was good thoughts, the second was good works, and the third was good words. His answers were apparently satisfactory, and he went off into the wilderness to live the life of an ascetic and recluse, meditating and fasting.

The general pattern of the great religious leader or prophet is again pursued in the realm of temptation. A female daeva, Spendarmad, appeared before him and tempted him with her charm, her companionship, her conversation and her cooperation. Zarathushtra, however, was not to be attracted by her beautiful frontal appearance, and he demanded to see her back view, which was hideous and loathsome. A further temptation was to reject the righteousness and perfection that he had already perceived in his dreams, to abandon the Good Law, and to receive instead worldly power. Zarathushtra rejected this final temptation. For the rest of his life he was subjected to poverty and a great deal of persecution. Throughout it all, however, he felt certain that God would vindicate him in the next life. So he continued to walk around the country teaching his doctrines to all who were interested. His death remains as much a mystery as his life; one account suggests that he was murdered by hostile priests when he was praying near an altar fire. Another, perhaps less reliable account, holds that a flash of lightning enveloped him and he was borne up to heaven.

3   The Teaching of Zoroaster

Zarathushtra set out largely to reform religion as it already existed in Iran. It was one of his aims to eradicate the grosser elements that seemed to dominate animism and the fertility cults, and to give some sort of order and organization to the current polytheism. He established a firm dualism between God and the Devil, between Good and Evil. God was Ahura Mazda (Ormuzd), the Lord of Light or Wise Lord.

He was God of wisdom, holiness, purity and righteousness, the first and the last, and as he unfolded his power so the world was filled with his goodness. Ahura Mazda was an entirely moral being, and through personal contact with him men received Right Thought. In this respect Zoroastrianism was very much a psychological religion, seeking to change the direction of man's thinking from evil to good. God was the Creator of all, and he regulated the course of nature. Thus, Zarathushtra was not propounding a dualism between God and Matter – rather Matter itself was being protected by God from the Devil, and from the attacks of his evil spirits. Ahura Mazda was supported by six holy angels or Amesha Spentas, namely:

Asha Vahista:	Right Knowledge, Truth, Righteousness, Supreme Virtue
Vohu Manah:	Right Thought, Wisdom
Khshathra Vairya:	Right Kingdom, Order, Dominion
Armaiti:	Right Religion, Piety
Haurvatat:	Right Health, Well-Being, Prosperity
Ameretat:	Immortality

These Amesha Spentas were projections of the characteristics of God. In addition, Sraosha (Obedience) was guardian angel of the world, and with Mithra (Truth) and Rashnu (Justice) he would be one of the judges in the next world.

Coexistent with Ahura Mazda, as a sort of dark twin, was the Devil or Evil Spirit known as Angra Mainyu (or Ahriman). He was the enemy of God from the beginning, being the Lord of Darkness, and preferring impurity and death to perfection and life. His great aim was to defraud mankind of a happy and pure life, and in this purpose he was supported by his daevas. The chief of these daevas was the Druj or the Lie, who perpetually sought to deceive mankind. Sometimes Angra Mainyu appears to have been identified with the Druj, perhaps in very much the same way as the Amesha Spentas were regarded as projections of God. Ahura Mazda and Angra Mainyu are specifically referred to as 'twins' in certain passages of the Zoroastrian scriptures, as for example:

> The two primeval spirits who revealed themselves in vision as twins, are the Better and the Bad in thought and word and action. And between these two the wise ones chose aright, the foolish not so[1].

According to Zoroastrian belief, this world was connected to the next by a bridge called *Chinvat*, that is, a bridge of Separation. This implied, simply, that after death there was a process of selection or separation as the souls of the good and those of the evil passed over the bridge. There was a sort of divine calculus at work whereby the evil and the good performed by the individual were measured against each other. To those who had an excess of good the bridge appeared broad and easy to cross. Attacks by the daevas were warded off and the good were assisted across to heaven by the six Amesha Spentas. To those with an excess of evil, the bridge was like a razor-edge, and they were assisted over that edge by daevas and so fell into Hell, which was filled with boiling lead and a variety of tortures. Heaven, on the other hand, was a place of beautiful thoughts and beautiful people. If an individual survived the divine calculus with an exact balance between good and evil, he went to a place between the earth and the stars, a sort of limbo or possibly purgatory. Here he or she could purge their sins before going to heaven. In the process of 'weighing the soul' to discover the extent of its goodness or evil, morality in terms of thoughts, words and deeds was of paramount importance. In some of the Zoroastrian mythology, Mithra was the guardian of the bridge and the final arbiter of the destiny of the soul. But there is a very real sense in which man was regarded as working out his own salvation – he personally was responsible for the way he lived and behaved, and in the end he really decided upon his own destiny.

Death was obviously a period of great danger when the daevas would do their utmost to gain possession of a soul. It was very important, therefore, to ensure that all the necessary rituals were performed, from washings to prayers and exorcisms. A sacred liquid, haoma, was poured into the mouth and ears of the dead person. Haoma was regarded, in the old Iranian religion, as the blood of the bull-deity, and it conferred immortality upon the drinker. In the preparation of the dead soul to walk the bridge of Chinvat, this liquid was regarded as a sort of protection on the path to immortality. The room in which the dead person lay was thoroughly disinfected, and a fire and incense were kept burning. Because the earth was sacred, and fire equally so, no body could be buried in the earth or cremated. In a large Zoroastrian community, therefore, a *dakhma* or tower of silence would be erected in an unclean place far from the town. This was a stone structure about twelve feet in height, hollowed out in the centre. Bodies were placed inside it and vultures would pick off the flesh, leaving only the skeletal bones. Eventually these would be pushed through a grating in the centre of the floor of the structure. After a person's death, there would be mourning for three days during which time prayers would be said and sacrifices would be made to ensure the safe passage of the soul across Chinvat on the fourth day. If these proved successful, the good man would eventually be led through the three courts of Good Thoughts, Good Words and Good Works into Everlasting Light.

Over the years Zoroastrianism developed an eschatology, or doctrine of last things. There has always been a strong feeling in most religions that Good must triumph in the end, followed by a wonderful Golden Age of purity, peace and love. One of the grave dilemmas of Zoroastrianism has been the apparent equal balance between Good and Evil in the eternal twins, Ahura Mazda and Angra Mainyu. Certain Magi suggested that these two forces were, in fact, simply emanations of a primeval principle of space-time, called Zurvan[2]. The principle of Zurvan would ultimately resolve the tension of Good and Evil (or Better and Bad) expressed in the twin forces and Good, Right and Justice would finally prevail. This would be brought about by three *saoshyants*, or saviours, who would each appear after an interval of a thousand years. The third *saoshyant* would be born supernaturally – once more of a virgin – and he would usher in the age of the Reign or Kingdom of Righteousness. This would, in fact, be the Kingdom of Ahura Mazda, whilst Angra Mainyu and his followers would in some way be eternally burked, if not destroyed. The material world would itself become immortal, and the *fravashis*, or guardian spirits, of the dead would protect all men and all things.

The concept of Zurvan certainly helped to preserve the unity of the godhead, and disposed of some embarrassing questions concerning the origin of the twin spirits of Good and Evil. But in the long run the teaching was suppressed as heresy, for in a sense it made Ahura Mazda's victory a rather hollow one. It was one thing to provide a *deus ex machina* to resolve man's insoluble problem; it was quite another thing to provide one to solve the problem of God, Ahura Mazda, himself.

4 The Subsequent History of Zoroastrianism

Zoroastrianism was for a long time the official religion of Persia, from 521 BC on the accession of Darius I. Eventually, however, the Muslims destroyed the Persian kingdom in AD 642, and they somewhat forcibly converted the majority to Islam, and persecuted those who were loyal to their religious faith. Many of the latter decided to emigrate to Western India in order to pursue their beliefs and forms of worship without opposition, and they settled mainly in the area of Bombay (Mumbai). Today there are only a very small remnant (possibly some 10,000) of Zoroastrians left in Iran, and they are usually referred to as Gabars, or infidels. They live apart from the rest of their society and are mainly agriculturalists and traders. Those who settled in India are called Parsis (Parsees), that is, 'the people of Pars' (ie Persia). Others have, over the years, moved from India in order to develop commerce and trade in East Africa.

Wherever they have gone the Parsis have built for their worship fire-temples, which they refer to as the 'doors of Mithra', that is, the doors which lead to truth and, with it, obedience and justice. They do not allow any outsiders to enter these holy places, for the fire which burns eternally within them must be kept free from any contamination. The temples themselves are decorated with stone, and fire is the chief feature in them. This is always kept burning in the inner sanctuary, and the priests are responsible for ensuring that it never goes out. Worshippers bring sandalwood daily to the temple, and this the priest uses for fire and applies some of the sacred ash upon the foreheads of the worshippers. There are no images in the sanctuary and there is no form of animal sacrifice, which is regarded as quite unnecessary. Worshippers visit the temple weekly, and some of the more devout even daily. They remove their shoes before entering, present their sandalwood offerings to the priest and then recite prayers, which are couched in the ancient ritual language. The priests wear white robes, and they normally cover their mouths with white masks in order not to defile the fire.

The religion of the Parsis is not a missionary one, so that they have to maintain their numbers (possibly in the region of 270,000) through procreation alone. Their view is that each person should pursue the religion of the country in which they were born. Their priests (*mobeds*) are hereditary, and Zarathushtra – referred to as Zartusht – is regarded as a divine saviour or *saoshyant*, very much akin to the Hindu concept of the *avatara*.

At the age of seven, the child of the Parsi family receives the sacred cord and shirt, which together symbolize initiation (*naojate*) into the total Parsi religious community. Such an initiate is pledged to pursue and inculcate all good thoughts, good words and good actions. He or she may now become fully involved in the fire rituals of the temple. Each day prayers are said in the home, every morning and evening and on certain special occasions. Each day the Parsi pledges his allegiance anew to the religion of Zartusht which is regarded as the greatest and the best of all the religions that have flourished in the past and which are likely to flourish in the future.

The dead of the Parsis are exposed on the dakhmas as previously mentioned in section 3. In some of the smaller Parsi communities, however, this method would be inconvenient so that stone chambers or lead coffins are used instead. In this way the earth does not suffer defilement, and the bodies are not left exposed. Usually a furrow is made in the ground around the burial place in order to ward off evil spirits. Once a year, sometime before the celebration of New Year's Day, a feast of the dead is held in honour of Favardin, who is the divine being presiding over the fravashis or spirits of the ancestors of the Parsis. The fravashis, who return in a guardian role, are given a welcome in front of the dakhmas. The most important celebration of the year, however, is that of New Year's Day when everyone bathes meticulously, puts on new clothes, and goes to the temple to burn sandalwood, to give alms to the poor, and to exchange greetings.

In Bombay (Mumbai), a regular feature of worship occurs at

sunset when Parsis gather in their numbers by the beach. They then dip their fingers in the waters of the ocean and, anointing their forehead and their eyes, they raise their hands in prayer to Ahura Mazda. This is done in the presence of the setting sun which is to them a symbol of the 'righteous, shining and undefiled spirit of the waters' that must never be defiled by their activities.

Parsi communities are successful and very well-organized; they are prosperous, even wealthy, active and westernized. Whilst it is true that the older and more conservative Parsis wear traditional dress (robes and hard hats), most of them today don European or modern Indian dress. Parsi women are held to be amongst the most emancipated in the world, and Parsis generally are prominent in all forms of social and educational work. There is, in their teaching, considerable emphasis upon ethical monotheism both in theory and in the practice of the 'Good Life'.

5   The Sacred Literature

Zarathushtra held that Ahura Mazda presented the holy scriptures to him when he met God face-to-face in his dreams. The main scriptures are *the Avesta*, which is basically a collection of fragments, including stories, hymns and prayers, but without any really continuous theme. Included in the *Avesta* are the *Yashts* which provide specific regulations for ritual and practical life, and some hymns to accompany certain sacrifices. Also added as a part of the *Avesta* are the *Gathas* (cf the Aryan *Gita*), which are a collection of moral and metaphysical odes or songs. In the *Gathas*, Zarathushtra rejects all other gods, who become daevas, and he holds to Ahura Mazda alone. Finally, the *Zend Avesta* is a commentary upon the *Avesta*.

6   Hinduism

1   The Historical Background

India is made up of a great diversity of peoples, with a considerable variety of races and ethnic stocks. These have gradually been welded into a major society, possessing a basic cultural unity through the religion of Hinduism. The aboriginal inhabitants of India appear to have been negroid types of small stature referred to as Negritos. Aborigines of a similar type are still to be found in the Rajmahal Hills of Bihar as well as in the East Indian islands of the Andaman group, in Malaysia and in SE Asia generally. The Negritos were followed by the Australoid peoples, who are to be found among the tribal populations of central and southern India, among the lower or 'exterior' castes generally, and among the Veddas of Ceylon. The next to arrive were the Mongoloids, represented by many of the tribal peoples of the North who inhabit a broad expanse of Himalayan country from Kashmir in the North West to Bhutan in the East. The Caucasoids followed the Mongoloids and were of the Mediterranean sub-type, dark in complexion, of slight build, moderate in stature, and dolichocephalic or long-headed. This type is dominant in northern India and among the upper classes generally. Finally, about 1500 BC an Aryan group of pastoralists entered northern India from the northern plateau of Iran; they were tall, fair Caucasoids referred to as Proto-

Nordics, and they are now found mainly between the Indus and the area in the north of Madhya Pradesh known as Bundelkhand.

Excavations by Sir John Marshall in the 1920s revealed a pre-Aryan civilization in the Indus Valley at the two cities of Harappa and Mohenjodaro (the Mound of the Dead), in the North West of India. This culture dates from circa 3000 BC, and it continued to flourish until circa 2000 BC, when it began to wane. In fact, when the Proto-Nordics entered India, this ancient Indus civilization had already decayed and disintegrated. The Harappan culture was essentially an urban one, with something like forty sites scattered over the Indus plains. According to O H K Spate[1], the general impression provided by the remains is that of 'a utilitarian business culture', whilst the high standard of drainage appears to have been one of its most striking features. Professor E O James[2] has suggested that, although the cities were well-planned, the bare, red-bricked, two-roomed cottages were 'devoid of any semblance of ornament', and bore every indication of a 'utility' motive. Professor Stuart Piggott[3] has compared them to 'contemporary coolie-lines'. It seems clear, however, that this utilitarian culture had accomplished a great deal in the way of irrigation farming; that barley, wheat and the date palm were cultivated; that craftsmen were involved in the working of gold, silver and bronze; that cotton was manufactured; and that the inhabitants excelled in the domestication of animals such as the dog, sheep, pig, buffalo, elephant, hen, bull and camel. There was also a flourishing trade between the Indus civilization and the people inhabiting the areas around Mesopotamia and the Persian Gulf. The many clay seals, usually small, flat and rectangular with pictorial motifs, may well have been tokens used by the merchants of the Harappan culture.

It is now considered mistaken to suggest, as some scholars did in the past, that the invading Indo-Aryans or Proto-Nordics were responsible in any way for destroying a superior civilization. The 'bourgeois mediocrity' of Harappa, to use Piggott's phrase, was already over; the light-skinned, cattle-breeding *aryas*, or noble ones, began to settle in small forest clearings where they established villages and gradually developed agriculture. They were essentially a simple society based upon a family unit, and wherever they went they developed the village type of life. Although they increasingly expanded their interest in agriculture, they still reared cattle, and the cow was regarded as a measure of value and of wealth, and so became a valuable commodity. Gradually they subdued the indigenous peoples of North India, the cattle-thieves called Panis, and the land-workers called Dasas. The latter, in particular, were despised because of their darker colour and their somewhat flat features, compared with the Aryan clear-cut features and fair skins. Eventually the Dasas found themselves enslaved by the Aryans, and the very word *dasas* was used as an expression of contempt for those belonging to a lower and menial element in society.

2   The Caste System

The story of the gradual evolution of the caste system over a period of a millennium cannot be fully entered into here. When, however, the Aryans first came into India it would seem that they themselves were divided into three social groups. There were their warrior-leaders and rajahs who represented the aristocracy; then there was a group whose purpose it was to ensure the fertility of families, herds and flocks, namely, the priests; and finally there were the herdsmen and general workers, or commoners. This social division was also an economic one, and the power of the aristocracy derived from their wealth and their control of the weapons of war. Generally speaking, when the Aryans conquered the indigenous peoples of India, they themselves assumed the status of the three upper castes, whilst the non-Aryans became the fourth caste. It is significant that the Sanskrit word used for caste (ie *varna*) literally means 'colour'; and the dark *dasas* became the lowest caste within the hierarchy.

There were obviously many sustained struggles for power, particularly between the aristocracy and the priests; and there were long periods when first one, and then the other, appears to have been in the ascendancy. Eventually the priests won the day because they had the power of passing on divinity to the kings and rulers, or of withholding it. Thus, the three upper castes were established in the main from Aryan stock. They were the *brahmins* (*brahmanas*) or priestly caste; the *kshatriyas* or warriors; and the *vaishyas* or agriculturalists. The conquered *dasas* formed the lowest caste and were the labourers, the herdsmen, the serfs and slaves, and were called *shudras*, and their function was to be subservient to the three upper castes.

These four broad divisions, however, do not by any means constitute the total complexity of the caste system. Taya Zinkin[4] states that there are over two thousand *jatis* or sub-castes among the brahmins alone, so that altogether there are literally thousands of sub-castes and kin-groups. The ramifications of caste structure are so many and complicated that the most that can be done here is to make one or two generalizations about it.

According to orthodox Hinduism, inter-caste marriage was strictly prohibited; in fact, a caste has been defined as

> a group of families whose members can marry with each other and can eat in each other's company without believing themselves polluted.[5]

But despite this, one form of inter-caste marriage seems to have been permitted, namely, that form which is termed *anuloma* marriage in which the bridegroom is of a higher caste than that of his bride. Children born of such a marriage have usually belonged to their father's caste. Today, however, marriage customs vary with caste and sub-caste, and the orthodox ideals of non-intermixture of caste are rapidly becoming modified. It is also true, as Zinkin[6] emphasizes, that colour does not decide caste, nor is it any longer of much help in discriminating one caste from another:

> A Brahmin is no less a Brahmin if he is born jet-black; an Untouchable is no whit less untouchable if she happens to be fair.

This brings us to the whole question of 'untouchability'. One group remains permanently outside the caste system and is referred to as 'outcastes', and they number approximately ten percent of the Indian population. Formerly known as 'untouchables' or pariahs (*paryas*), these people were not only without a caste, they were also social outcasts without opportunities of labour or of contact with members of the caste system. Their chief occupation was that of begging and ensuring that they 'did not pollute their benefactors by personal contact'. K M Sen maintains that there is no certainty about the idea of the origination of untouchability; and although the scriptural support for it is indeed slender it does not seem to be of recent origin. Sen[7] states that

> Quite conceivably, some form of untouchability might have
> existed in pre-Aryan India. It is perhaps of some significance
> to note that untouchability is strongest in South India and
> that it applies not merely to low castes vis-à-vis higher ones, but
> sometimes even between low castes.

Thus, virtually every group, caste or *jati* appears to be in a state of 'untouchability' in relation to another group, caste or *jati*.

Mahatma Gandhi continually worked very hard on behalf of the untouchables during his lifetime, and he refused to accept that any sort of contact with them incurred ritual pollution. We are told that his wife had considerable problems with drinking vessels and toilet facilities in her menage because her Gandhiji would invite into their home, and at the same time, people who in normal Hindu society would have avoided one another because of the danger of pollution. These would include, of course, not merely untouchables but also members of different *jatis*, or sub-castes, of the same main groupings who had specific avoidance laws or dietary tabus. Outcastes were first referred to as *harijans* by Gandhi – that is, they were 'children of God'- and this name has remained with them. Today, there exist laws against the deliberate practice of untouchability; but one cannot, by legislation, change overnight the habits and customs of three or four millennia.

There is, of course, a strong link between the historical and social fact of the caste system and the traditional religious beliefs of the Hindus. Myth and historical reality are inevitably mingled in religious faith, creed and dogma, and this is clearly so in respect of caste. A hymn in one of the oldest of the Hindu scriptures, the *Rig-Veda*, poses both questions and answers:

> When the gods made a sacrifice with the Man as their victim....
> When they divided the Man, into how many parts did they
>   divide him?
> What was his mouth, what were his arms, what were his thighs
>   and his feet called?
> The brahmin was his mouth, of his arms were made the
>   warrior.
> The thighs became the vaishya, of his feet the shudra was born.[8]

This hymn, composed probably a millennium before Christ, provides a presumption concerning the position and role of each of the castes. The brahmins were intended to become priests or the mouthpieces of the gods; the kshatriyas were to become the warriors, using their arms to promote the will of their gods and to increase their territory; the vaishyas would bear the weight and burden of the work to provide both the gods and their highest servants with sustenance. The shudras would perform the laborious work of fetching and carrying under the direction and control of the vaishyas.

This mythical view, however, has never remained unchallenged even within Hindu religious literature. Thus, for example, one of the Puranas[9] argues that

> since members of all the four castes are children of God, they
> all belong to the same caste. All human beings have the same
> Father, and children of the same Father cannot have different
> castes.

Such an argument is difficult to combat even for a Hindu; but the fact is that he is faced with a *fait accompli* in the established and formalized caste system itself. It is a system which has operated socially as well as religiously for several thousands of years. A myth which provides a rationalization of what actually exists is likely to be preferred to a philosophy of what might or ought to be, however noble and altruistic. It is true that the average Hindu really believes that his religion demands the observance of caste, and that many of the evils of his world have arisen as a result of the pollution caused by caste intermixture. Even in the *Bhagavad-Gita*, 'The Song of God', there is an explicit acceptance of caste and all that caste implies, as for example when Arjuna says to Krishna:

> We know not what fate falls
> On families broken
> The rites forgotten,
> Vice rots the remnant
> Defiling the woman,
> And from their corruption
> Comes mixing of castes:
> The curse of confusion
> Degrades the victims
> And damns the destroyers.[10]

But, implicitly, there is also an acceptance throughout, in the words of the Lord Krishna, that caste like war is really incidental to life in the body; the only true reality is the indwelling Godhead, the *atman*, which ultimately is the same for all men. In other words, caste itself is unimportant in absolute terms, viewed *sub specie aeternitatis*, provided one understands the nature of It, the *atman*, in all Its wonder.

3 Sacred Scriptures

(a) Vedas
Among the earliest of human documents, whether religious or

secular, are the *Vedas*. *Veda* is a Sanskrit word meaning 'knowledge', and there are four books of knowledge – Rig, Sama, Yajur and Atharva. We shall here concern ourselves only with the *Rig-Veda* which is the Hymn Veda containing over a thousand hymns arranged in ten books. Like most hymn and song collections, the *Rig-Veda* was undoubtedly in the form of oral tradition for many years and possibly centuries, and was eventually written down probably at about the same time as the oldest books of the Hebrew Old Testament.

In the *Rig-Veda* many gods are referred to, the most exalted of whom was Varuna, the great sky-god, who was responsible for giving moral laws to men and for hearing their most urgent prayers. Among the many other gods in this polytheistic scheme was the great Indra, controller of cosmic law, a hard-drinking warrior and storm-god who staggered across the heavens at times, regurgitating over the earth, thus producing rain and fertility to the soil. Agni was lord of the ritual order and the sacrificial fire, without whose presence no sacrifice was valid or acceptable. Soma, the god of immortality, was associated with the sacred drink and food of the gods – *soma* – which the priests drank in order to induce an hypnotic state wherein the god took possession of them and gave them revelations. Yama was the god of death and was naturally invoked at funerals and cremations. Originally one of the minor gods was Vishnu, who later became one of the greatest of all the Hindu deities. Behind all the gods of the Vedas was the changeless cosmic order referred to as *Rta* which, being impersonal, was under the personal guardianship of Varuna. Thus the Vedas present a moral universe always sustained by the gods and the ritual systems which they in turn have given to man. But there does arise the question as to whether the *Rig-Veda* is really and basically polytheistic. For example, *Rig-Veda* I. 164, 46 states that 'The real is one, though wise men give it various names.' This verse, though regarded by many scholars as of late origin, suggests that the Hindus possibly in Vedic times saw their God as ultimately One, just as the *Bhagavad-Gita* (Chapter IX) much later says, 'Some bow to the countless gods that are only my million faces'. More certainly the Vedas eventually give rise to philosophical speculations such as, for example, those expressed in the 'Song of Creation' (*Rig-Veda*, X. 129):

> Who verily knows and who can here declare it, when it was
>   born and whence comes this creation?
> The gods are later than this world's production,
>   who knows, then, whence it first came into being?
> He, the first origin of this creation,
>   whether he formed it all or did not form it.
> Whose eye controls this world in highest heaven,
>   he verily knows it, or perhaps he knows it not.

This is moving towards the concept of the One Being in the *Upanishads*, the 'One without a second', Brahman; and although it still lacks any real certainty, it is clearly asking the questions.

(b) Upanishads

Between about 800 BC and 600 BC the *Upanishads*, which are a collection of thoughtful speculations, were compiled by hermits. The word *Upanishad* itself means 'sitting down near', and it really connotes the lessons learned by sitting down at the feet of a guru. These writings number over one hundred, possibly more than two hundred since some are still being discovered, but only a dozen or so are really considered important[11]. They seek to establish a way of knowledge, mainly through meditation which leads eventually to complete identity with the Ultimate Reality. This ultimate form of existence is referred to as Brahman, which includes all previously worshipped gods as well as man himself.

Brahman is identified with the supernatural power which is operative in the spoken words of the Vedas, and in the cosmic activity of *Rta*. The gods, or representations of Brahman, all reduce to this one Being, the Mind which exists behind all creation, for 'In the beginning the world was just Being, one only, without a second'[12]. Brahman is a neutral power, spirit or force, and is the sustenance of all. He is at the same time indescribable and immaterial; he is not this, nor is he that (*neti*, neti), for all things are but the effects of Brahman's self-consciousness – 'In the beginning this was Brahman. It knew itself.' Man must not be waylaid by the vagaries and the fleeting phenomena of life, but he must seek That which is behind and beyond all appearances.

> Lead me from the unreal to the real,
> Lead me from darkness to light,
> Lead me from death to immortality.[13]

Brahman is without a second. This is the philosophy of non-duality or *advaita* and, in consequence, to know peace, to know Brahman, one must eradicate all sense of separation. The individual soul is the atman; and as the *Chandogya Upanishad* emphasizes there is nothing outside Brahman, so that when the atman is ultimately identified with Brahman there ceases to be separation or separate existence. The atman then becomes what, in fact, it already is – one with the essence of the universe; and *tat tvam asi*, 'That thou art'.

> He is the innermost Self. He is the great Lord. He it is that
> reveals the purity within the heart by means of which he, who
> is pure being, may be reached. He is the ruler. He is the great
> Light, shining forever.[14]

The individual soul, Self or atman, eventually will realize its identity with all the gods and with the unqualified and unqualifiable Absolute, Brahman[15]; and it is henceforth free from the destructive and frustrating forces of life – it has *moksha* or liberation. This liberation is release from the round of rebirths, from *samsara*. It is a state whereby, following the realization that the individual is one with Brahman, the influence of karma is transcended and there is no more rebirth. All of this represents a concept of the universe which is entirely spiritual: Brahman, or God, pervades everything and everybody. We make a gauche attempt to characterize and categorize religious concepts and ideas by such terms as polytheism, monism, pantheism and so forth, but Hinduism refuses to be so pigeon-holed. There are within it aspects of every stage and every category, but the essence of Hinduism transcends all our attempts at description, just as Brahman does.

(c) Ramayana

The *Ramayana*[16] is a Hindu epic collected sometime between 200 BC and AD 200, and it was composed originally by the poet Valmiki in 24,000 couplets. Rama was an *avatara,* a descent or incarnation of the god Vishnu, and therefore divine; and the *Ramayana* is an account of the way in which Rama was cheated of his inheritance and went into exile with his wife Sita. They lived in the forest but Sita was eventually stolen by the demon-king of Ceylon, called Ravana. Rama finally, with the help of his brother and the monkey-god, Hanuman, crossed from Southern India into Ceylon, where together they defeated Ravana, and brought Sita back home to India by means of a *vimana* or 'aerial car'. Rama, now fully exonerated and justified, had his throne restored to him.

(d) Mahabharata

The great Bharata epic, or the *Mahabharata*, is an account in over 100,000 couplets in Sanskrit of the struggle of the Bharatas, a group of tribes in Northern India; and India itself was later known as Bharata. The book is a compilation of a considerable amount of material gathered over a long period of time, including the stories and legends about various heroes, and myths concerning the gods. The most interesting and important part of the book concerns a discussion between the god Krishna and a kshatriya called Arjuna, which we shall consider separately. Krishna himself was born in Mathura in North India. He was probably an old culture deity of the Indus civilization, but in the *Mahabharata* he appears as an avatar of Vishnu whose purpose it is to rid the country of a demon. As a small child he delivered his parents from the tyrant, but as a boy and adolescent he was full of mischievous pranks, stealing butter, milking cows, upsetting milk pails, and becoming involved in endless sporting pranks with cow-girls. All this seems to emphasize his identity with man and his love of humanity. Eventually he was shot in the foot by an arrow of a careless hunter, and as a result he died, since this – as with so many mythical deities – was his one vulnerable spot. Krishna has often been referred to as the 'Christ of India', the incarnation or avatar who brought peace, love and grace to mankind, and who is perpetually recollected in the Hare Krishna chant.

(e) The Bhagavad-Gita and Yoga

The *Bhagavad-Gita*, or 'Song of the Lord', is the gospel of Krishna and the Hindu equivalent of the gospel story of the New Testament. Its date is generally placed somewhere between the fifth and the second centuries BC, and the 'Song' was probably not originally a part of the *Mahabharata*. The situation is described as one in which the hero, Arjuna, finds himself faced with the possibility of fighting friends and relations, on the battlefield, on the plain of Kurushetra, which was a sacred place of pilgrimage. Arjuna has a personal charioteer who turns out to be none other than Krishna himself. Arjuna is hesitating before engaging in battle and asks himself what is the use of killing or of victory? Should one fight one's own kinsmen, whatever the cause of their disagreement?

The *Gita* is a discussion between Arjuna and Krishna concerning these problems, and Krishna emphasizes the importance 'of performing caste duty – and that of the warrior princes or kshatriyas is clearly to engage in battle and to seek to destroy the enemy. Nevertheless, such duty must be performed without attachment to the results whether good or evil. All men should perform their role, their duty, their particular function, without fear of punishment and equally without any hope of reward. But, additionally, talk of death indicates a lack of understanding of the very nature of the atman; the soul cannot be destroyed for – like Brahman itself – it is immortal. Man's life on earth has really only one purpose, namely, to identify himself with this immortal Self, and so to come to a unitive knowledge of Brahman, the Divine Ground.

The *Gita* goes on to teach the various ways of life and conduct through different forms of yoga. The West has learned about yoga mainly through popular advertisements and demonstrations showing devotees in sometimes strange and awkward positions. But this particular form of yoga, known as *hatha yoga*, is merely one aspect which tends to emphasize control of the body by the mind. The word 'yoga' has the same origin as the English 'yoke' and the Latin *iugum;* it means a discipline, a way, a union. The man who pursues the way is a yogi, or one who has yoked himself and is pursuing a path of union. When Jesus said to his disciples, 'Take my yoke upon you and learn from me', he implied that knowledge of God demanded a certain discipline. In Hinduism, the guru yokes himself (metaphorically speaking) to the disciple. The discipline and the goal are one.

Interestingly enough, among the relics of the Harappa civilization, archaeologists have discovered sculptured figures in a variety of yogic *asanas*, or positions. And there is certainly a presumption among many writers on India and Hinduism, that at least the physical practice of yoga is of greater antiquity than the Aryan invasion. Although there are several distinct schools of yoga, with differing practices and techniques, the aim of yoga is one – to find union with Brahman. E W F Tomlin[17] states that

> When sometime between 300 and 150 BC, the sage Patanjali composed the *Yoga Sutras*, he was probably engaged in the codification of many ancient traditions. Men who devote a lifetime to the practice of ascetic meditation must evolve a great variety of techniques; but the comparative simplicity of Patanjali's rules must not blind us to the elaborate metaphysics upon which they are based. The practice, however scrupulous, of such rules of posture, breathing etc, by the enthusiastic Westerner can scarcely do harm; but abstract gymnastics are no substitute for the arduous consecration of a lifetime to reflection, *askesis*, and worship.

And this admirably sums up the whole business and difficulty of yoga. It is a way of life, it is the totality of living, it is the perpetual practice of the presence of Brahman. As in the Chinese religion of Taoism, the Tao is the Way, the goal and the way-goer, so in Hinduism yoga is the discipline, the end and the practice. The yogi is not an exhibitionist displaying to the world his conquest of space, time and consciousness, but one whose sole, all-consuming aim is to reach the state of *samadhi*, or union with Brahman. If his intensification of consciousness should result in what we are pleased to term 'supernormal' experience, or psi-phenomena, he will certainly not reject them; nor, on the other hand, will he seek to exploit them. Such phenomena are but extensions and diversifications of Brahman within Its creation and, in particular, within the atman. Patanjali[18] held that

> The student whose mind is steadied by meditation obtains mastery which extends from the atomic to the infinite.

The *Bhagavad-Gita* provides a synthesis of at least three forms of yoga: the path of knowledge, or *jnana*; the path of works, or *karma*; and the path of devotion, or *bhakti*. The way of the yogi is the way of knowledge of the Absolute Ground, of the Truth, of the Reality, of the Self. Knowledge of the Self is increased and developed by being yoked to a great Master – and for Arjuna the Master is Krishna. Self-knowledge is also assisted by meditation. Patanjali once described the mind as being somewhat akin to the activity of an inebriated monkey, suffering from some nervous disease (like St Vitus' dance), and stung into uncontrolled fury by a wasp. Patiently and gradually no matter where his restless and unquiet mind may wander, the individual must free himself from all mental distractions and fix his mind upon the atman; always, however much his thoughts may scatter, he must bring them back to this focal point[19].

Such a practice of meditation does not imply inaction, but only non-attachment to the results of action. The true yogi must be fully involved in life and its problems, since freedom from activity can never be achieved by abstention from action. Actions, however, must be disinterested and must be performed sacramentally[20]. This view is summed up in the statement of Krishna[21]:

Brahman is the ritual,
Brahman is the offering,
Brahman is he who offers
To the fire that is Brahman.
If a man sees Brahman
In every action,
He will find Brahman.

Such a union with God is both the end and the means; to reach Brahman one must be absorbed into Brahman; and this absorption is achieved by devotion (*bhakti*) to God, or to Krishna, his avatar, or indeed to any deity the devotee may choose to worship[22]. Men may bow to countless gods, but they are all only Brahman's million faces[23]. In all this, the *Bhagavad-Gita* emphasizes the vital importance of human relationships: one must be friendly and compassionate to all, and one should not hate any living creature. One should no longer think in terms of 'I' and 'mine' for these are delusions[24]; there is only Brahman. Pleasure and pain must be accepted with tranquillity and equal equanimity – for they cannot change or affect the essential and eternal Self. Only if the devotee will set his heart upon his Lord in this way, and will take him for his ideal above all others, will he come into the Being of God.

The *Gita* provides a message for every man in every age. In the words of the Lord Krishna[25]:

When goodness grows weak
When evil increases,
I make myself a body.
In every age I come back
To deliver the holy,
To destroy the sin of the sinner,
To establish righteousness.

Every age has its avatar of Brahman, its divine incarnation and saviour. This avatar is there to point the way to the Eternal Brahman, so that in loving him, and showing our devotion to him through the acceptance of all men equally, we may eventually find Brahman himself, for

> To love is to know me,
> My innermost nature,
> The truth that I am:
> Through this knowledge he enters
> At once to my Being[26].

But, says the *Gita*, the light which illumines every man that comes into the world is essentially and ultimately the light that is within himself. Thus, the *Gita* firmly asserts that the kingdom of heaven is within us. We must, therefore, look inward and find the truth in ourselves, in our innermost being.

> The Lord is everywhere
> And always perfect:
> What does he care for man's sin
> Or the righteousness of man?

> The Atman is the light:
> The light is covered by darkness:
> This darkness is delusion:
> That is why we dream.

> When the light of the Atman
> Drives out our darkness
> That light shines forth from us,
> A sun in splendour,
> The revealed Brahman[27].

4 The Nature of Brahman or God

In the beginning was Prajapati, or Brahman,
With whom was the word;
And the word was verily the Supreme Brahman[28].

Ultimately Brahman, the Absolute and Supreme Reality, can be expressed only by the sort of negation implicit in the word 'incomprehensible', used in the Athanasian Creed of the Christian Church. Brahman cannot be defined, It can be expressed only as *neti, neti* – It is not this, not that. One can exhaust the universe itself in seeking this identification of Brahman; and everywhere one goes one has to admit that Brahman is not this, Brahman is not that. But, like St Athanasius, the Hindu realizes that man cannot live long in the realm of the incomprehensible. St Athanasius went on to define the indefinable in some attempt to comprehend the incomprehensible and to give concretion to the purely abstract. One must, he said, worship God in Trinity, Unity in Trinity and Trinity in Unity – until gradually the hardened dogmas began to emerge and to end with 'life everlasting' or 'everlasting fire'.

Hinduism, too, has its unity and diversity, the One and the Many, and even a form of trinity. The reader will find that Hinduism, or Hinduism at varying stages of its development, has been placed into every conceivable category of religious belief: it is pantheism or monism[29]; it is monotheistic[30]; it has a kathenotheistic tendency at the Vedic stage[31]; it is a dualism and a polytheism[32]. It is, in fact, none of these but rather panontism[33] or panentheism. One cannot, without going into all the nuances and niceties of distinction between these terms, assign Hinduism here to any particular philosophical-cum-theological position. Nor, of course, is it very important, since there is room in it for almost every shade of belief. Its own 'honest to God' reformation led to an intellectualization of Brahman, the Impersonal, the Transcendent, the Infinite and the Absolute. At the same time, It was not 'out there', but 'in here', within every man at a deep spiritual level. At the somewhat warmer and personal, though still transcendent level, Hinduism produced Ishvara, an object of worship and love.

Brahman, as we have already seen, is 'not this' and 'not that' because Brahman is *advitiyam*, 'without a second'; Brahman is the sum-total of all that exists; Brahman is ALL-Being (hence the use of the term 'panontism'). Yet all things consist in Brahman (hence 'panentheism'), and are permeated by It. This is something that all great mystics and poets have understood for many centuries.

> With bliss ineffable
> I felt the sentiment of Being spread
> O'er all that moves and all that seemeth still.

This 'sentiment of Being' that Wordsworth experienced was similar to, if not the same as, the Hindu's experience of the all-pervasive Brahman. It was the same consciousness of 'the All', the totality of Being that moved the author of the third century Gospel of Thomas, discovered in 1945 at Nag Hammadi, to exclaim:

> I am the All;
>   (from me) the All has gone forth,
>   and to me the All has returned.
> Split wood: I am there.
> Lift the stone, and you will find me there[34].

Hinduism possesses some interesting psychological as well as spiritual insights. According to Carl Jung, the concept of the trinity or triad is an archetype existing preconsciously and forming a structural dominant of man's psyche in general; and he traces the existence of triads of gods at very primitive levels and in the religions of Babylonia, Egypt and Greece[35]. Ishvara, the personal god, became a triad of gods or Trimurti, each being a representation of a particular function of the Supreme God. The three-faced God incorporated Brahma the Creator, Vishnu the Preserver, and Shiva the Destroyer or Dissolver. Brahma was originally Prajapati, or God in creativity, who was responsible for the projection of the universe as an extension of himself. Vishnu's function was to preserve the world from evil and destruction, and to make personal intervention in the cosmic process. This he has done through a variety of avatars, such as fish, tortoise, boar, man-lion, dwarf, brahmin, Rama, Krishna, Buddha; and finally Kalki who is yet to come in order to restore the Golden Age. Shiva's function was closely associated with the destruction of evil so that the natural cycle of creation, preservation and re-creation might be maintained.

There is no precise equation between the Christian concept of the Trinity and the Hindu concept of the Trimurti; but there is an obvious similarity in the context of the role or function. Brahma is God the Father bodying forth creation; his popularity has declined over the years and very few temples have been built to celebrate his worship. Vishnu, for many Hindus the sole god, is God the Son and man's perpetual saviour. His worship is performed in temples dedicated to him by his followers, the *vaishnavas*. Shiva is God the Dissolver, that is, the spiritual element in the Trimurti which discerns good and evil and divides them asunder in order to destroy the evil; and his worship is supported by the *shaivas*. He is sometimes referred to as the dancing lord, Nata-raja, shaking the world with his activity. All this underlines a similarity of function between the Hindu Trimurti and the Christian Trinity, but it clearly must not be pressed too far in theological terms, even though it may provide some preliminary 'common ground' for discussion between Christians and Hindus.

But, like the Christian, the Hindu is not content to leave his God either at the impersonal level, which is also absolute, or at the personal level, which is also transcendent, nor yet at the level of mystical triunity. God must still, for him, find expression in human (and sometimes animal) form in incarnation. The avatars are regarded as mediators between God and man: saviours who reject the ultimate joy of union with Brahman in order to assist mankind to find the union for themselves. Apart from the 'descents' of Vishnu already referred to, including the Buddha, and in particular his form as Krishna in the *Bhagavad-Gita*, two of the most recent additions have been Mahatma Gandhi and Sri Aurobindo.

God, Brahman, is the Absolute and the undifferentiated; but within every man is the atman, the soul or inner Self. The atman is God immanent in each and every one, and this fact is expressed in the *Chandogya Upanishad*[36] in the statement 'tat tvam asi', 'Thou art That'. The Brahman and the atman are one and the same, and this doctrine provides for a non-duality (*advaita*) in the concept of God. Man does not stand over against Him, for when Brahman projected out of Himself the universe He entered into every being – indeed, into every single thing, and 'All that is has its Self in Him alone'[37]. The *Chandogya* goes on to identify Brahman with everything that exists – with earth, food, fire and sun. In fact, just as formerly it was said that Brahman was not this, not that (*neti, neti*), now it is equally affirmed that Brahman *is* this, He *is* that (*iti, iti*):

> He who glows in the depths of your eyes – that is Brahman,
> that is the Self of yourself. He is the Beautiful One, he
> is the Luminous One. In all the worlds, forever and ever, he
> shines[38].

Only when the individual has a realization of this ultimate inner identity between himself and God does he obtain release from the illusion (*maya*) of life. Then he reaches the stage of *moksha* or liberation from all illusions. This is a stage of passionless peace, the emancipation of Nirvana. Nirvana is not here seen as a place but rather as a different dimension or state of consciousness, as an awareness of union with God, who is finally seen and experienced as the only Reality. Brahman is described in one word as *Sacchidananda*, a word involving a triune concept of God as *sat* or Infinite Being and Goodness, as *chit* or Infinite Consciousness and Knowledge, and as *ananda* or Infinite Bliss and Happiness. To enter into His Being does not imply being snuffed out like a candle; it is to cease to operate as a small, infinitesimal, discrete and partial being and to extend one's consciousness and beingness to the infinite dimension of Brahman.

In the words of Krishna[39]:

> For I am Brahman
> Within this body,
> Life immortal
> That shall not perish:
> I am the Truth
> And the Joy for ever.

The whole essence of Brahman is summed up in this single stanza: immortal life, truth and everlasting joy.

5   Reincarnation and Salvation

> To be born here and to die here,
> To die here and to be born elsewhere,
> To be born there and to die there,
> This is the round of existence[40].

The caste system may be accepted at different levels and for different reasons by different Hindus; but the end-result is the same. There is a resignation to what is God-ordained, socially acceptable and sanctioned, or perhaps even adventitious. But this resignation results from an inner realization that this present life is but a brief incident and time-span within eternity. The fact that one is born into a particular caste, and that there is no possibility of advance up the caste scale in this present life, pales into insignificance when one realizes that there is a virtual inevitability about return after death. Such return and its nature are entirely contingent upon the sort of life one has lived here and now. This is the important thing in the philosophy of caste – not the fact that I may have been born as a humble *shudra*, but the fact that, if I want to return next time in a more favourable position in a higher caste, I must live as near a perfect life as possible in my present condition.

The philosophy of *samsara*, or reincarnation, is far-reaching and capable of an ever-developing sophistication. It is not to be confounded by mathematical arguments about increasing or decreasing population, or by the discovery of other planets and their possible habitation. The Hindu, at least the thinking Hindu, regards his present span of life as merely an episode in a long succession of lives, some already lived, some yet to come; some human and some possibly animal; some here on this earth, and some elsewhere on other planets or in other dimensions. The universe is his oyster. But he is also part and parcel of its physical, spiritual and moral causation – he cannot escape his total participation in all that happens throughout the universe.

The concept of *karma* (action, work) involves complete personal responsibility for what the individual does. Every embodied being, in close connection with its environment, is the product of its own past. None can avoid *karma*; it is the debt that we have to pay, the work and the deeds that we have to do in order to elicit our own personal salvation (*moksha*). Just as we have complete responsibility for our own actions, so also we have freedom of will, since our present joy or sorrow is contingent upon our freely chosen activity in the past – back to the first conscious choice we ever made for good or ill. Nor is this doctrine of 'we reap what we sow' peculiar to Hinduism. The Jewish prophet Jeremiah, in the sixth century before Christ, stated that 'each shall die for his own sin, and he who eats the sour grapes, his own teeth shall be set on edge'[41]. And Ezekiel, who also flourished in the sixth century BC, and supported the doctrine of individual rather than collective retribution, maintained that the evil-man was as responsible for his own dying and death as the good-man for his own living and life: 'The soul that sins, that soul shall die'[42]. Nor did the Christian philosophy change anything in this respect for St Paul when he wrote his letter to the Galatians[43]:

> Make no mistake – God is not mocked – a man will reap just what he sows; he who sows for his flesh will reap destruction from the flesh, and he who sows for the spirit will reap life eternal from the spirit.

Ultimately, the individual will be released from the apparently ceaseless round of *samsara*, or rebirth, only when his karmic debt is fully paid, and his personal purification leads to an acceptance of the *dharma*, or universal law of goodness, truth and righteousness. The final goal is one of 'no return'. This will occur when the chains of desire and of the illusion (*maya*) of life are broken, and *moksha*, salvation or liberation, is attained.

7 Jainism

1 Mahavira (fl 500 BC)

Jainism, like Sikhism and Buddhism, arose within the religion of Hinduism itself in the form of a reaction to certain of its beliefs and practices, just as within Christianity sects and schisms have developed during nearly two thousand years. These sects have had their effect upon the main streams of religion and upon society as a whole. Hinduism and India are different today because of the Jains, the Sikhs and the Buddhists, however small their present number of followers might be. The Jains claim that their religion goes back beyond the time of Mahavira to that of an earlier teacher, named Parsva, whose doctrines were later developed by Mahavira himself, and there is some support by scholars for this possibility.

Vardhamana, later referred to as Mahavira ('the great man'), was born during the sixth century before Christ near Vaishali in Bihar. His father was a very wealthy kshatriya chief who, with his wife, practised extreme forms of fasting in the hope that eventually rebirth might be averted through starvation and suicide. In fact, both his father and mother eventually succeeded in their efforts and left their son to his devices at the age of thirty-two. Mahavira became depressed about the whole business of life and death, and he began a serious, intellectual search for truth, knowledge and understanding. He renounced the wealth and social position which he inherited from his father, and he began to withdraw from all the splendour of the rich kshatriya life to which he himself had been accustomed, despite his parents' nihilistic views.

Tradition claims that for twelve or thirteen years Mahavira wandered around the country of Western Bengal, during which time he practised extreme forms of asceticism and rejected every sort of property, including personal clothing. Perpetually seeking liberation (moksha) from the illusions of life, he finally sat under a tree by the side of a river where he meditated and, ultimately, attained the liberation he sought.

Mahavira held that eternal truths were revealed to him during this critical period of meditation. These truths were conveyed in this way only to the *jinas*, the conquerors or saviours of the world who appeared from age to age, and he was one of them. The function of a *jina* was to reform the older, orthodox teaching and to highlight its essence. Mahavira began to preach and draw around him followers who accepted his call to asceticism, and discipleship brooked no barriers of caste or gender. His disciples were, and still are, known as Jains, that is, those who conquer and are victorious over the evils and distractions of life. The Sanskrit word *ji* means 'to conquer', and there is in this religion a consciousness of the conquest of karmic matter. The body was, for the Jain, no longer in command. As E O James[1] has indicated, as far as Mahavira was concerned the 'fundamental ill' was the association which existed between the soul and the body. The body was the product of karma; the elimination of karma would result in liberation from the prison of the body.

After Mahavira attained to his perfect spiritual knowledge, or *kevala*, he continued his wanderings for thirty years during which the religion or sect of Jainism became established.

2   The Essence of Jainism

The Jain took five vows based upon the three 'jewels' of right faith, right knowledge, and right action. These three jewels were essential possessions if the devotee were to reach the everlasting peace and inaction of moksha or nirvana. For the Jain the latter state meant a complete dissociation from karma and all that it implied. Karma was regarded as a sort of substance that adhered to the soul and gave it concrete form in the shape of a body. The soul was thenceforth coloured by the deeds of the individual; if he were pure it would be white; if cruel it would be black, and so on. The growth of the body around the soul could be eroded by asceticism; hence the Jain lived a very strict life.

The Jain's first vow was concerned with the preservation of all life, since killing, or *himsa*, was the worst possible action, whether the object of the action were a human being or an insect. The concept of non-killing, or *ahimsa*, went further than the mere action of killing; it involved thought, word, and all deeds including eating and drinking which resulted in the deprivation of life. The principle of ahimsa excluded the Jain from all forms of industry that involved the destruction of any sort of life. Thus, the Jain could not engage in agriculture, hunting or fishing. For this reason a strict Jain will avoid disturbing the earth in any way; he will sweep in front of him wherever he walks in order not to tread upon an insect; and he will strain his drinks and wear a cloth over his mouth for the same reason.

The second vow was concerned with the jewel of right knowledge and truth: there was to be no uttering of a lie. Actually, once more, the vow concerns more than the mere telling of a lie – there is to be no lie in the soul, no deceit, no rejection of what is intuitively known to be the truth. The third vow involved an attitude to property: no Jain could take that which belonged to another unless it were clearly a gift. According to his fourth vow, the Jain must not indulge in any sensual pleasures, particularly sexual intercourse. But, if all Jains made and kept this vow, the whole sect would rapidly doom itself to destruction. And so, as in other religions, there remain two levels of discipleship: those who are completely involved in the asceticism of the religion and all its rigours; and those who in any case are unable to go to such extremes but who, nevertheless, are responsible for the continuance of the sect physically speaking. His fifth vow involved the renunciation of all interests in worldly affairs: he must have no personal attachments in this life.

During the first century AD, the Jains developed two schisms – the *svetambaras*, or white-robed ones; and the *digambaras*, or sky-clad ones. Whilst the former wore a simple white robe, the latter insisted upon the rejection of all forms of ownership including clothes, and so went about naked. Both groups, however, practised much the same sort of austerities, involving intense meditation, and physical and emotional control. The concept of God is completely denied in their scheme of things, and the Hindu's search for Brahman is considered useless. This does not mean that Jainism is purely materialistic: the very concept of the *jiva*, or soul, which is the equivalent of the Hindu atman, is opposed to this. Moreover, any belief in reincarnation implies a spiritual dimension within the universe. When, however, the soul is finally liberated from material obstacles, the jiva is referred to as *jivanmukta,* and it reaches a state of omniscience or perfect knowledge (*kevala-jnana*). As it rises, it reaches the top of the universe (*lokakasa*) where it remains eternally. There are some individuals referred to as *arahats* because, although they have reached a stage of enlightenment and sainthood, they have not yet attained liberation (*moksha*); yet they live without amassing any further karma. Women, and even the 'gods' themselves, must become men before they can attain to final sainthood.

The whole philosophy of the Jains is summed up in their *Akaranga Sutra*[2]:

> He who knows wrath, knows pride. He who knows pride, knows deceit. He who knows deceit, knows greed. He who knows greed, knows love. He who knows love, knows conception. He who knows conception, knows birth. He who knows birth, knows death. He who knows death, knows hell. He who knows hell, knows animal existence. He who knows animal existence, knows pain. Therefore a wise man should avoid wrath, pride, deceit, greed, love, hate, delusion, conception, birth, hell, animal existence and pain.

True knowledge will so inform a man that henceforth he will avoid all those things which result in karma, and consequently the continuance of rebirth or samsara. Only when nothing is deliberately desired or sought after will the individual disciple reach the state of 'beyond good and evil', in which the jiva remains unmoved, unaffected and eternally unchanged.

The Jains, because of their peculiar position in relation to the sanctity and inviolability of all life, are naturally vegetarians and pacifists. But, in addition, because they cannot hunt, fish or participate in agriculture, they have become a race of bankers, merchants and landowners – a prosperous community representing probably about one-third per cent of the Indian population. Their contribution to Indian culture, through their brilliantly carved and decorated temples, their fine white marble images which represent the jinas, and their whole ethos of *ahimsa*, cannot be overestimated. It is clear that Mahatma Gandhi was considerably influenced by their thought and action – or, perhaps more accurately, their inaction or passivity in the face of violence. Moreover, much of the reform spirit of Jainism in regard to such practices as vegetarianism has affected a large body of Hindus.

8   Sikhism

Today there are some twenty million Sikhs, the greater proportion of whom live in the Punjab. When India was partitioned in 1947, the Sikhs combined in an attempt to gain complete independence for themselves, with a state of their own. There resulted a bloody struggle in which Hindus, Muslims and Sikhs were all involved, and eventually the Sikhs were drawn out of the Pakistan area of the Punjab and finally settled in India.

During the fifteenth century AD there were several reform movements within both Islam and Hinduism. Kabir (1440-1518), a Muslim weaver who lived in Varanasi (Benares), became a disciple of the Hindu teacher Ramananda, and he composed a large number of mystical hymns, songs and poems. He made a strong impact upon his hearers, many of whom persecuted him for his heresies. When he was eventually expelled from Varanasi he began to wander around the country with a number of ardent disciples, seeking to convert others to a more tolerant and universal belief in God. Kabir accepted that there was truth in all religions, and that the God known as Allah or Krishna or Rama was in fact one and the same God. He went further and developed the theme that God was in the hearts of all men and that, wherever one looked, God could be found. His attitude towards all living creatures was that in some way, however small, they were an expression of God. Therefore, pain which was inflicted upon any creature, whether human or animal, was pain inflicted upon God. Those who pursued the path of Kabir, who sang his songs, and who practised his doctrine of ahimsa, or non-hurtfulness, were referred to as *Kabir-panthis*. His general belief in God is summed up in his statement:

> O God, whether Allah or Rama, I live by thy Name. The difference among faiths is only one in names; everywhere the yearning is for the name of God.

Nanak (1469-1538) was clearly influenced by the broad approach of Kabir's teaching and its acceptance of all men of goodwill. Nanak was born in a rural environment near Lahore in the Punjab; his parents were Hindus, and he himself married and had two children. One day he decided to leave his family in search of the truth, and he became an ascetic, joining the Sufis who were a mystical sect of the Muslims. He experienced and seemed to understand the deep conflict between Hinduism and Islam; and whilst touring the subcontinent of India he attacked the priesthood for their ostentation and encouragement of idolatry, and also the caste system which was responsible for so much division in society. At the age of thirty he resolved the dilemma of sectarianism by the dictum, 'There is no Hindu, there is no Muslim, but only one human being; he is the Sikh'. The 'Sikh' is simply 'a disciple' of God.

Nanak believed in the fundamental, innate goodness of man: if only he were set free from the domination of conventional and sectarian beliefs, he would find God everywhere and in every man. He believed that rituals came between God and man, not as a mediation of God's grace, but as an unwarranted intrusion and obstacle between man and his ultimate realization. And so Nanak did not hesitate to ridicule brahmanic rituals; but equally he flouted the religious customs of Islam and other religions. It is said that on one occasion he was reproached for sleeping with his feet towards Mecca. This to him was one of the puerilities of pettifogging religious convention, and he replied in kind: 'All right, put my feet in a place where God is not.'

In his view there was no real divorce between man and God, and there should be no separation between man and man either. Caste was criminal to him simply because it erected barriers – social, personal and religious – between God's children. All men were equal in God's sight; there were no kings or kshatriyas, no serfs or shudras, no outcastes, only people. In his simple and uncomplicated way, he saw society as possessing the possibilities of the primitive socialism reflected in the life of the early Christian Church – all wealth was to be divided evenly among all people according to their basic needs.

Not surprisingly the Sikhs became the object of some persecution. Nanak, however, determined that the reforms that he had begun should continue, and so he nominated his successor who was referred to as a guru, or teacher. There followed a line of gurus who were peaceful men refusing to participate in any form of violence or warfare. All was well until one guru was put to death by an invading Mogul emperor, after which the Sikhs developed a strong sense of self-preservation. The tenth and last guru, Govind Rai, organized the sect of the Sikhs into a strong, militant group who were able, should the occasion arise, to defend themselves and to destroy the aggressor.

Guru Govind decided before his death that the reign of the gurus was over. In future the essence of Sikhism would be the holy scriptures of the Sikhs, the *Adi Granth* or the 'Original Book', written in Punjabi. This book is an anthology of compositions by a variety of authors, including poems and songs by Ramananda, Kabir, Nanak, Govind Singh, and the Muslim Sheik Farid. It includes the morning prayer, or *Japji*, which is recited by all Sikhs daily and which begins, 'There is one God, the creator, omnipresent, immortal'. The poems and hymns composed by the gurus have been set to classical Indian music, and they are sung somewhat in the manner of plainsong.

Govind regarded his disciples as the elect or pure ones, the *Khalsa*, who should model their lives upon the ten gurus who had been their leaders. His male disciples were lions in the battle for truth and right, and henceforth they were to be called 'Singh' or 'lion'. Female disciples were to receive the appellation 'Kaur', meaning 'princess'. These names were to be added at a baptismal rite called *pahul*, normally performed by several devout Sikh laymen some few years after the birth of a child. The ritual involved the sprinkling of the child's eyes and hair with *amrita*, a concoction of sugar and 'holy' water.

The Sikhs, the Khalsa, were committed to a way of life which would ensure their spiritual purity. They were permitted by Govind to eat meats, except beef, provided the animals were killed at one stroke. They were strictly forbidden to smoke tobacco, and most Sikhs soon dispensed with alcoholic beverages. There were five visible signs of membership of the Khalsa, known as the 'Five K's': *kesh*, or beard and uncut hair covered by a turban; *kangha*, or comb to keep their hair clean; *kirpan*, or short sword to be used if necessary in self-defence; *kara*, or steel bangle representing the law of God to which the wearer is bound; and *kachha*, or short pants worn beneath the trousers. All these elements are symbolic in much the same way as crosses, crucifixes, rosaries and clerical collars.

Sikhism is a deliberately syncretistic religion, seeking to bring together the best in Islam, Hinduism and Buddhism with their various sectarian groups. It is monotheistic in essence: there is one God called 'the Name' (Nam), who is the creator, eternal, omnipresent, absolute and formless. But although absolute, God is also personal; although transcendent, he is also immanent in man, and he reveals his presence and his will through the gurus and the *Adi Granth*. There is no need to become a priest or a monk in order to find God. As the guru says, 'Why dost thou go to the forest in search of God? He lives in all, yet is ever distinct; he lives in thee too'. As in Hinduism, there may be use of words or sounds for God other than that of *Nam*, but God is One, and there is no second. There is also a firm belief in reincarnation, obviously derived from Hindu philosophy.

The sacred city of Sikhism is Amritsar where there exists the small but impressive Golden Temple in the midst of a large artificial lake. But for Sikhism generally worship in a temple is not essential for communion with God. Since God is everywhere, worship can occur wherever man seeks that presence. There is, however, a meeting-place where communal religious observances may take place, and where members are taught the elements of their faith. This is the *gurdwara*, or place of the guru, which is a simple, bare hall without chairs or stools, but with a platform and lectern to support the *Adi Granth*. The congregation, who are all equal in God's eyes, sit or squat on the floor. Most gurdwaras are open for short services every day and for longer services once a week; but they are also social and community centres where Sikhs meet to discuss their problems, share experiences, learn more about their faith, and even share meals.

Sikhism is a religion which believes that as far as possible the course of nature should not be disturbed. The *kesh* or uncut hair, for example, is a symbolic expression of the continuity of nature, which must not be opposed in its prolific development except for the sake of human survival. The Sikh is opposed to all forms of selfishness, immorality, cruelty, greed or excess; and in this respect he obviously has a great deal of common ground with both Judaism and Christianity, as well as with Buddhism. In fact, despite that at first sight Sikhism appears to be a minor syncretic sect, it does in fact offer a major contribution to unity in religious philosophy and thought, and it possesses something of that 'perennial philosophy' which has always attracted some of the world's greatest minds. Sikhism is open to all people. They must first believe in the ten gurus and the sacredness of the *Adi Granth*. If they faithfully practise the gurus' words, they will find themselves at one with the gurus. In fact, the true Sikh has incorporated the gurus, and more specifically the guru Nanak, within himself.

9 Buddhism

1 Gautama (563-483 BC)

The Northern Buddhists and most Western scholars date Gautama between 563 BC and 483 BC; the Southern Buddhists favour an earlier dating between 624 BC and 544 BC; the Chinese Buddhists have given a date as early as 1000 BC; whilst other scholars involved in Buddhist research have placed him as late as the fourth century BC. That such a person as Gautama existed most scholars today would agree; they would also agree that time has resulted in a vast accretion of myths, legends and apocryphal sayings and writings.

The bare facts of Gautama's birth, life and death are intertwined with interesting and piquant stories about his physical prowess, his amazing endurance and fortitude, his miraculous gifts, and his intense compassion for mankind. Gautama Siddhartha Shakyamuni was born in North East India, in the foothills of Nepal, at Kapilavastu (now called Piprava). His father, Suddhodana, was a great king who ruled over the Shakya tribe; he was a wealthy kshatriya who wielded great power and influence. One cannot ignore the various accounts of Gautama's birth, which was regarded as some sort of 'immaculate conception'; and such accounts reflect that wisdom which so many religions have in retrospect, feeling as they do that such incredible leadership and insight could result only from supernatural or supernormal powers. Legend has it that Maya, the wife of Suddhodana, lived for thirty-two months of her marriage in

135

total asceticism. One night she had a dream that an elephant pierced her right side, and that as a result of this she conceived. She informed her husband who regarded this as a sign of some unusual event, and he restricted himself to intercourse with his other wives. Ten months later, in Lumbini Park (possibly the present village of Rummindei), Maya gave birth to a son who came out of her right side whilst she held onto the branches of an overhanging fig-tree.

The *Jatakas*, or Birth Stories, are a collection of legends which reveal the sense of awe and wonder which always seemed to accompany the life of Gautama. They provide accounts of the 547 previous existences of Gautama as a bird, animal and man. There were, apparently, many supernatural manifestations both at the conception and at the birth of Gautama, some of them comparable with those in the gospel accounts of the life of Jesus. They speak of the way in which, as the cosmos became aware of this great historical event, the world was flooded with light, the blind received their sight in order to share the vision of his glory, and the deaf and dumb freely conversed in the ecstasy of expectation. Even the fires of hell were temporarily quenched and the crimes of the beasts were hushed as the peace of Brahman encircled the earth. Mara, the Evil One, alone refused to rejoice.

In due course Gautama was presented at the temple of the god, Abhaya. It was discovered that he had the thirty-two large marks and eighty smaller marks on his body of a great and unusual man. A wise man, named Asita, who came down from his seclusion in the mountains, prophesied that Gautama would in due course become a powerful emperor (no doubt as the inheritor of his father's kingdom), or that he would become an ascetic who would provide mankind with some form of deliverance from the dreadful evil, pain and suffering of the world. His mother, Maya, died seven days after his birth.

Tradition has it that Gautama grew up to a very luxurious life in his father's palace, and that at the age of sixteen years he married a princess called Gopa Yasodhara. His father presented him with three large and beautiful palaces and four gardens. Yasodhara bore him a son, Rahula, and it seemed that his happiness would be complete. By the orders of his father, Gautama was perpetually protected from the evil, dirt and ugliness of life: he was not permitted to have any contact with sickness, old age or death; and always, when he went out walking or riding, he was admonished to go only in certain directions and along certain paths. Moreover, he was always shielded by a court entourage provided by his father. But Gautama was discontented with the life that he was living, despite the perhaps exaggerated accounts of the palaces and forty thousand dancing-girls which Suddhona thoughtfully provided for him.

It was contact with the realities of life which first made Gautama aware of his utter ignorance of the deeper, spiritual levels of being. Somehow one day he escaped from his over-protective entourage, and he experienced the 'Four Passing Sights' of old age, disease and death, as well as withdrawal from life. He observed an old man, broken and bent, leaning upon his stick, ugly, decrepit and in despair. Then he saw what must have always been a common and unavoidable sight in India – a disease-ridden body and a corpse nearby, rotting in the heat and the sun, and overrun with insect life. Finally, he encountered a monk with his head shaven, wearing a single threadbare robe and carrying a begging-bowl. Here was a man who had withdrawn from life with all its personal problems and involvements. Gautama began to reflect upon this new vision of the world as a place where life was tortured and subject to death. He, therefore, posed the question:

> Since life is subject to suffering, old age and death, where is that realm of living where suffering, age and death no longer have any dominion?

So, at the age of twenty-nine, one night Gautama left his sleeping wife and son, his palaces and all their possibilities of pleasure, and rode out on his horse, Kanthaka, accompanied by his faithful servant Chhandaka. Some distance from the palace he changed his garments, cut off his hair, and dismissed his servant with his jewels, his clothes and his horse. For six years Gautama appears to have learned everything he could from anyone who had anything to teach. He became a mendicant, meditating, fasting and practising yoga.

One day, after considerable wandering and agonizing, Gautama eventually rested under a bo-tree (a bodhi-tree, pipal, sacred fig tree, tree of enlightenment, or *ficus religiosa)*, at a place now called Bodh Gaya in Bihar. As he sat in meditation under this tree, he was presented with three main temptations by Mara. The first temptation was at the level of desire, and here Mara seems to have been somewhat unperceptive – a man who had not been imprisoned by a delightful wife and thousands of dancing girls at home in his palace was hardly likely to succumb to the three daughter-goddesses whom Mara presented to him. The second temptation was to destroy himself. During periods of incredible misery and torment, in which he experienced hurricanes, rain and darkness, Gautama saw the whole of human suffering presented before him. The temptation here was to invite, or accept, death in order to escape from the whole catena of life's sorrows. But again, Gautama did not succumb and it was, apparently, at the end of this temptation that he reached enlightenment *(bodhi)*, and became the 'Enlightened One' or the Buddha – the one who is awake.

But it is one thing to know the truths and realities of life, to become enlightened, it is quite another to be able to mediate the truths one knows to others. Mara, in his third and greatest temptation, emphasized the sheer immensity of the task that the Buddha was setting himself. Why not, then, accept his own enlightenment and keep it to himself because of this awful sense of the impossibility of transmitting to others such ineffable knowledge? He could immediately attain to nirvana, and all his fears, anxieties and doubts would be over. The Buddha, however, whilst fully aware of all the problems that were likely to face him – after all, he had been facing them continuously for the past six years – accepted that there would always be some, perhaps the few, who would understand what he was trying to say. And so, for the remaining forty-five years of his life the Buddha wandered around India teaching what he felt had been vouchsafed to him through his own personal enlightenment.

His first converts were among his own kshatriya and Shakya friends, but his disciples gradually extended to people of every caste and every type of religious thinking. Among his followers was his great friend Ananda who served the Buddha until the latter died. His cousin, Devadatta, also became a follower and something of a Judas. He greatly envied the spiritual power of the Buddha, and so he sought to arouse the monks against him. Failing in this he sent hired assassins against him. But they fell before the Buddha as soon as he approached, blinded by a great light. Then Devadatta tried to cause a stone pillar to fall upon him, but the Buddha stopped it so that it rested in mid-air. Finally, a drugged elephant was driven into the path of the Buddha, but when it saw him it kneeled and adored him. Devadatta was thus finally defeated and sent into hell.

The Buddha strongly advised his monks, however endowed they might be with supernormal powers, not to work miracles, for true conversion should not be the result of such constraints but rather the outcome only of moral conviction. Despite this admonition at least seventy-seven miracles are ascribed to the Buddha, who healed the sick out of his great compassion for man, roused and calmed storms, performed miracles of bilocation by preaching in different places simultaneously, multiplied his own image and terminated outbreaks of disease and plague.

The Buddha taught suffering and the end of suffering; he attacked the caste system and the conventional rites, celebrations and prayers of the Hindu religion and of the Brahmanist system generally. He was opposed to the concept of collectivity which Brahmanism seemed at every point to involve, and so he sought to undermine it. He saw a people who, desperately needing spiritual release, were chained by the oppressive and obscurantist teachings of traditionalists. To these people he said, 'Be lamps unto yourselves'. They were not to accept unreflectingly what their teacher taught them; they were not to accept what they heard by report through tradition or scripture; they were to search within themselves, for enlightenment came from within. They had to walk the path themselves, no one could walk it for them, for the Buddha could only show the way. They had to work out their salvation with considerable concentration and diligence. Just as Jeremiah (circa 626-586 BC) appealed to the individual rather than to the group, so also did the Buddha, and his dying words were, 'All composite things are doomed to extinction. Exert yourselves in wakefulness'.

2   The Four Noble Truths

The Buddha taught the Four Noble Truths, the Middle Way, and the Noble Eightfold Path, and his starting-point was suffering – that fact in life which had shaken his youthful innocence and joy. All life is suffering or *dukkha*; life is out of joint or off-centre, just like a wheel that has slipped off its pivot. This is the first noble truth. The stress, strain, pain, misery, sorrow and unhappiness of life were all an expression of this friction caused by dislocation. Healing could occur only when the cause of this dislocation had been discovered.

The second noble truth is the recognition that desire, or *tanha*, is the cause of all suffering. *Tanha* is a selfish or blind craving or demandingness; it is the desire to find fulfilment in the fleeting pleasures as they arise, in a *part* of the self. The fact of *tanha* is best illustrated by a circle. Perfect integration of the personality occurs when life operates from the centre; there is then no friction, no suffering. When, however, life operates from off-centre, a partial self is set up. It is this new and partial self that proceeds to take over and to become fulfilled; but the mere fact that only a part of the self is being satisfied causes suffering, disappointment, frustration, friction and pain. This partial fulfilment leads to 'self-centredness', and in the extreme pathological state this can mean, as with some psychotic patients, a complete solipsist existence in which no communication may be made with another person for many years. As Anthony Storr[1] remarks:

> And so we have the paradox that man is at his most individual when most in contact with his fellows, and is least of all a separate individual when detached from them.

To get back on-centre implies an extension of the self; it implies a recognition that we are members one of another, and that all others are extensions, in some way or another, of ourselves.

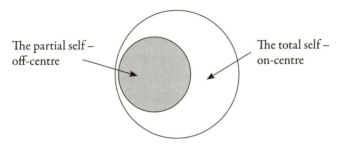

The partial self – off-centre

The total self – on-centre

And so we come to the third noble truth which is expressed simply and explicitly in the sentence, 'We must overcome desire'. We can become free from suffering and torment only if and when we become released from the narrowness of our self-interest (inevitably partial) and extend our interest to all of mankind. This is man's search for his original wholeness; it represents his recognition that only as he gets back on-centre can he really *be* himself.

The fourth noble truth is the actual overcoming of desire and the techniques involved in doing so. What the Buddha proposes is certainly not 'instant salvation'; anyone who looks for an easy or immediate conversion or salvation would assuredly have to look elsewhere. To become integrated or 'total' one must practise integration; and this involves the Eightfold Path. But before one can even begin upon this path one has to create a right association, that is, one has to develop the right *guru-chela*, or master-disciple, relationship.

3   The Eightfold Path

The way, the truth and the life were for the Buddha one and the same; they are called the *dharma* (Sanskrit; *dhamma*, Pali). The Buddha was in a unique position to give the *dharma* because he was himself one 'who had fully come through': he was *tathagata*. The *dharma* was expressed in the Middle Way of the Eightfold Path – a middle path between the extremes of complete self-mortification and the quest of emancipation through knowledge and works. The Path begins with *right knowledge* or right views: one must understand what one is about and have a correct view of things. We must, in fact, know ourselves in order to rule ourselves, and our self-knowledge must be based on a complete acceptance of the four noble truths already discussed, and a pure vision of those truths.

Right knowledge of the self will provide a plan for living, an understanding of what is yet required to attain to wholeness. We must then consider what we really want from life, since without a *right aim*, hope, aspiration or determination we shall make no progress. For progress, there must be a consistency – a consistent acceptance of our identity with all mankind and our involvement in the welfare of all. We must continually reject our separateness, our discreteness. We must hitch our wagon to the star of perfection and never look back.

In this progression towards the goal of integration, our speech and speech patterns are vitally important. What we say is some indication of what we think and what we are. It is an index of our being and of our character; and there should clearly be some correspondence between what we think and say and do (Cf Zoroastrianism). If we deviate from the truth we should understand what element in the self is seeking private satisfaction and bring our partial self under control. Our efforts to deceive others harm not only them but also ourselves – they reduce our very being. Plato once remarked that the mask an actor wears is apt to become his face; our behaviour patterns eventually become our *selves*, for we are judged by them, and our whole activity is predicted by them.

> Better than a thousand words is indeed one single word that gives peace. Better than a thousand useless verses is one single verse that gives peace[2].

This is the path of *right speech*, and it is one in which slander, gossip and lack of charity are alien to the whole concept of union with others. We cannot have identity with others if we are forever driving a wedge between ourselves and them. The principle of *noli me tangere*, whether practised by forms of isolation or by means of verbal attack, is in the long run self-destructive.

Right behaviour can be achieved only by self-examination, by a careful reflection upon our daily activity, and by a very close look at our motives in whatever we may do. And so,

> Make haste and do what is good; keep your mind away from evil. If a man is slow in doing good, his mind finds pleasure in evil.....Neither in the sky, nor deep in the ocean, nor in the mountain-cave, nor anywhere, can a man be free from the evil he has done[3].

But, in more specific terms, there are some things that no one on the path can find it within himself to do. He cannot kill, for all life is sacred. He cannot steal, for such activity reflects the very covetousness of the soul and the very deprivation we seek to bring upon others. He cannot lie, for lying presupposes a lack of integration within the self, a hiatus between thought and word, and between word and action. It is not simply that others may be deceived by such activity; in Platonic terms the 'lie in the soul' is destructive of the individual self. He cannot be unchaste, for this involves the rejection of the total self in favour of a lower and partial self. And, finally, he cannot drink intoxicants or take drugs, for these lead to a lack of control by the central consciousness of the self and, once more, a partial element of the self takes over. A man who travels on the path must, at all times, be aware of who is travelling, of the destination, and also of the nature of the journey. Man's behaviour involves the four great virtues of Buddhism[4]: *Maitri*, or love, friendliness and goodwill; *Karuna*, or compassion for the sufferings of others; *Mudita*, or joy in the good and happiness of every being; and *Upeksha*, or forgiveness.

It is important that the traveller should have the *right livelihood*, the right occupation in life. There are some things which the Wayfarer cannot honestly and sincerely engage in, for if his work pulls in a direction opposed to spiritual progress then that work is deleterious. Life in all its fullness must be promoted by whatever labour one is involved in, for labour is but the means to the ultimate goal of the spirit in Nirvana. Nirvana is the state of supreme enlightenment beyond the conception of mind and thought; it is the annihilation of the personal or *separated* self, although not annihilation *per se*, for the Buddha was not nihilistic.

Once the right occupation has been chosen, the individual must perpetually engage in making the *right effort*. This is not a question of wishful thinking, it is a matter of enormous personal effort which each one on the path must exert steadily and daily without intermission. Life is a serious business; it demands the fullest possible identification with the end in view and an unrelenting participation in the effort of will required to reach the goal. At the same time, as Juan Mascaro[5] has pointed out, when one is involved in right effort there is also right relaxation:

> In concentration it means the right attention to something whilst there is a relaxing of everything not connected with the object of attention. All effort is right in the sense that we never think it is an effort.

Man *is* essentially what he thinks, and his thoughts go out to others and affect them for good or ill. We must be concerned to fill our world with loving and sympathetic thoughts since we may thus participate positively in the lives of others. *Right mindfulness* demands that we should closely examine our selves, our minds, our thinking and our personal relationships. This self-analysis is not a selfish or unhealthy introspection, but a purposeful consideration of one's thoughts in relation to others and an acceptance that, with Tennyson's Ulysses, 'I am a part of all that I have met'. Our lives, which are essentially our thoughts, go out towards and into others. We must, therefore, always be on our guard, to watch and to remember, for:

Watchfulness is the path of immortality: unwatchfulness is
the path of death. Those who are watchful never die: those
who do not watch are already as dead... .The wise man who by
watchfulness conquers thoughtlessness is as one who free from
sorrows ascends the palace of wisdom and there, from its high
terrace, sees those in sorrow below; even as a wise strong man
on the holy mountain might behold the many unwise far below
on the plain... .The monk who has the joy of watchfulness,
and who looks with fear on thoughtlessness, he can never be
deprived of his victory and he is near NIRVANA[6].

If the disciple follows the path with complete determination and
right absorption, he cannot fail to reach the end, for the end and the
way are one. The techniques of *raja yoga*, the royal yoga, will lead
ultimately to the realization of the fact that Being itself is infinite,
eternal, cosmic and within ourselves. It is beyond description and
analysis[7] for all words are limiting, especially those that seek to
express the endless infinitude of cosmic consciousness. 'When the
traveller has reached the end of the journey, he has attained to the
state of nirvana'[7], or union with nirvana. Then

> In the freedom of the Infinite he is free from all sorrows, the
> fetters that bound him are thrown away, and the burning fever
> of life is no more... .he is free from *Samsara*, the ever-returning
> life-in-death. And he who is free from credulous beliefs since
> he has seen the eternal NIRVANA, who has thrown off the
> bondage of the lower life and, far beyond temptations, has
> surrendered all his desires, he is indeed great amongst men[8].

4 Karma, Reincarnation and Anatta

The Buddha appears to have denied the ultimate reality of a permanent
soul or atman. This doctrine is referred to as the doctrine of *anatta*,
or the unreality of the self. This 'not-self' doctrine was not easy to

reconcile with the idea of reincarnation, or the transmigration of souls. Apparently it was karma that survived death, not the self. The human being was an aggregate of five elements or *skandhas*, namely: the body and its senses, feelings and sensations, sense-perceptions, volitions and mental faculties, and reason or consciousness. These *skandhas* were certainly not fixed and permanently definable in relation to any particular individual; they were, in fact, changing daily. Thus, what we term the soul, or ego, has no real or continuous existence, for our personality is no more than the sum of its changing parts. E O James[9] has put it this way:

> What transmigrates is a 'stream of energy clothing itself in body after body' as the flame from one wick lamp may be passed on to another wick. All we really know or observe within ourselves, or in the world around us, are these ever-changing states of consciousness or awareness. Therefore, since everything is in a state of endless 'becoming' there is no eternal 'Being', no underlying Unity or Brahman as an Absolute, no permanent personality human or divine. Indeed, the permanency of the ego, or of the world of appearances, is the great illusion which must be renounced if deliverance from the wheel of perpetual becoming is ever to be attained. The will to live and to have, the thirst for sentient life with all its pain and misery, desires and fleeting pleasures, must be abandoned.

Thus the aim and end of existence is the cessation of pain, sorrow and suffering, and release from the aggregate of *skandhas*. The individual who, like the Buddha, has discovered truth, will attain to the peace and perfection of Nirvana, and to that highest state of all, Parinirvana, from which there is no return. The Buddha believed that Nirvana could be attained in this life by those path-goers who were highly advanced. The Buddha himself took 547 lives to reach that level, and then rejected it in order, as a *bodhisattva*, to serve mankind and show the way. The state of Nirvana was reached as a result of the cessation of all personal craving for pleasure, for desirable objects, and for life itself. In this way the individual passed beyond karma and beyond rebirth. This state was not annihilation; at the same time there was no way whereby language could describe it. To this extent the Buddha was agnostic, and he frequently resorted to the expression of opposites in order to demonstrate the ineffableness of certain concepts. The asking of questions, such as 'How was the world created?' and 'Who created?' was a waste of time, because the answers were not available. One could go on propounding theories *ad infinitum* because, with each new discovery, one had to change or modify the theory. But action was more important than theory. If a man were struck by a poisoned arrow, it is unlikely that he would ask – before he consented to any treatment – who shot the arrow, from what type of tree the wood of the bow was taken, what the horse was like with whose mane the bow was bound, and what the caste and colour were of the archer. His one and only concern would be that he should be healed in the best and most expeditious manner.

The Venerable Kapilavaddho Bhikku[10] has expressed it all as follows:

There was once a man looking into a very deep pool of water. A stranger approached and said, 'What is this at which you are looking, Sir?' 'This is water' replied the man. 'Water' said the stranger, 'What is water?' 'Water' replied the man 'is a liquid.' 'Liquid' asked the stranger, 'What is liquid?' 'This liquid is composed of two gases, oxygen and hydrogen, and is wet', replied the man. 'Gases, hydrogen, oxygen, wet. I don't understand' said the stranger. 'Well, it is not dry', said the man. 'I came to you and asked a simple question as to what you were looking at and all I get is a long list of words, but no answer. It would appear to me that you yourself do not know at what you look', said the stranger. The man replied, 'I do verily know at what I look. I know its very substance, essence and taste, but I cannot impart this wisdom to you by words. However, I think that your questioning is sincere and I am going to do you a great kindness.' He then thrust the stranger into the water. He then KNEW with a real KNOWING.

The Socratic dialectic is followed here by a certain Socratic irony, and the message is clear. If you really want to know what water is like, get into it. In Buddhist terms, if you really want to know what the path is all about, you must tread it; samadhi and Nirvana can only really be understood by making the effort to experience them through the practical and the contemplative life. Ultimately, the answer is expressed in the words:

> I go to the Buddha for refuge,
> I go to the Dhamma (doctrine) for refuge,
> I go to the Sangha (monastic order) for refuge[11].

5   The Subsequent History of Buddhism

In 270 BC Ashoka Maurya became king and emperor of most of the subcontinent of India and, like his father Bindusara, and his grandfather Chandragupta, he continued to campaign in order to extend his empire. Thus, ten years after his ascension to the throne he became master of virtually all India, having completely routed his remaining enemies, the Kalingans. The destruction was ruthless and terrible, involving thousands of Indians; and Ashoka, eventually revolted by the horrors of the wars and battles in which he had participated, was filled with remorse and sought consolation in Buddhism and its doctrine of ahimsa, or non-violence.

Ashoka succeeded in uniting his people in the Buddhist dharma, and Buddhism became the established religion of India. Romila Thapar[12], however, emphasizes that the Buddhism which Ashoka inculcated and developed was not simply a religious belief, but 'a social and intellectual movement at many levels', which in consequence had an influence upon all the ramifications of society. Ashoka was, in a very real sense, a humanist desiring that his people should be non-violent and should uphold the dignity of man. He issued a whole series of edicts in which he positively forbade violence and bloodshed, and enjoined upon all his people a pursuance of religion and, in particular, of morality. These edicts were inscribed upon many blocks of stone, rocks and pillars throughout his empire, and a large number of them are still to be seen, particularly in central and northern India. Ashoka forbade killing for sacrifices or for food, and there was to be no hunting or fishing. More positively, he taught respect for parents, and obedience to their commands, as well as respect for the laws of the land and for those entrusted with the duty of keeping order. He built many rest homes and hospitals, for both human beings and animals. His edicts were signed by 'the king, the Beloved of the gods, Piyadassi', the latter term meaning 'The Humane One'.

Soon after Ashoka died, about 232 BC, the empire began to break up. The fundamental loyalty to the person of the king had so far held it together; but after his death brahmanic teachings gradually returned within the national religion, and Buddhism itself became fragmented. By the end of the seventh century AD it became clear that, as far as India was concerned, Buddhism was a dying religion. G Parrinder[13] remarks that Buddhism

> remained a cultural force till the twelfth century AD, and
> so had almost as long an influence on Indian culture as
> Christianity has had on Europe to date.

By the time the invading Muslims had entered India with the message of Islam, Hinduism had already absorbed, in principle at least, some of the finer elements of Buddhism; whilst what little remained of Buddhism as a separate religion had become, to some extent, infected by baser Hindu practices. Indeed, by about the eleventh century AD, Buddhism *per se* was virtually non-existent in India. But its spirit still remains even in modern times, for the Maha Bodhi Society, which Anagarika Dharmapala of Sri Lanka founded in 1891, is very active throughout the whole of India; whilst Gautama the Buddha remains for the Hindu the great 'Enlightened One' who enlightened, as an avatar of Vishnu, and continues to enlighten others. He also remains for his followers the supremely 'Compassionate One', filled with compassion (karuna) for all suffering humanity.

There have been a number of Buddhist Councils since the death of the Buddha: the first (circa 483 BC) decided upon the rules of monkish discipline; the second (circa 383 BC) discussed the relaxation of these rules; the third (in 250 BC), held by Ashoka, decided that only orthodox monks should be admitted to the Sangha; the fourth was held in Sri Lanka during the first century BC; the fifth, held in 1871 AD in Mandalay, Myanmar, had the sacred texts inscribed upon 700 marble slabs; and the sixth took place at Rangoon in 1956. The Sixth Council was held to celebrate the 2500th anniversary of the Parinirvana of the Buddha, and it set out specifically to collate the Buddhist scriptures and to ensure that satisfactory arrangements were made to have them translated into many languages. It must be understood that the Buddha himself wrote nothing at all as far as we know; and further, that none of his teaching was written down for at least four hundred years after his death.

We cannot consider here all the great variety of Buddhist sects and developments, but the main groupings are as follows. The oldest school, variously known as the Hinayana ('the Little Vehicle') or the Theravada ('the tradition of the elders'), developed in South India, Sri Lanka, Myanmar, Thailand, Turkestan, Cambodia and Laos. In Sri Lanka it captured in particular the Sinhalese, who are the majority race, whilst the Tamils, who reside mainly in the north of the island, remain Hindu. It has a more conservative and somewhat negative philosophy as represented in the *Tripitaka* (Pali, *Tipitaka* or 'three baskets'), the canonical Buddhist scriptures. Ashokan missionaries took Buddhism to Thailand, where it became the official state religion. The Hinayana School believes in an intense self-development through a monastic regime, and the mendicant members of the Sangha (the *bhikkus*) are permitted five possessions only – a robe, an alms-bowl, a razor, needle, and a water strainer. The scriptures of this School are in *pali-bhasa* or Pali language, and they are therefore referred to as the 'Pali Canon', as distinct from the scriptures of the Mahayana School which are in Sanskrit. This literature, based upon oral tradition, was codified under King Ashoka in about 250 BC.

The Mahayana ('the Great Vehicle') School developed in North India from where it travelled to places such as Tibet, China and Japan. Tibet eventually developed its own peculiar form of Buddhism which we shall look at briefly in a moment. These northern Buddhists considered their doctrine as the one true 'vehicle' through which the Buddha would save all beings and eventually bring them to Nirvana. Thus, the Buddha has been gradually changed from an avatar and bodhisattva into a saviour-god able to save all mankind. Salvation is by faith and by the grace which may be transferred from more enlightened beings to those who are struggling on the Path. One of the chief of the northern buddhas is Amitabha (Amita or Amida), the Lord of the Pure Land or the Western Paradise. The buddha who is to come is known as Maitreya.

Mahayana Buddhism became a state religion in China during the latter part of the fourth century AD, and Kwanyin, the Goddess of Mercy, became a prime example of spiritual motherhood. Buddhism reached Japan during the sixth century AD, and here the main Shinto goddess was identified with one of the buddhas, whilst the Prince Shotoku was regarded as the male incarnation of Kwannon (or Kwanyin). The Pure Land sect was the largest to preach that Amida was the only saviour; the Nichiren sect goes back to the original Buddha, and accepts that the only scripture that is essential to an understanding of the Buddha's doctrine is the Lotus Sutra. The Nichiren sect as well as the Zen School will be examined later when we consider Japanese religion.

The Buddhism of Tibet has always been a peculiar form of Buddhism, often referred to as Lamaism. It would appear to combine a great variety of elements of Buddhism – from the best to the worst – with a considerable element of pre-Buddhist religion and superstition referred to as *Bon*, in which the shaman reigned supreme. Tibetan Buddhism has gradually established itself into two main sects, the Red

Hats and the Yellow Hats. The Red Hats are the older, 'unreformed church', in which the lamas often are allowed to marry and are generally more close to the common people who support them. The Yellow Hats, or Gelugpa sect, form what might be regarded as the 'established church', with reformed teachings and practices. The chief lamas, known as the Dalai and the Tashi, belong to this sect. The Dalai Lama formerly lived at the Potala Palace in Lhasa, surrounded by lamas or 'superior ones' – then almost one-third of the population. He is regarded as the incarnation of the bodhisattva Chenresi, or Avalokiteshvara; whilst the Tashi Lama is seen as an incarnation of Amitabha. The general feudal system of Tibet was somewhat rudely interrupted by the Chinese invasion in 1959. The Tashi Lama had already gone to China, but the Dalai Lama, and a supporting number of his followers, managed to escape to Delhi in India, where these Tibetan Buddhists are allowed the freedom to pursue their religious beliefs and practices. Despite the varieties and differences in the Buddhism of Tibet, all seem to agree that:

> in the beginning was THAT, the nameless Absolute which
> all Hindus invoke as Aum, contracted to Om, the first
> syllable of the Tibetan formula Om Mani Padme Hum, the
> outer meaning of which is merely 'Hail to the Jewel in the
> Lotus', and its inward meaning the meaning of the Universe.
> Within the One there stirs desire, the First Cause of which
> must ever remain unknown and is not in Buddhism even
> the subject of speculation. The One divides and is two, but
> two is inconceivable save as Three; hence the Trikaya, the
> Trinity in all its forms. In manifestation there is Mind-Only,
> and the appearance of Mind. This relative world is subject
> to interrelation or causation, and the law of Cause-Effect
> controls all manifested things. Morality is the cleansing and
> development of the vehicles through which the individual
> expresses the Absolute within; psychology an understanding
> of the mind. The Goal is Nirvana, the end of separation, the
> return to the One, to THAT[14].

In general terms, the Mahayana School regarded the Theravada School as a somewhat cold and passionless philosophy devoid of religious teaching and lacking in joy and enthusiasm. The Hinayana School ignored man's spiritual gropings for something higher and so 'wronged the spiritual side of man'[15].For the members of the Mahayana School the Hinayana beliefs were incomplete, restricted and somewhat superficial, since they regarded them as merely the introduction to some of the deeper and more important truths of the Mahayana which was in no way bound by the Pali Canon. Through such scriptures as the *Mahavastu*[16] they began to deny any reality in phenomena as such. This sutra was compiled by a group of the sect called *Mahasanghika*, who are generally held responsible for the development of this School. Through their teaching, Gautama Shakyamuni became less and less of a historical figure, whilst 'the Buddha' became increasingly a spiritual being or principle.

The whole question of Nirvana and its nature is raised in the *Lankavatara Sutra*. Nirvana, it suggests, cannot be understood by reason alone. According to the Theraveda School, the individual reaches this state when he has conquered all obstacles in his path to liberation. But there are bodhisattvas who turn back again to share in the sufferings of the world and to help others. These can never really enjoy the attainment of Nirvana, yet they have proved to be the most worthy. But, says this Mahayanist sutra, the state of Nirvana is in reality just what these bodisattvas are experiencing. It is the state in which compassionate identity with others and their sufferings transcends any thought of the individual as a separate entity. The very fact of being a bodhisattva is a demonstration that Nirvana has been reached, and that there can be nothing outside it. Thus, the very renunciation of Nirvana for the sake of others is in itself the real discovery of Nirvana[17].

10 Chinese Religion

1 General Background

The powerful Chou dynasty existed between the eighth and third centuries BC. During that time there was almost perpetual war among the States of China – in particular the period from 403 BC to 250 BC was known as the time of the 'Warring States'. In 250 BC, however, the dynasty finally collapsed after a time in which there was great cruelty and during which hundreds of thousands of Chinese were executed in mass murders simply for being on the wrong side. It is hardly surprising that a period such as this should have produced some of China's greatest thinkers and religious philosophers.

In more general terms, there was throughout China a belief in animism, ancestor-worship, superstitious rituals and sacrifices, shamanistic magic and practices, and pantheism. Each Chou king himself was regarded as *t'ien tzu*, or 'the son of heaven', and he therefore commanded absolute obedience, respect and worship. *T'ien* was heaven or the dome of the sky, sometimes referred to as *Yang*, the male creative process, and sometimes personified as *Shang-ti*, the supreme ancestor. *Yin* was the name given to the earth, the passive female process which had to be fertilized by *Yang* each year to make it productive.

But religion and morality were never completely divorced in the Chinese philosophical scheme; religious custom and social mores were indissolubly bound together so that habitual actions were closely related to the ancestors and the gods who were worshipped. During the fifth and sixth centuries such social mores were undergoing radical abuse and attack in the Chou dynasty. There was an increasingly rational approach to the problems of State and, therefore, of society generally and finally of the individual. Some outstanding thinkers arose during this time, and although the historical proof of their existence, and of the exact period of their lifetimes, is somewhat tenuous, their ideas and thoughts have been gathered into books attributed to certain particular individuals.

2   Confucius (circa 551 BC – 479 BC)

One of these philosophers, and until recent years probably the best known in the Western world, was a man called K'ung Fu Tzu ('Confucius' in its Latinized form), or the Master K'ung. He was born in the feudal state of Lu in Shantung Province, most probably of poor parents who seem to have died within a few years of his birth. Thus his upbringing was modest, he married early and had a son and daughter. He became a tutor and instructed in a wide range of subjects, including divination and sports, and before long he became noted for both his eloquence and wisdom. He seems to have had a love of poor students and a great deal of personal sympathy with the peasants in his society.

Although he was undoubtedly a learned man, he was probably in the main self-taught, and he remained humble throughout his life. It is likely that many of his students were far more successful than he had ever been with regard to obtaining good posts in public administration. After some minor advisory appointments in one or two States, he set off at about sixty years of age to seek a prince who would employ him, but the advice he gave was not always welcome so he eventually returned home to the State of Lu, and there he began to collect a variety of sayings and discussions which eventually became the *Analects*. In fact, this book is our principal source for the teaching of Confucius, and it was probably collated years after his death by some of his disciples and admirers. The collection is largely in anecdotal form and is a discussion of moral, social, religious and political questions put in a very epigrammatic way.

3 The Teaching of Confucius

Confucius was clearly a man who deplored the disruption and decay which he saw in society. He always seems to have had a feeling that somehow T'ien, or Heaven, was inspiring him in the statements he made, and was giving him special protection. Whilst he believed that society required stabilizing and ordering through custom and tradition, he was opposed to extreme measures. For example, he was not in sympathy with the idea of savage punishment for crimes committed, however 'useful' it might appear to be. On the other hand, the idea that love alone was the answer to all social problems found no positive response with him. However idealistic it might be, it was certainly not always pragmatic. One had to take a *middle course* between extremes. It is worth noting that other great thinkers have suggested something similar, although not in the same context (e.g. the Buddha's Middle Way, Aristotle's Golden Mean, and St Paul's 'moderation in all things'). Confucius argued that one should answer hatred with justice and love with benevolence; that the way that one should follow is constantly in the middle between life's extremes; that we should seek to acquire a harmony and balance in life, and that there should be nothing in excess – 'enough is enough, but enough is necessary'; 'excess and deficiency are equally at fault'[1].

Confucius had a great belief in tradition at a time when custom and social mores were failing. He believed, therefore, that it was necessary deliberately to attend to the traditions that were considered valuable and to do one's best to reinforce them. This meant making citizens more conscious of the traditions and habits of their society, even if the basic reasons for such mores were changed in our thinking. There were always new elements to be absorbed, and new factors to be assimilated.

For Confucius there were unquestionably certain virtues which were desirable for any society and its individual members. Firstly, there was *li* which meant propriety, correct conduct or behaviour; the way things should be done. There was a true and appropriate way for all people to behave in the context of their 'station and its duties', and this always involved a certain courtesy, even reverence, in behaviour. There were for Confucius five basic relationships in social life: between ruler and subject, husband and wife, father and son, elder brother and younger brother, and between friend and friend. The healthy ordering of society demanded that these relationships should be properly constituted, and should be harmonious. Duties were mutual and reflected the cosmic harmony of Yang and Yin.

In all this the family unit was the basic unit of society, and Confucius saw the family as a reflection of the social macrocosm – if the family were in a healthy and harmonious state, so also would be society at large. Children needed to respect their parents, and parents were required to fulfil their duties towards their children. In this interaction there was obviously a need to speak the same language, to communicate, to have dialogue. We are all painfully aware of the rate at which current language and meanings can move away from us, until we are no longer 'with it'. Confucius argued that semantics were of prime importance in the family, for 'when the meanings of the father are no longer meaningful to the son, civilization is in danger'. Equally, of course, one might suggest that when the meanings of the son are no longer meaningful to the father, civilization is in danger. There is need for one generation to communicate with another, in order that there might be some sort of continuity and understanding. New lifestyles are perpetually developing and changing, and it is important that one should fully apprehend such changes, or life will cease to be ordered for us, and we shall see only chaos. The mere courtesies of life demanded that we should at least communicate and seek to understand one another. It was for Confucius all a part of the *tao* or system of life, of social order and cosmic harmony.

Secondly, *jen* represented the ideal relationship between people, whether one calls it love, compassion, benevolence or goodness. It meant that empathy for others whereby one could finally gauge and discriminate their feelings so as not to hurt them in any way. It was that compassion whereby one identified completely with others both in their failures and in their successes, and in the exercise of which one did not seek to blame others for one's own failings. Confucius said: 'I have yet to meet a man who, on observing his own faults, blamed himself'[2].

Thirdly, there was a great variety of reciprocity, or *shu*. This was expressed in a somewhat negative form, although like the Golden Rule of Jesus it was positive in application: 'What I do not wish others to do unto me I also wish not to do unto others'[3]. Indeed, for Confucius this was the beginning and the end of the Law, which consisted solely of loyalty, as already expressed in the five human relationships, and in reciprocity[4]. In fact, reciprocity was the one word that would keep all people on the path to the end of their days[5].

Fourthly, there was the virtue called *chun-tzu*, which appears to have embraced a large number of qualities. It was an expression of manhood-at-its-best, true manhood, in which the total Self found its fullest exploration. It is perhaps best described in the words of the *Analects* in the following aphoristic passages [6-13]:

> Great Man, being universal in his outlook, is impartial;
> Petty Man, being partial, is not universal in his outlook.
> Great Man is conscious only of justice; Petty Man, only of self-interest.
> He who concentrates upon the task and forgets about reward may be called Man-at-his-best.
> Wisdom has no doubts. Manhood-at-its-best has no concerns. Courage is without fear.
> The achieving of Manhood-at-its-best must come from you yourself; one does not acquire it from others! Great Man is accommodating, but he is not one of the crowd. Petty Man is one of the crowd, but he is also a source of discord.

> Great Man is dignified but not proud. Petty Man is proud but not dignified.
>
> Great Man reaches complete understanding of the main issues; Petty Man reaches complete understanding of the minute details.

Thus, the virtues of Manhood-at-its-best are an understanding with humility, magnanimity in all situations, sincerity in all utterances and actions, diligence and single-mindedness in work, and a certain graciousness in all relationships with others[14]. The really Great Man puts himself at the disposal of others, is concerned with the wellbeing of others, and is not self-seeking.

Fifthly, there is the quality called *te*, or power. For Confucius this meant the power of moral example and its effect upon people generally. It was no use for a ruler to tell his subjects to be virtuous if he himself were a mean and unworthy person. Indeed, Confucius argued that only the truly reluctant ruler, without personal ambition, was really fit and worthy to rule. Leaders, in fact, led not so much by law as by personal qualities and charisma; they had to inspire people by their very character and its power. And this meant, inevitably, that the leader must first establish order within himself and must be a living exponent of that stability which he looked for in society at large. High position should never be sought for its own sake:

> Do not worry about holding high position; worry rather about playing your proper role. Worry not that no one knows of you; seek to be worth knowing[15].

Finally, there was the quality of *wen*, or high culture. Art, aesthetics, poetry, music, philosophy – these were all preferable to the martial arts, and were to be cultivated for their own sake. But this did not mean for Confucius the loading of the memory with mere factual data, for 'Learning without thought brings ensnarement. Thought without learning totters'[16]. True learning and culture involved an understanding and appreciation of the whole field of knowledge, and not the inculcation of insignificant trivia, for knowledge 'is to know what one knows and what one does not know'[17]. It was, in effect, a sensible awareness of how little we really do know. And, at the end of the day, true knowledge was to know and to love one's fellow men[18]. Moreover, true culture was something that went into the individual to make up the total person and all his qualities. Ultimately, the moral power and culture achieved by Manhood-at-its-best had come from himself, for 'one does not acquire it from others!'[19]. 'The Master is his own path'[20].

The approach of Confucius to religion in general was one largely of acceptance of heaven, earth, ancestors and living people as a sort of inseparable continuum. If he did not elaborate upon religion and religious concepts, it was not because he had none, but rather because he accepted the importance of living to the full in the here and now. We are told that he did not discuss 'anomalies, feats of strength, rebellions or divinities'[21]. When someone enquired about the proper treatment of spirits and divinities, he replied:

> You cannot treat spirits and divinities properly before you are able to treat your fellow-men properly.... You cannot know about death before you know about life[22].

Confucius saw the cosmic order as a totality in which the Supreme Ancestor (*Shang Ti*) ruled over ancestors (*Ti*) and all the peoples and spirits of the universe. There was no break between the divine and the human, and there was a cosmic communion between all beings expressed through the traditional rituals and cults of society. Confucius clearly did not distinguish between ethic and religion – they were one and the same; and he may well have agreed with the statement of Jesus that 'the kingdom of heaven is within you'.

4 Some Other Chinese Philosophers

In discussing other Chinese philosophers in relation to Confucianism, one is always faced with the dual problem of whether such philosophers existed and, if so, when. *Mo Tzu*, for example, according to some historians, was a contemporary of Confucius, whilst according to others he flourished in the fifth century BC after the death of Confucius. Of Mo Tzu's 'Works' fifty-three chapters survive, but generally speaking his critics considered him too intellectual. He has been classified both as an idealist and as a utilitarian. Mo Tzu proposed love, not force, as the answer to society's problems – 'love without discrimination'. This certainly seems, at first blush, to be idealistic, and it probably is, but to Mo Tzu it had an extremely utilitarian basis. Universal love and mutual aid were, in fact, the only way of eradicating war, which was useless. Love paid in the long run, and when all people loved one another the strong were no longer able to overpower the weak, the wealthy could no longer mock the poor, and the cunning would no longer prey upon the simple, for such conditions would no longer obtain.

Mo Tzu may well have begun as a Confucian, but the Doctrine of the Mean eventually appeared to him as being too discriminatory, and he became dissatisfied with it. Certainly a man should love others as himself, in the Confucian sense of reciprocity, but love had to be without any discrimination whatsoever. *Shang Ti* was for him more in the nature of a personal god who loved the whole world universally, and mortal man should follow the example of *Shang Ti*. The utilitarianism of Mo Tzu (or Mohism) was such that he argued, 'If it were not useful, even I would disapprove of it. But how can there be anything that is good, but at the same time not useful?'

Meng-Tzu (Mencius), who flourished during the fourth century BC, was a member of the Confucian School. He spent many years travelling from one State to another seeking to find any ruler who could be persuaded to follow his philosophy. His advice to all rulers was to love and protect the common people, to seek after righteousness and to live simply and humbly. He had a great loathing of war and violence and was virtually a pacifist. He believed strongly in the basic and fundamental goodness of human nature, and that man was born with a moral consciousness which distinguished between good and evil, right and wrong. When he did evil, man realized that he had not lived up to the best that he knew, and he consequently felt guilty and ashamed.

Han Fei Tzu lived during the third century BC, and he was a member of the royal house in the State of Han. He was a proponent of a form of realism coupled with legalism, and he was certainly not a supporter of the Mohist doctrine of love without discrimination. If people did not behave, he suggested, one should deal with them so rigorously that they would never dream of violating the Law again. The purpose of rewards was to encourage people to live in accordance with the Law; the purpose of punishments was to prevent illegal activity, and the heavier the punishments were, the greater the deterrent would be. If anyone should think that such a view was hardly in accordance with that of human nature as propounded by Mencius, then they would of course be right. The fact is (suggested Han Fei Tzu) that, far from being good, human nature is evil, and one cannot compromise, for 'ice and embers cannot lie in the same bowl'. Things are what they are; people are the way they are; we cannot change them fundamentally, but we can put the brakes on them, we can control them:

> No lake is so still but that it has its wave;
> No circle so perfect but that it has its blur.
> I would change things for you if I could;
> As I can't, you must take them as they are.

Han Fei Tzu wanted his society to accept its failures, but at the same time to suppress and punish all its criminals by severe punishment, even death. In this way the best in society as a whole would be preserved and society itself would become stabilized.

5 Lao-Tzu and Taoism

Lao-Tzu, or the Old Man, is usually considered to have been a contemporary of Confucius, although there can be no certainty that he ever existed. In any event, the work *Tao Te Ching*[23] is vastly more important than the author or compilers. There are many legends about Lao-Tzu which are largely of the symbolic variety. One story suggests that he was immaculately conceived by a shooting star and was carried in his mother's womb for sixty, or for eighty-two years. When he was finally born he was already a wise old man with white hair; he continued to live until he was one hundred and sixty years old. Lao-Tzu lived a very simple life as a keeper of State archives, until he found that he could no longer put up with the corruption in society. He set out, therefore, to travel to the mountains in the West, but on his journey a gate-keeper asked him to set down his teaching in writing. This he did and was then taken up into heaven in a cloud. The work he wrote, entitled 'The Book of the Way and Its Power' (*Tao Te Ching*) was composed in two volumes, totalling eighty-one chapters of about two hundred stanzas written in rhymes. Some scholars have suggested that, in fact, this work probably dates from the third century BC, and that it was a composite effort. In Chinese it is represented by about five thousand characters.

The *tao* is such a mystical concept that words are inadequate to define it or to describe it. It is ineffable, and at the same time it is both immanent and transcendent. It has been translated perhaps most frequently as the path, reason, word, God and system. The system usually means the Cosmic System, and it is the equivalent of the Greek *logos*. It thus has a number of connotations, from the way the universe itself works to a method, principle, doctrine or just a way of doing something. It permeates everything and is both 'within us and around'. It is the dynamic, the driving force behind all life; it is Bergson's *élan vital* or vital force, Shaw's Life Force, the physicist's Energy, and the psychologist's *hormé*. If a man wishes to be in harmony with the universe he must himself have *tao*, or order, within. As we look at the plurality of objects and people around us, we find that there is a unity at the back of them all – it is the *tao*; and the supreme end of life is to attain to oneness with the *tao*:

> There is a Being, wonderful, perfect;
> It existed before heaven and earth!

How quiet it is! How spiritual it is!
It stands alone and it does not change.
It moves around and around, but it does
    not on this account suffer.
All life comes from it.
It wraps everything with its Love as in a garment.
Yet it claims no honour, it does not demand
    to be Lord.
I do not know its name, and so I call it
    TAO, the Way, and I rejoice in its TE,
    or Power[24].

Thus, the *tao* is the integrating principle of all life, to be found within the universe itself, within man, and within the whole of life around him. Within the Self it maintains a certain identicality with the reality of the external world; but it is not something that can be delineated in words. It can be known only by experience and by acquaintance, for

Those who know do not speak:
Those who speak do not know[25].

There is, therefore, something quite incommunicable about the nature of the *tao*, and the only way to know it is to have personal experience of it. We can know about and about something, and yet never *know* it, never have complete and perfect apprehension of it. There is the story of Chuang Tzu, who was strolling over a bridge with another Chinese, Hui Tzu. Chuang Tzu said, 'Look at the little fish darting hither and thither at will. Such is the pleasure that fish enjoy.' Hui Tzu answered, somewhat reprovingly, 'You are not a fish; how can you possibly know what gives pleasure to a fish?' Chuang Tzu immediately responded, 'You are not I. How do you know that I do not know what gives pleasure to a fish?' There is a subjectivism, according to Taoism, about all experience; so that what gives pleasure and immediate apprehension to one may leave another quite cold. Chuang Tzu saw a validity in all points of view for the very simple reason that, without a very deep empathy with the persons concerned, one could not possibly share their immediate perceptions and understanding.

Again, the *tao* is disclosed only to those who are prepared for its conditions. There is much that we have accumulated through life which we must shed, in terms of misinformation, misconstruction, prejudice and partiality. The *tao* is already there within us; what we have to do is to allow it to escape by opening up a way for it through the layers of accreted prejudice, hatred and fear. Once the dams have been broken down, the *tao* flows like water – gentle, taking all shapes, filling all emptiness, finding a natural level, and wearing down the toughest opposition:

> Man, at his best, like water,
> Serves as he goes along:
> Like water he seeks his own level,
> The common level of life.
>
> What is more fluid, more yielding than water?
> Yet, back it comes again, wearing down the tough strength
> Which cannot move to withstand it.
> So it is that the strong yield to the weak,
> The haughty to the humble.
> This we know, but never learn[26].

The *tao* is finally demonstrated in the interaction of Yang and Yin and in their unification. The Yang is the positive, male, active and light element in the universe, whilst the Yin is the negative, female, passive and dark element. These two elements are not so much in opposition to each other as in a state of tension or complementarity. The circle of the *tao* embraces them both; at the circumference and at the centre they must, therefore, be one. Moreover, each is to be found in the other's domain as a permanent reminder that life is not composed of entirely discrete elements: they all intertwine and are interrelated. It is only when we seek to separate things, to analyze and categorize them, that we lose their totality and essential unity.

The quality *te* means virtue, dominion, sway or power, and it is in essence that moral power which holds society together; it is the very nature of any thing, 'because it is in virtue of its *te* that a thing is what it is'[27]. Through meditation one can get to know one's own deepest nature and its inbuilt power so that ultimately, through a thorough understanding of the Self, one can begin to imagine creatively, and to move mountains.

One of the main concepts of Taoism is that of *wu wei*, or actionless activity. This does not mean an ideal of *no* activity at all, but rather of no unnecessary or unnatural action. Thus, taking the image of water again, it does not attempt to flow uphill or through hard rock; nevertheless, in taking the line of least resistance it manages somehow to insinuate into every crevice and fissure in the rocks, and to wear down the strongest blockages in its path. All this may take time, but there is no hurry – 'as water finds its way, gently, effortlessly', yet somehow manages to touch all points, 'so does the superior man conduct himself'[28].

Wu wei implies relaxing and letting go. Most people have found, at some time or other in life, that the more tensed up they get, and the more consciously they attempt to do things, the less they manage effectively to accomplish. Yet 'to the mind that is still the whole universe surrenders'; it cannot be taken by storm, but it gives itself up freely to those who are prepared mentally and spiritually to accept. The more we agonize and resist mentally, the less we seem to accomplish. How many really creative people have had their greatest inspirations when they ceased to beat their brains and allowed the *tao* to flow through them in creative quietude! The truly sensitive reed bends with the wind and so never gets broken. Similarly, the teacher or leader who anxiously rushes round in a futile fulness of activity may, in the very long run, wear himself out and accomplish little; but

> A leader is best
> When people barely know that he exists.
> ...Of a good leader, who talks little,
> When his work is done, his aim fulfilled,
> They will all say, 'We did this ourselves'[29].

Taoism rejected the hostility and self-assertion so evident in society. There was a great need for humility coupled with simplicity. The utility of both objects and people depended more often on what was absent, on the intrinsic nothingness, rather than what was present, which was often complicated.

> Thirty spokes will converge
> In the hub of a wheel
> But the use of the cart
> Will depend on the part
> Of the hub that is void.

> With a wall all around
> A clay bowl is moulded;
> But the use of the bowl
> Will depend on the part
> Of the bowl that is void.

> Cut out windows and doors
> In the house as you build;

But the use of the house
Will depend on the space
In the walls that is void.

So advantage is had
From whatever is there;
But usefulness rises
From whatever is not[30].

Just as space is functional in art, architecture, building and pottery, so also is 'emptiness' functional in relation to people's minds. Our minds are so often cluttered with half-remembered dogmas and ideas that they close up at the mere suggestion of something new or different.

A humble attitude towards nature, with its incredibly intricate composition, will eventually reveal more, and keep it intact, than will the aggressive attempt to conquer all, for:

Those who take over the earth
And shape it to their will,
Never, I notice, succeed;
The earth is a vessel so sacred
That at the mere approach of the profane
It is marred.
And when they reach out their fingers it is gone[31].

Moreover, there are many different descriptions of the universe, all of which may have some sort of validity; and, of course, our descriptions have their vogue and are gradually, or even suddenly, modified out of existence. But the 'Reality' is still there to be described, even though that Reality itself may have changed. Indeed, our descriptions sometimes come full circle, so that we find ourselves using terms and analogies that are virtually identical with those of ancient times[32].

The quietism of Taoism was supported by an opposition to all externally imposed rules of morality, which it regarded as artificial.

True morality was self-engendered from within the individual. Such morality would accept no violence against another person, and therefore wars and civil strife were wrong:

> One who would guide a leader in the uses of life will warn him against the use of arms for conquest. Even the finest arms are an instrument of evil: an army's harvest is a waste of thorns[33].

Taoism was thus pacifist in outlook, its morality was personal and came from within the innermost being, and the *tao* itself was identified with heaven, or *T'ien*. Union with *T'ien* through the *tao* gave immortality to man's spirit.

Although little is known about the life of *Chuang Tzu*, he is generally accepted as one of the greatest Taoist philosophers, and that he flourished during the latter part of the fourth century BC and the early part of the third century BC. The book of *Chuang Tzu*, although compiled mostly by Kuo Hsiang and his School, enjoys a status second only to the *Tao Te Ching*. Chuang Tzu held a view of evolution which was circular rather than linear – it was a process of endless return within a closed circle. There was a certain tolerance about his philosophy, and there existed for him the possibility of many different points of view on almost every topic. Indeed, he went on to suggest that there was equal validity, or invalidity, in all points of view and judgements. One had to reach a higher point of impartiality in relation to such 'antinomies of reason'. In a sense there was nothing untypical about Chuang Tzu's thought – China has always been a world of opposites, of positive and negative, of Yang and Yin, of being (*yu*) and non-being (*wu*), of movement (*tung*) and quiescence (*ching*), of activity (*wei*) and non-activity (*wu wei*). These opposites may seem paradoxical, and at times even illogical, to the Westerner, but to the Chinese they represent the very fibre of the cosmos; and if one follows current physical descriptions and nomenclature it is almost like reading a piece of Chinese philosophy. This philosophy shows considerable interest in the psychological problem of the control over mental activity by sense-perceptions, and sees the human mind as the counterpart in the individual of the *tao* in the universe at large.

6 Mahayana Buddhism

The main schism in Buddhism between the Mahayana and Hinayana Schools has already been mentioned under the Religions of India (Chapter 9 on 'Buddhism'). The Mahayana School was probably to be found in China as early as AD 65 during the time of the Emperor Ming-Ti, and the Buddhist scriptures had been brought to China by some visiting monks. At first there was some resistance to the teaching of the Buddha, particularly in relation to the concept of reincarnation, which seemed to eliminate the possibility of any form of ancestor-worship, since ancestors probably no longer existed as such. Mahayana Buddhism, however, appeared to have a lot in common with Taoist teaching, particularly in the more mystical approach of meditation and quietism. In addition, the concept of universal salvation and the potential buddhahood of all men, appealed very much to the humanistic approach of Chinese religious and moral teaching.

During the fourth century AD, the Pure Land School (*Ching-Tu*) was founded by a Taoist called Hui Yan. Chinese were now allowed to become monks, and Amitabha (or Amida) was regarded as the buddha at the centre of their worship. Later on the *Tien-T'ai* School was founded, and this sect, named after a sacred mountain, sought to synthesize all the different sects and their scriptures. In AD 520 an Indian monk, Bodhidharma, travelled to China and emphasized the importance of *dhyana*, or meditation, which became an all-important technique with some Chinese Buddhist groups who called it Ch'an, which later became the Zen Buddhism so well-known in Japan. In line with Mahayana Buddhism generally there developed a strong belief in the bodhisattvas, those individuals who had reached the state of bodhi, or enlightenment, but who had deferred their own transition to nirvana in order, out of their great compassion and sacrifice, to help all other beings to become enlightened and saved. Kwanyin became the great symbol of mercy and compassion in China, and has been worshipped as a goddess and giver of children. She was the equivalent of the Sanskrit Avalokita, the Tibetan Chenresi, and the Japanese Kwannon. The 'Buddha to come' in Chinese belief was Maitreya – the fat, jolly and laughing Buddha.

7   The Subsequent History of Chinese Religion

Writing in 1947, Chiang Monlin[34] said:

> As I stood by the Confucian Temple in Peiping, I felt as if Heaven , earth and myself merged in one vastness. Nature and man are one and inseparable.

Confucianism became a State religion during the Han dynasty (206 BC – AD 220), and its general morality and code of conduct became a basic training and discipline for all State officials. In AD 59 the Emperor decreed that sacrifices should be made to Confucius at least in every urban school in China. During the succeeding centuries, shrines and small sanctuaries were erected to him in every part of the Chinese Empire, whilst his collection of Sayings (the *Analects*) became the basis for all education. By the sixteenth century most homes had a small ancestral tablet to his memory, before which food offerings were made, prayers were said, and incense was burned.

In AD 1934 the birthday of Confucius was declared a national holiday; but since the advent of Communism in China in AD 1949, the State cult of Confucianism has ceased to exist. Mao Zedong (Mao Tse-tung) was once reported as saying, 'I hated Confucius from about the age of eight'; nevertheless, although Confucius was regarded as a traditionalist and supporter of the feudal system of his times, many of his sayings have found a new guise in the Maoist philosophy. There is something about the Chinese character and nature that manages to assimilate all thoughts, things and people that come within its orbit. They have managed to absorb all their conquerors and to retain some of the better qualities that they have introduced; they have themselves imported Western ideas and infused them with Chinese culture and ideology. They certainly could not eradicate at one stroke the influence and ideals of such a person as Confucius, any more than the Western world could erase the indelible influence of Jesus.

Taoism had certain principles that were fundamental to Chinese life and philosophy that, once more, it would be impossible to dispose of them completely. This is partly because they are adaptable to virtually any system. If Chuang Tzu was right when he argued that all viewpoints had relative validity and merit, then it was possible to argue that communism had validity as seen from a particular and temporal point of view. Such a theme fitted in comfortably with the classic *I Ching* (the Book of Changes), for 'whatever is born or done this moment of time has the qualities of this moment of time'. One can change one's position or point of view according to the time and the necessities of the Age, for life itself is like a dream in which one changes one's own being, just as a kaleidoscope's pattern may be changed by a sudden movement. As Chuang Tzu[35] remarked:

> I dreamt I was a butterfly... now I do not know whether I was then a man dreaming I was a butterfly, or whether I am now a butterfly dreaming I am a man.

Like many other teachings which seek to rise above the discrimination between good and evil, Taoism found its purity of purpose eventually transformed into a relativity of behaviour and judgement that resulted in all sorts of abuse. It turned to magical practices and alchemy. Lao Tzu himself was deified and worshipped along with other gods. There developed a 'hygienic school' concerned with breathing practices similar to those of yoga, with panacea and longevity pills, herbal and quack medicines, and a vast number of odd superstitions. In the second century AD, a Taoist church was formed with missionaries, and during the T'ang dynasty (AD 618-907) Taoism came into full imperial favour. Eventually its leaders became celestial masters, or 'popes', and they lived on sacred mountains. They formed secret sects and societies (one such being the 'League of Righteous Energy') which were very violent and anti-foreign, and were in fact representative of everything that classical Taoism rejected. The Boxer rebellions were led mainly by these renegade Taoists. In 1927 the revolutionaries evicted them from their lands which they divided up amongst the peasants. The Communist government eventually crushed the Taoist societies and, with Buddhist monks and Confucian priests, they were made to work like all other Chinese subjects, with reference neither to belief nor religious persuasion.

Whether the question of one Chinese religion or three is really any longer relevant or merely academic one really cannot say. Communism has mixed attitudes towards the pursuance of religion by any of the people, unless the situation is something that can be manipulated to their own advantage. Certainly prior to the Communist Revolution it might have been difficult, in most cases, to identify particular Chinese as Confucianist, Taoist or Buddhist. They were most likely pursuing elements of all three. As C K Yang[36] has said:

> A person may pray in a Buddhist temple of the God of Medicine (Hua T'o), for health, depending on the magical power desired for the occasion. He goes to a temple, lights candles and incense; mumbles a prayer for the benefit or benediction desired, burns papers, pays the priest (if there is one) for the incense and for the oil for the 'everburning lamp', and leaves the temple without further obligation. When one hires Buddhist or Taoist priests or professional magicians to pray and perform magic at home or elsewhere, the obligation also ends at the conclusion of the service. Such a relationship between the worshipper, on the one hand, and the temple or priest on the other, is an 'over-the-counter' deal, and the worshipper is free to shop in the religious market according to his taste and convictions.

11 Japanese Religion

1 Shinto

The indigenous religion of Japan is known as Shinto, a word derived from the Chinese Shen-tao, meaning 'The Way of the Gods'; the Japanese equivalent is Kami-no-Michi. The original inhabitants of Japan were known as Ainus, some of whom still live in the northern island of Hokkaido and in Sakhalin, which is now Russian territory. Their early religion was a form of animistic nature worship, with an element of totemism in it. Much of the cultus was involved with fertility and its maintenance, but it developed gradually into a firm belief in the divinity of kingship. The sun was worshipped as the physical expression of the sun-goddess, Amaterasu, whilst the general polytheistic beliefs embraced the moon-god, Tauki-yomi, and the storm-god, Susa-no-wo. The Japanese islands themselves were, according to legend, created by Izanagi, 'the male who invites', and Izanami, 'the female who invites'. These two were really the Japanese equivalent of the Chinese Yang and Yin. All gods had their own particular functions – the sun-goddess, Amaterasu, ruled over the whole world; Susa-no-wo was responsible for damage done to the harvest, in particular the rice paddy-fields, and rituals were enacted which demonstrated the victory of Amaterasu over Susa-no-wo. This triumph over all enemies, including the most powerful, was represented in the victories of the Mikado or Emperor, who was the earthly descendant and representative of Amaterasu. The Mikado himself was worshipped as divine, and the first duty of all his people was to be loyal to him in every circumstance, and to support him faithfully against all of his enemies.

Mt Fuji was regarded as the centre of Shinto worship, the very home of the sun-goddess. Japan itself has been known as the 'Land of the gods (kami)', and its 800,000 kami have had shrines erected to them all over Japan where they are supposed to dwell, either permanently or temporarily when summoned during the various local and seasonal rites. In general, there is no congregational worship in Shinto, but all followers participate in rituals carried out in the environs of the shrines. There are two main shrines in Japan, namely, the Grand Imperial Shrine of Ise, which was served originally by the daughter of the Emperor as the high priestess of the religion; and the Great Meiji Shrine of Tokyo. In all shrines the mirror is a sacred symbol of the god concerned.

The kami really represented anything unusual in nature, such as mountains, trees or stones of peculiar shape or size, or in some odd position. So that virtually anything in nature could be representative of kami, or divinity. They might be regarded as superior, miraculous or divine; and as good or evil. Sometimes they represent great heroes of the past who have become deified and kept in the memory of the common people. In their homes people would erect small shelves on which to place their gods, called *kami-dana*. Kami, in fact, is such a general term that it virtually has the same connotation as mana, or power; and it is this mana in the kami that is contacted and manipulated by Shinto priests in order to obtain health, wealth, a good harvest and fertility generally. State Shinto, with Emperor worship as its very core and *raison d'etre*, led to a view of the divinity of the Emperor which meant that he could do no wrong, and that death in his service would lead to an immediate entry into the realms of the heavenly Amaterasu as kami, demi-gods or heroes. After the Second World War, the Emperor Hirohito officially repudiated his own divinity, and in theory at least State Shinto was abolished. In practice, however, many Shinto sects have survived, in some instances combined with Buddhism in one or another of its many forms.

2 Buddhism

Buddhist sects, such as the Kusha, Kegon and Hosso, infiltrated into Japan from China during the sixth, seventh and eighth centuries, but today they are little more than a memory. Other sects, such as the Jo-Jitsu, proved to be insufficiently practical and active, and too literary. In AD 804 the Tendai sect, with its chief scripture 'The Lotus of the True Law', and with its ascetic discipline, entered Japan. Broadly speaking, it attempted to integrate the essential beliefs of Mahayana and Hinayana Buddhism and to reconcile their differences. It employed forms of yoga and meditation (*dhayana*) in order to develop powers of concentration and controlled behaviour. Another sect, the Shingon, 'Mystery' or 'True Word' sect, regarded the kami of Shinto as expressions or emanations of the Buddha. It took up many of the Shinto rituals, and combined them with Tantric incantations and divinations; it claimed to control the weather, increase fertility, ensure good luck through its charms and rites, cure physical disease, and rescue people from hell itself.

During the latter half of the thirteenth century a Buddhist monk called Nichiren (1222-82), a member of the Tendai sect which had its headquarters on Mt Hiei in the hills above Kyoto, became thoroughly dissatisfied with both the Tendai sect and other forms of Buddhism. He suddenly conceived the idea that he alone could save Japan, and saw himself as the incarnation of the Bodhisattva, or the Saviour-Buddha, who was foretold in the sutra of the 'Lotus of the True Law'. With considerable prophetic fierceness and zeal he denounced all other sects and all other Buddhist scriptures. The Lotus Sutra alone was for him the true and inspired scripture, whilst all other scriptures were superfluous or positively harmful. Nichiren derived his apocalyptic mysticism from Mahayana Buddhism, and identified his religion with the national life of his country. We shall see some of the developments of this sect in modern Japan when we consider other religions in Section 4 of this chapter.

The Jodo, or Pure Land Sect, was founded in 1175 by the scholar Genku; it held that the Lord God Amida (or Nembutsu) desired all men to be saved, to ascend towards the Pure Land, and to attain to buddhahood. Salvation was achieved not by effort, not by faith, not even by works, but by the repetition of the mantra, 'Namu-Amidam-Butsu' ('Hail Amida Buddha'). The Jodo sect gradually became the chief Buddhist sect in Japan, mainly perhaps because it held out salvation to all with a minimum of real effort. In most Japanese homes, certainly before WW2, there was (in addition to their *kami-dana*) a *butsu-dana* or Buddha-shelf, on which there stood almost invariably an image of Amida.

During the Tokugawa regime (AD 1600-1868) the Shoguns, or State dictators, made use of Buddhism to isolate the Japanese Emperor, as well as Japan, from the West. This regime developed the cult and code of Bushido, or the 'warrior-knight way'. The *Samurai*, or warrior class, had to combine the loyalty to the Emperor and country which was inculcated by Shinto, the devotion to ancestors and the general rules of morality taught by Confucius, with the rigorous discipline which permeated all Zen instruction, in order to formulate a code of conduct and action for *every* situation that might arise. The virtues embodied by the Samurai, and expressed in principle by Bushido, were honour, loyalty, justice, truthfulness, politeness, gratitude, reserve, and above all courage. Any Samurai who failed to maintain these virtues, or in any way disgraced the Bushido caste, had one option only open to them – they had to commit *seppuku* (more vulgarly known as *harakiri)*, or suicide. There was also a form of suicide which was a virtue in itself, not simply the only way out for one who had lost face. This was the sort of suicide enacted by the *kamikase* pilots during the WW2, for the sake of their divine Emperor and country, when they flew their bomb-filled planes directly at enemy targets. As a result of their sacrifice they immediately became kami, heroes and gods.

3 Zen Buddhism

The great path has no gates,
Thousands of roads enter it,
When one passes through the gateless gate
He walks freely between heaven and earth[1].

Tradition has it that when the Buddha preached his 'Flower Sermon' all that he did was to hold a golden lotus aloft, and then said nothing, and he continued to say nothing. Out of this grew the concept and practice of *dhayana*, or meditation. In AD 520 Bodhidharma took the method to China, where it was called *Ch'an* and in the twelfth century, under the influence of the Rinzai Sect, it reached Japan where it was called *Zen*. The belief was that continuous meditation developed illumination by an intuitive process or immediate insight, but it all required a very vigorous and unrelenting self-discipline.

To explicate Zen is very much like the attempt to analyze Taoism. There is a sense in which it is inexplicable in terms of reason and logic, and as soon as we begin to use words we lose it. As always in these matters, the artist, the poet or the musician stands a far better chance of getting the message across than does the philosopher or the theologian. But the attempt must be made; and in one sense, at least, it is encouraging to note that one of the greatest masters of Zen, Daisetz Suzuki, was a prolific writer on the subject; in another sense, however, when one reflects on his brilliance and level of awareness, it is no great comfort. In the end Zen has to be experienced, it cannot be taught. It can, nevertheless, be subtly communicated by those who have undergone its discipline and illumination. Dylan Thomas[2] expressed something akin to its spirit in the following lines:

Light breaks on secret lots,
On tips of thought where thoughts smell in the rain;
When logics die,
The secret of the soil grows through the eye,
And blood jumps in the sun;
Above the waste allotments the dawn halts.

It is when we cease to agitate our minds, or to use logic that, suddenly, the truth dawns like a light that 'breaks where no sun shines'.

One is always reminded somewhat of the serious-minded Charles Dodgson who managed to write numerous books on logic, and yet was able to compose the classic *Alice's Adventures in Wonderland* and *Through the Looking-Glass*. We are introduced to a mad world in which, after our initial acceptance of its universe of discourse, nothing seems impossible. The very simplicity of Zen is itself deceptive, for behind this apparent simplicity lies the profundity of the mysteries of the universe. The whole of our life seems to be bound up with tensions and a sense of dualities and paradoxes. Zen aims, by a variety of mental (and sometimes even physical) shocks to relieve these tensions and to bring the individual into a state which is beyond all duality. This is the state of *satori* or enlightenment, the mental awareness of the 'suchness' (*tathata*) or essential nature of all things.

We know only too well the embarrassment sometimes caused by people who attempt to describe their religious experience. It is not necessarily a fact that we are sceptical concerning their experience: it is just that we ourselves have never had it, and we are not in any way able to subject it to any known tests that will validate it either as a real experience or as something that we ourselves might have, It is, in a very real sense, ineffable and incommunicable. They *know* that they have had the experience: we can neither know that they have had it nor know that we too can experience it. Moreover, the words used to describe the experience in retrospect are so painfully inadequate and uncharged that, as a result, they usually fall flat in the repetition. Truth and Reality go beyond all human language and transcend our deepest thoughts. 'It is as foolish to tie labels round the neck of Truth as to throw adjectives at the sunset'.[3]

The Zen Buddhist, then, is obviously not interested in creeds, canons and dogmas; these can no more give us reality than a description of a New Guinea jungle can give us the experience of it. There are people who recite creeds weekly, if not daily, who have hardly ever given a second thought as to the essential meaning of what they are reciting. One is reminded of the words of Jesus, 'Not every one who says unto me, 'Lord, Lord', shall enter the Kingdom of Heaven'; because the Kingdom is not a matter of creeds, confessions or avowed allegiances, it is a question of inner experience and enlightenment. The Zen Buddhist argues that one can theorize about God and perform mental gymnastics to prove his existence – or even his non-existence – but the truth and reality of the matter lie not in logic or dialectic, but in personal 'knowledge' and experience in terms of one's total being.

All this does not mean, of course, that Zen does not have its own techniques. In *zazen* one sits in meditation, with unfocused gaze, in a *zendo* or hall for meditation, or in the quiet of one's own room. Meditation is an art which requires repeated and daily practice, and which obviously does not come easily to everyone. But the theme, as with Taoism, is that 'to the mind that is still the whole universe surrenders', and 'be still and know'.

Another technique of Zen is the setting of problems or the statement of paradoxes which are, logically speaking, insoluble. These problems or riddles are termed *koans*, and their object is to shock the mind into a state beyond tension and duality. 'What was the appearance of your face before your ancestors were born?' 'A man kept a goose in a bottle, and it grew larger and larger until it could not get out of the bottle any more. He did not want to break the bottle, nor did he wish to hurt the goose; how would *you* get it out?' 'We are all familiar with the sound of two hands clapping, but what is the sound of one hand clapping?'

We have become familiar in the West with many of these koans, and some people still make a literal attempt to solve the problems; but the whole spirit of Zen is against any verbal solutions – the answers lie ultimately in action and experience. Thus, one master simply raised one finger when anyone ever enquired concerning the meaning of Zen; another would hit the enquirer on the head; yet another would immediately take up some apparently irrelevant activity. But in Zen no activity is really irrelevant. The theme is perhaps most straightforwardly represented by the story of the novitiate monk who said to his master, 'I have just entered your monastery; would you kindly give me some instruction?' 'Yes – have you eaten yet?' 'I have.' 'Then go and wash your bowl.' Anyone looking for instant miracles is doomed to disappointment, for these are not of the essence of Zen, which somehow only the poet manages to capture:

> Miraculous power and marvellous activity –
> Drawing water and hewing wood[4].
> Sitting quietly, doing nothing,
> Spring comes, and the grass grows by itself[5].

In *sanzen* the pupil sits down beside the Zen master in meditation. The master may be used as a sort of sounding-board or agitant in order that the pupil may develop his sensitivity and awareness with some help and guidance. There are limits here, of course, since there is basically nothing to teach, nor does the Zen master seek to teach anything. He himself has already trod the path, and in some indescribable way and charismatic manner he may well transmit something of reality and truth through his own beingness and personality. Moreover, it is in this one-to-one situation that the Zen master may agitate the mind of the pupil into some intuitive awareness of himself and his world through the posing of paradoxes and problems as exemplified in the koans.

Satori is the sudden illumination of one's own inner consciousness by a new and previously unconsidered truth; or it may be by an idea or thought previously considered but left half-digested in the unconscious. Professor W I B Beveridge[6] has referred to intuition as an 'inductive leap', which is not unlike the sudden diversion of an electron from one orbit to another, leaving no clear trace of its path to demonstrate its continuity. It is a mental and spiritual explosion through which the individual may find identity with all others, and indeed with the universe itself. One who has this experience may describe it thus: 'Zing! I entered. I seemed to lose the boundaries of my physical body with all of its limitations. I was standing at the very centre of the universe, and I saw myriads of people coming towards me – but they were all the same being, namely, myself. I was myself the universe, and no individual had ever existed.'

Life itself becomes different after such an experience as this: nothing can ever be the same again. One may do relatively the same things, but the individual is now fully in harmony with them; one may see the same things, but they possess a different, fuller depth and quality. This was expressed by Ch'ing-yuan[7] in the following way:

> Before I had studied Zen for thirty years, I saw mountains as mountains, and waters as waters. When I arrived at a more intimate knowledge, I came to the point where I saw that mountains are not mountains, and waters are not waters. But now that I have got its very substance I am at rest. For it's just that I see mountains once again as mountains, and waters once again as waters.

For the Zen Buddhist *this* is life eternal; the here and now in which all things and all life may be experienced. Eternal life does not *begin* at all since this would be a contradiction in terms. It is in everything that we do and are. This timelessness of consciousness has repeatedly been expressed by poets, such as T S Eliot in 'The Love Song of J Alfred Prufrock'[8] and by Rupert Brooke in his poem entitled, 'Dining-Room Tea'[9]:

> Under a vast and starless sky
> I saw the immortal moment lie.
> One instant I, an instant, knew
> As God knows all. And it and you
> I, above Time, oh, blind! could see
> In witless immortality.
> I saw the marble cup; the tea,
> Hung in the air, an amber stream;
> I saw the fire's unglittering gleam,
> The painted flame, the frozen smoke.

> ... Dazed at length
> Human eyes grew, mortal strength
> Wearied; and Time began to creep.

And so, for the poet, 'the broken syllable was ended', and he returned from a million miles, after a million years, to the unbroken laughter around him. In similar fashion, for the Buddhist, Eternity flashes into Time as we know it and destroys its linearity. Like Henry Vaughan[10], he sees Eternity in a moment and the discrete elements of linear time are swallowed up.

And just as Time becomes a whole so, to the Zen follower who seeks satori, the Mind and Consciousness are indivisible. Nothing and no one can be excluded from the totality of this experience. We live in an age when logic, analysis and categorization are all-important. We are outstanding in the art and practice of differentiation – 'We murder to dissect'. But for the Zen Buddhist the most important thing in life is to see people whole.

Zen has entered a whole range of Japanese activities – *ikebana*, or flower arrangement; *origami*, or paper cutting; poetry, especially in the form of *haikus*, which require both inspiration and discipline; *chado*, or tea preparation; *kendo*, a tough form of duel with bamboo poles; archery[11]; *bonsai*, or landscape gardening in miniature; black-ink landscape painting; and *judo*, in which the opponent's own force is harnessed and used against him, whilst one's own force is employed with economy and subtlety. But in all things Zen sits loosely; it has no abiding-place, it has perfect freedom – for the mind abides where there is no abiding. It seeks ultimate enlightenment, but it is as much unattached to the aim of satori as to anything else, for satori is not something to be grasped at will; rather it comes with profound humility. Thus, fully involved in life, the Zen Buddhist remains unattached. Should he lose all of his possessions in life, even though an intruder should rob him of all his valued objects, he still says with resignation:

> The thief left it behind –
> The moon at the window[12].

4 Some Other Current Religions

It has been estimated that there are well over 170 religions in Japan, about one-third of which have a Shinto base, whilst another third are centred on some form of Buddhism. The remainder are a mixture of Shinto, Buddhism and Christianity. Most of them have a religious headquarters as a sort of holy temple and place of pilgrimage. Their creeds and doctrines are, in the main, simple and easy to understand, free of archaic jargon, and lacking that esotericism which acted as a closed door to all but the thoroughly initiated. In the main they are concerned with the establishment of peace in their own society, and some regard themselves as mediators for the rest of the world. The Kingdom of God is not some 'far-off divine event', but rather something which is to be established here and now. Life, therefore, is one whole, and religion is in no way to be divorced from everyday activity. Thus, many of them have become politically-orientated, and their doors are open to all, thus seeking to provide for man a sense of personal dignity, serenity and uniqueness. Most of them, apart from such sects as Soka Gakkai, accept the relativity of all religions:

> We are all climbing Mt Fuji, some from one starting-place, some from others, so we cannot see each other now because the mountain is between us, but we will all see the same moon when we finally arrive at the top[13].

(a) Tenrikyo

This religion was founded by a woman named Nakayama Miki in 1863, when she decided to destroy her house and to give all her personal property to the poor. The name Tenrikyo means 'the teaching of divine wisdom', and Miki, who was originally brought up as a Buddhist, acted as a spiritualist medium and as a mediatrix between Divine Wisdom and man. Miki developed dance, ecstasy or trance, and faith healing in her religion. Whilst she herself brought considerable comfort to her devoted followers, she died in 1887 at the age of eighty-nine after enduring considerable persecution, poverty and terms of imprisonment. Today her descendants are in charge of the religion, whose headquarters are at Tenri City, the City of Divine Wisdom. The devotees of the religion, currently numbering more than two million, hold services twice daily, at sunrise and sunset, and periodically reproduce or re-enact their conception of the creation of the world in the Kanrodai Dance. Their sole deity is the god Tenri-o-no-mikoto, the Lord of Divine Wisdom who was the creator of all things. All people have sinned and need salvation, which is freely granted to those who enter the sect. There is a firm belief in an after-life and some form of reincarnation. All members of Tenrikyo are expected to be missionary in their outlook and to propagate the gospel of Tenri.

(b) Kurozumikyo

This sect was founded in 1814 by the Kurozumi family and it is interested only in Japan and things which are specifically Japanese. Its followers, numbering in the region of a million, are mostly farming people who are still traditional Shintoists at heart; in fact, Kurozumikyo is one of the thirteen main Shinto sects still in existence. For them, the Sun-goddess, Amaterasu-o-mikami, is still supreme, and the eight million gods who originally formed a part of Shinto polytheism are regarded as manifestations of the Sun-goddess. All creatures are sons of God, or rather of the Goddess, and man must give up his selfishness and be outgoing towards others – again, strictly within the context of Japan. Healing is very important in this religion, and a variety of therapies, including hypnotism, are employed. Its main concern is with life in the present, and so it concentrates on how to live here and now rather than in some after-life. There is a oneness between the deity and man, and death becomes irrelevant in much the same sort of way as it was to Confucius – there is utter and complete continuity between heaven and earth.

(c) Konkokyo

This religion was founded in 1859, and it has a close connection with Shinto. Elements such as magic, exorcism or divination find no place in its beliefs and practice, but there is a considerable emphasis upon self-criticism, social interest and piety. Because of its social interest it has a great concern for education which takes a high place in its general organization. Daily life, including religious practices such as prayer, is all-important, and the sect demands absolute belief in God with sincerity and thoroughness. Faith, it says, 'polishes the jewel of your heart', and so the individual believer must have great faith, surrender all selfish desires, and develop harmony within society and throughout the universe. Konkokyo believes that all people are God's children, and it is entirely monotheistic in its worship of the One Great Father of the Universe, Tenchi-kane-no-kami. It accepts that there have been, and are mediators between God and man, and it is very tolerant of other religions such as Buddhism and Christianity. Its followers number in the region of three-quarters of a million, all of whom find some identity with the Father through their philosophy of suffering and salvation:

> Our suffering is God's affliction too,
> Our salvation is God's joy.

(d) The Nichiren Group: Soka Gakkai

The main religious sects in this group are Reiyukai, Rissho Kosei Kai and Soka Gakkai. We shall briefly mention the first two, but our main concern will be with Soka Gakkai. *Reiyukai*, which was founded in 1925 by Kubo Kakutaro, is the 'Association of the Friends of the Spirit'. It has been the perpetual victim of division within its membership, which has resulted in at least eight splits from the main group. Its headquarters are to be found in a large hall in Tokyo. A mandala composed by Kubo is the centre of its worship, and meditation upon it is claimed to give direct communication with all bodhisattvas and buddhas, whether past, present or future. There is no separate doctrine of any Supreme Being – all the power of the universe is centrated in the mandala. For all believers there are six essential rules of conduct, referred to as *Rokuseigyo*: (1) every day they must read selected portions of the Lotus Sutra; (2) they must possess a personal copy of the Sutra; (3) they must carry a rosary; (4) they must wear a shoulder band; (5) they must have a copy of the mandala; and (6) they must erect an altar in their homes, which must be a replica of the altar at headquarters, and they must worship their ancestors in front of it. Reiyukai is very much a personal religion of self-realization, and it lacks something of the usual fanaticism of the Nichiren sects. Its missionary activity is of a gentle nature, called *michibiku*, that is, to give guidance along the way. Moreover, it is not exclusive in its approach, but is prepared to make contact with other religious groups.

Rissho Kosei Kai means the 'Society for the Establishment of Righteousness and Friendly Intercourse', and it has proved its success by gaining over two million followers since its foundation in 1938. It is essentially a religion of laymen, without an organized clergy, and especially of the working classes. Its main hall in Tokyo is dedicated to the Buddha Shakyamuni, and all members of the sect pay homage here. It also has a new Grand Temple, or *Daiseido*, which is capable of accommodating over fifty thousand worshippers, and is one of the largest religious buildings in the East. The sect has communal worship, and among its many deities is to be found the Sun-goddess, Amaterasu-o-mikami. Morning service is followed by *hoza*, or group counselling, with study groups and leaders who give guidance in the faith and in daily living. Originally, Rissho Kosei Kai was a breakaway sect from Reiyukai, but today it claims to be a revival movement of original Buddhism as transmitted through Nichiren. They have faith in the Buddha and in Nichiren as exponents of the ultimate truth, and this faith is expressed through the Daimoku, or Lotus Sutra, and the mandala. They believe that man is bound by the karmic law of causation and transmigration, but that the effects of this law can be broken by true repentance (*zange*) and a perfect life of service to one's neighbours. Because of its intense interest in social service, the religion is able to propagate itself through its many nurseries, kindergartens, middle schools, high schools, homes for old people and hospitals.

Finally, we come to what has proved to be one of the most important religions in Japan, both in terms of religion and of political influence, namely, *Soka Gakkai*, or the 'Value-creating Association'. It was originally founded in 1930 as a lay movement of the sect of Nichiren Shoshu, developed by Nikko after the death of Nichiren (AD 1282) as the Orthodox Nichiren sect of Buddhism. The sect has always been noted for its fanaticism, exclusiveness and intolerance; yet despite these facts it is still one of the fastest growing religions in the world.

Soka Gakkai was refounded after WW2 by Toda Josei in 1946, and under his direction it developed at a fast rate. Its headquarters are at the foot of Mt Fuji, where in 1958 a super-modern Grand Kodo was erected for worship. The Soka Gakkai has always held a fanatical conviction that it possessed, in its own organization and teaching, the answer to the problem of the future of the Japanese people, and it has sought to promote both the religious and the political activities of the sect through active methods of propagation and propaganda.

In 1959 Soka Gakkai sponsored six candidates for the Upper House in the government of Japan. All six were elected, making a total of nine members altogether. In the election of 1962 anther six members were added, making a total of fifteen. It has gone on from strength to strength, and in its political endeavours Soka Gakkai has entered the arena of the trade unions, and has fought successful battles with such unions as those controlling the employment and pay of coal-miners. And, because it has identified itself closely with the nation of Japan and its welfare, it has been prepared to do battle with any political organization in the interests of the promotion of health, wealth and happiness.

Soka Gakkai regards the Lotus Sutra as the ultimate revelation of the Buddha, whilst Nichiren and the universe are one. It is the ultimate religious authority, and in this it is completely uncompromising. Its three mystic laws are to be found in the Gohonzon, which is the chief object of worship; and in Kaidan, or the place in which to receive correct instruction. The Gohonzon is a mandala which is a graphic presentation of the universe organized in terms of the Eternal Buddha, the other buddhas, and the bodhisattvas. Only the names of these beings are presented and are written vertically in *kanji*, that is, in Chinese characters. In the centre of the Gohonzon is the Daimoku, meditation upon and recitation of which brings to the worshipper satori, the power to heal sickness, to create wealth and to bring about peace.

In Soka Gakkai there is considerable emphasis upon faith-healing. It is the belief of devotees that their religion can positively prevent disease, and for some time one of their great slogans was, 'Don't waste your money on medicine and doctors, just join Soka Gakkai'. The responsibility and implications of such a slogan, however, eventually proved to be too great, and today it is more often expressed in the modified form of 'Consult your doctor first, and if he fails you or cannot help you, then come to Soka Gakkai'. The Daimoku appears to possess unlimited power, and provides a way towards the salvation of unbelievers. The Kaidan is the very centre where instruction and ordination are performed and where the mandala, Gohonzon, is located. The Kaidan will ultimately, so it is believed, become the national temple of Japan; and Soka Gakkai, under the leadership of a returned Nichiren Shoshu, will become the Japanese national religion, if not also the religion of the world.

The three great values which Soka Gakkai seeks to promote are goodness, beauty and benefit. At the same time it is actively opposed to the anti-values of evil, ugliness and harm. This is a practical religion which believes that it already has the truth enshrined in the Lotus Sutra and its doctrines. The devotee already has the truth within himself; what is then important is to create values based upon such truth:

> The fallacies inherent in the usually quoted conceptions of truth, goodness, and beauty as the substance of value that have existed since the philosophy of Kant are refuted in the *Kachiron* (An Essay on Value), an epochal philosophical work that explains the difference between truth and value, and advocates a system of value based on new concepts of goodness, beauty, and benefit. It dissolves the confusion existing in the contemporary world and closely examines the sources of happiness[14].

These are great claims, but there is a certain practicality about it all which appeals to the layman, as opposed to the usual metaphysical problems which surround Truth in abstract terms.

Worship takes place at Taisek-ji in a daily service known as the *ushitora*, which lasts for an hour and a half and has, according to tradition, never been cancelled for over seven centuries. During the service the Daimoku is recited, the Lotus Sutra is read, and there is a loud rhythmic beating of drums. The service takes place between midnight and 1.30 am, after which those who have participated are directed to their sleeping quarters.

Devotees of Soka Gakkai adopt a missionary or proselytizing method termed *shakufuku*, meaning 'to break and subdue'. By simple logic they seek to demonstrate the invalidity of all other religions[15]. All believers must practise *shakufuku* among relatives, friends and neighbours, and seek by every means to convert people to Soka Gakkai. There is a very vigorous Youth Corps for those under the age of thirty, and each detachment has its banners, sings the Corps song, and performs group exercises. This Corps is a valuable vehicle for exerting at least some moral pressure. Nationalistic, this religion claims to represent the universal desire for unity and peace, centred on the harmony of the universe through the Buddha and Nichiren Shoshu.

12 Judaism

1 Its Origin

The Hebrews, who have been identified by some scholars with a widely-dispersed group of people in Mesopotamia called the Habiru, were a wandering tribe of Semites who purported to have been descendants of Shem, one of the three sons of Noah. Some Hebrews had settled in South Babylonia, and it was here at Ur in Chaldaea that Terah and his sons, including Abraham, lived probably in the nineteenth or eighteenth century BC. Eventually Abraham and his family left Ur during a period of zeal on the part of King Hammurabi, who was forcibly reforming the religion of his kingdom into one of sun-worship. The Babylonians were animists and polytheists, and their ziggurat temples probably represented the mountains, with mountain-gods living at the top. Their chief god in the hierarchy was at first the moon-god, Sin, who was replaced by the sun-god, Shamash. They also worshipped Dumuzi (or Tammuz) who was born to the Earth Mother, Ishtar. Dumuzi died at the Spring Festival every year, was mourned by his mother and by women worshippers in particular, and then rose again. He was a prototype of the Dying God and Rising Saviour, and his influence was still felt among the Jews as late as 580 BC[1].

The Hebrews, according to Old Testament tradition, settled in Canaan under the leadership of Abraham. It is not easy to characterize the religion of Abraham and his family, but it is clear from references in the Jewish scriptures that it included a great variety of elements. There was animism[2] which included worship of sacred trees (terebinths), rivers, wells, stones etc; polytheism[3], in which almost every other place-name represented the name of a god; fertility worship involved with the *baalim* or local deities; totemism, as revealed from the tribal names such as Simeon (hyaena), Caleb (dog), Deborah (bee), and Rachel (lamb); animal cults involving the sacrifice of oxen, lambs, goats[4]; tabu[5], which listed animals that might not be eaten, and forms of action which were forbidden; magic[6], involving divination with the cup or the liver, the power of rain-making, and the use of the magic rod; and ancestor worship[7].

During the time of famine the descendants of Abraham, the children of Jacob or Israel, migrated to Egypt and were eventually enslaved there. During the reign of Ramses II (circa 1299-1232) the Israelites were oppressed and were made to build the great cities of Pithom and Ramses. One Hebrew, Moses, was trained in Egyptian beliefs and magic, but after killing an Egyptian overseer he fled to the land of Midian, where he received a revelation from the god of the Kenites. When he asked the god what his name was, he received the enigmatic reply, 'I am that I am', or 'I will be what I will be'[8]. This god also said to Moses, 'You must tell the Israelites that the Eternal (YHWH), the God of their fathers, the God of Abraham, the God of Isaac, and the God of Jacob, has sent you to them'[9].

2   The Various Influences

In their many journeys and sojourns the Israelites were invariably influenced by many other societies, cultures and religions, and they retained some elements of each despite their exclusivism and eventual monolatry and monotheism. In Egypt, although they set themselves apart from Egyptian beliefs and worship, they were impressed sufficiently by some forms of sacrificial ritual so that they wished to resuscitate calf, cow or bull worship, as represented by the Golden Calf which they made in the wilderness. This was possibly some vestige of the worship of Hathor, the Egyptian Cow Goddess. In the land of Canaan they were surrounded by a great deal of fertility ritual and human – usually child – sacrifice, and much of the animistic worship of the *baalim* ('lords' or 'gods', ie local deities) was from time to time taken over by them. Through intermarriage, such as that which occurred when King Ahab married the Phoenician Jezebel, a daughter of the King of Sidon, there developed worship of specifically alien gods, such as Melkart. A brief contact with a Syrian, such as Naaman[10], made the Israelites aware of the fact that their own God, Yahweh, was region-bound, and Naaman took back some of the Palestinian soil with him so that he might put it down in Syria when he got back, and upon it worship the Israelitish God.

During their exile in Assyria, the ten northern tribes came into contact with a culture of astrology and demonology, and in consequence there later developed a great deal of alien worship. The influence of the foreign ethos was experienced also in Judah[11], and under King Manasseh (circa 692-643 BC) there emerged a considerable amount of pagan and syncretistic worship. It was during the exile of the southern kingdom Jews in Babylonia that they saw the impossibility for them of any form of temple worship in a foreign land, and so they built small chapels, called synagogues, where they could gather together for prayer and hymn-singing. Thus, the synagogue pattern of worship was really established for the Jews between about 597 BC and 536 BC, when they returned to Palestine.

Persian influence was at its height during the period 536 BC to 333 BC. After Cyrus attacked and defeated the Babylonians, he had made it possible for Jews to return to Jerusalem for the rebuilding of the Temple[12]. Cyrus was even regarded as 'chosen by God' for this purpose[13]; and he certainly granted complete religious freedom for all of his subjects, and images and shrines of local gods were set up again.

There seems little doubt that, just as Babylonian aetiological mythology affected and influenced to some extent the presentation of the Creation stories in the book of Genesis, so eventually Iranian religious ideas affected Judaism. It may be that there was little direct effect until after the conquests of Persia by Alexander the Great in 331 BC, and the establishment of his rule over Palestine. Some twenty years after his death in 323 BC, Palestine came under the rule of the Ptolemies, followed in 198 BC by the rule of the Seleucids:

> It was at this time that a new type of Jewish literature, known as apocalyptic, began to emerge showing unmistakable traces of the principal doctrines of Zoroastrianism concerning heaven and hell, judgement after death and at the end of the world, an angelic hierarchy, a dualism of good and evil under two opposed forces with their respective leaders, Michael and Satan, together with a Messianic kingdom in which righteousness would prevail[14].

By the end of the second century BC, this sort of apocalyptic and eschatological writing had become thoroughly established among the Jews[15]. During the Seleucid Syrian rule, two extreme parties developed, namely, a priestly aristocracy of Hellenizers who sought to introduce everything Greek, and the Hasidim or 'godly ones', who were opposed to this policy of Hellenization.

In 168 BC, Antiochus IV (Epiphanes) plundered and desecrated the Temple in Jerusalem and he 'sent letters by the hand of messengers unto Jerusalem and the cities of Judah, that they should follow laws strange to the land'[16]. The worship of the Greek Olympian god, Zeus, was ordered in the Temple; this was 'the abomination of desolation' right at the heart of Jewish religion and culture. The Maccabaean Revolt followed after an incident involving an old priest, Mattathias, who had been ordered to perform an act of sacrilege but who slew the commissioner involved. The Revolt lasted from 166 BC to 160 BC, under the leadership of Judas and his sons, Jonathan and Simon; and political freedom was eventually gained until civil war broke out and Rome subjugated the country in 63 BC. It then became a part of the province of Syria. Generally speaking, the Romans tolerated other religions and cultures so long as they did not interfere with law and order. Fanatics, Zealots and Galilaeans were not so much members of an alien religion, so far as the Romans were concerned, as disturbers of the *pax Romana*, and that was unforgivable. The expectation and hope of a coming Messiah was considerable during the early days of the 'Christian era' and eventually the Romans, who had quelled rebellion after rebellion, destroyed the Temple of Jerusalem and its city in AD 70.

3   The Religion of the Prophets

To discuss in any sort of detail the development of the religious teaching of the Jewish prophets would require a very large book in itself. The great advances of Judaism as a religion were undoubtedly made by the insights of the great prophets, and the accompanying Chart is really a summary of their movement towards a period of crisis. However one may view that crisis, whether as the advent of the expected Messiah, or as the destruction of the centre of Judaistic religion in the razing of Jerusalem and its Temple to the ground, or as the culmination of the apocalyptic movement itself (even though most of it was regarded as extra- or non-canonical), there is very clear progression in the prophetic inspiration. What is perhaps of considerable interest to the student of comparative religion is the fact that during one of the great peaks of Judaistic propheticism, that is, when Jeremiah, Ezekiel and 'Second Isaiah' flourished, such great thinkers as Gautama Shakyamuni, Lao-Tzu, Zoroaster, Confucius and Socrates, are thought to have lived.

4   Judaism Today

(a) The Main Beliefs of Judaism
Judaism accepts, as do most advanced religions, that there is no way in which we can fully and ultimately describe the nature of God. God is ineffable; nevertheless, paradoxically, there seem to be some things that we can say about him. He is the perfect Creator of all that exists including man himself. And man is a co-worker with him

in the evocation of love and brotherhood in the world. God is one, spiritual and indivisible.

Judaism accepts the brotherhood of man without qualification, without any distinction of class or colour. There is a unity in man without uniformity, and Judaism looks forward to the time when all men everywhere will become united in their worship of and allegiance to the one God. Today Jews are more inclined to believe in a future Messianic Age, pervaded by peace and harmony, than in a personal Messiah either descending from the clouds in some apocalyptic fashion or being born into the world as a babe who will grow up to become a king and leader. In the past, it is true, many pious members of Judaism married young and brought up a large number of children in the hope that the 'Son of David', who would not come until all souls stored up for earthly life had been born, would appear all the more quickly. The *Talmud*[17] seems to support this Messianic view when it says:

> The birth of a male child causes universal joy... but the birth of a female child causes universal sorrow.

This is simply because a female child cannot become the Messiah. But however the Jew may interpret the Messianic concept, it is for him a matter of personal responsibility to help to usher in the Messianic Age.

Since man was created in the image of God, he has both a certain dignity and certain inalienable rights. All men are equal before God, and so all mankind is seen as a part of God's redemptive purpose. Jewish prayers are, therefore, outgoing and inclusive of all the peoples of the earth. Judaism does not accept any doctrine of Original Sin; on the contrary, man is born with a pure soul and is endowed by God with a double nature – a 'good inclination' and a 'bad inclination'. In respect of all our actions we are free, therefore, to make a choice[18]. In our choice of activity, and in the implicit freedom of such choice, we are responsible to God; and if we sin we must atone by showing our repentance both to God and to our fellows. Thoughout Judaism

The rise of the Jewish prophets

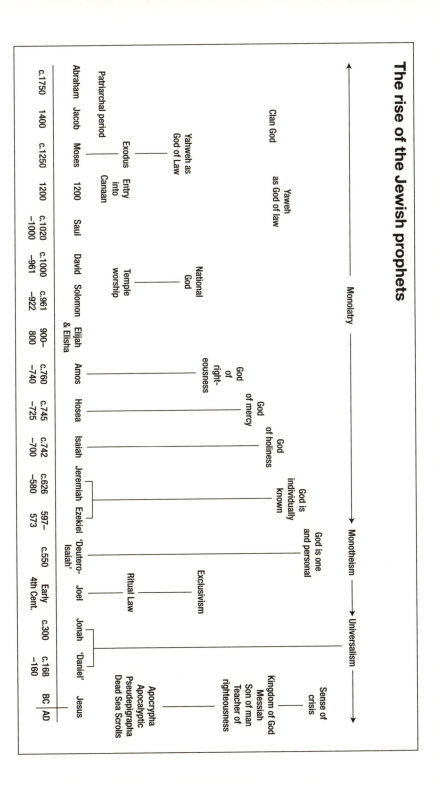

there is an emphasis upon human behaviour, upon morals and ethics, rather than upon the dogmatics of theology.

(b) The Creed
In order to belong to any religion there are obviously certain things that one must believe in. Some religions have long, and often involved and difficult, statements of belief, so that it frequently requires further elaboration and interpretation of those creeds by the theologians of the religions concerned. And this, in turn, is usually the origin of the development of sects and splinter groups. Perhaps the nearest approach to a creed in Judaism is what is called the *Shema*:

> Hear, O Israel, the Lord our God, the Lord is One. And thou shalt love the Lord thy God with all thy heart, and with all thy soul, and with all thy might[19].

To this may be added the statement in Leviticus[20] 'and thou shalt love thy neighbour as thyself'. It is worth noting that the word for 'neighbour' used here is the same as that used in other parts of the Old Testament for people such as the Egyptians[21]. It is also true that what Jesus referred to as 'the saying'[22] in his statement, 'You have heard the saying, "Thou shalt love thy neighbour and hate thine enemy"', is not something to be found in Old Testament scripture nor, indeed, in other Jewish scriptures of the time of Jesus. On the contrary we read:

> If thine enemy be hungry, give him bread to eat;
> And if he be thirsty, give him water to drink[23].
>
> Rejoice not when thine enemy falleth,
> And let not thine heart be glad when he stumbleth[24].
> To love each man his neighbour like himself;
> To grasp the hand of the poor, the needy and the stranger;
> To seek each man the welfare of his fellow[25].

The 'saying' referred to by Jesus was clearly one used currently in terms of attitudes towards the Romans rather than an accepted canonical view. There was no divine injunction laid upon the Jews to hate or destroy their enemies.

(c) The Afterlife

In the Old Testament there was a gradual development of the idea of life beyond the grave. Initially *sheol* was seen as a gloomy, dark and cheerless region beneath the earth to which all would eventually descend in a dull, semi-conscious existence[26]. It was the abode of the *rephaim*, the spirits or shades[27], and it was fully under the control of God[28]. Later, under the influence of Persian and Zoroastrian beliefs, the idea of a physical resurrection was developed and was accepted particularly by the sect of the Pharisees. Thus we read:

> O Thou Eternal, thy dead shall live again,
> Awakening from the dust, with songs of joy;
> For thy dew falls with light and life,
> Till dead spirits arise[29].

In the period between the Testaments, both in the Apocrypha and in the writings referred to as the Pseudepigrapha (that is, writings published under pseudonyms) the Greek idea of the immortality of the soul seems to have gained ground. We read, for example:

> But the souls of the righteous are in the hands of God,
> And no torment shall touch them.
> In the eyes of the foolish they seem to have died;
> And their departure was accounted to be their hurt,
> And their journeying away from us to be their ruin;
> But they are in peace.
> For even if in the sight of men they be punished,
> Their hope is full of immortality[30].

In modern Judaism there is no dogmatic belief concerning the afterlife; it is a matter of personal faith, and there is no doubt that individual Jews believe very different things about it. Nevertheless, most members of Judaism accept that in some way, and in some form, the soul survives the death and decay of the body. Their faith is expressed in the mediaeval hymn, the *Adon Olam*:

> My soul unto his hand divine
> Do I commend: I will not fear:
> My body with it I resign:
> I dread no evil: God is near.

With this supreme confidence in God's unfailing presence and succour, the Jew believes in the vital importance of doing his utmost to perfect this present life – the future can safely be left to God.

(d) The Special Mission of the Jews

The special mission of the Jews as seen by themselves is to promote, through their own actions and example, the Kingdom of God upon the earth. It is their objective to make it possible for all people of every nation to come to a knowledge of God. All the righteous of all peoples have the possibility of sharing in the world to come and in everything that this implies. Converts are accepted into Judaism after a long period of enquiry and instruction, although Judaism is not in itself a proselytizing religion. One of the reasons for this is the basic 'Noachist' belief that people outside of their faith may become 'sons of Noah' if not of the 'seed of Abraham'. That is, there are certain moral and ethical principles that they must follow if they wish to share in the faith of the Kingdom of God. They must abstain from idolatry, unchastity, the shedding of blood, the profanation of God's name, robbery, and the mutilation of animals. They must positively observe justice in all their dealings with other people. Thus, the non-Jew who sincerely pursues the highest teachings that he knows, and is moral in all his actions, may go forward to the greatest spiritual heights; for all the major religions have varying degrees of ultimate Truth within them; they all possess something of the core of perennial philosophy, and they already have implicit in their beliefs some of the high moral and ethical principles to be found in Judaism itself.

(e) The Attitude of Judaism to Jesus

Here one inevitably finds a great variety of belief, from total rejection of Jesus to a qualified acceptance of what he taught. The great Jewish scholar, Dr H J Schonfield, who has himself translated the New Testament[31], obviously has considerable respect for both Jesus and his teaching, but he certainly does not regard him as divine. The view of the Liberal Jews is that Jesus was one of the many religious teachers, preachers and prophets that the Jewish people have produced. They consider that Jesus was born a Jew and finally died as a Jew; he was certainly not God in the flesh. Such an idea is considered to be somewhat reminiscent of the Greek and Roman mystery-cults which were prevalent in the region of Palestine at the time of Jesus' birth.

Jesus claimed, or at least the evangelists claimed for him, that he was the 'Son of God' in a unique sense. At most, Judaism will accept that he was 'a son of God' in the same sense as we are all sons or children of God. The evidence concerning his personal life and conduct is insufficient to establish whether Jesus was more 'godly' or more good than anyone else who has ever lived and taught. He is certainly not, in their view, a Messiah or saviour sent by Yahweh to save us, whether as a personal sacrifice or as an atonement; and he is equally not the sole approach to God. It is also felt that Jesus did not really make these claims for himself – they were made for him by his disciples. Paul, for example, developed his theology largely from pagan and mythical elements, whereas Jesus was in fact a 'progressive' who fell foul of the more orthodox elements of his society. It is inevitable, with their uncompromising monotheistic views, that Jews should reject outright any idea of the Christian Trinity – there is one God and one God only, completely indivisible; anything else is idolatry and blasphemy. Even the oft-quoted 'Servant Passages' of 'Second Isaiah'[32], it is held (and most Christian scholars agree) do not refer to any individual person, Servant or Messiah, but rather to an Ideal Israel or a Faithful Remnant.

Whilst there may be considerable acceptance amongst Liberal Jews of the moral and ethical teaching of Jesus, there is a feeling, nevertheless, that much of the New Testament is polemical in nature and tends, therefore, to be somewhat exaggerated and overdrawn. J D Rayner[33] maintains that this is understandable; and he suggests that it is comparable to the exaggeration of the Old Testament prophets:

> Now when Moses declared that there was no truth, nor mercy, nor knowledge of God in the land, he was clearly exaggerating. And when Micah declared that the godly man had perished out of the earth, and the upright among men was no more, he was clearly exaggerating. And when Jeremiah declared that from the least of them even unto the greatest of them every one was greedy for gain, and from the prophet unto the priest every one dealt falsely, he was clearly exaggerating.... so also was Jesus, and for the same purpose, exaggerating when he condemned his fellow-Jews as concerned only with the letter and not the spirit of the Law, and with ritual purity rather than neighbourly love. Because, however, from the New Testament point of view, Jesus was the founder of a new religion, these denunciations of his appear in the New Testament as denunciations, not of human shortcomings prophetically exaggerated, but of the whole religious system which was to be superseded.

(f) Divisions in Judaism

Orthodoxy in Judaism for many centuries implied a rigid pursuance of the details of the Law, both in terms of ceremonial and ritual within the synagogue and in terms of daily activity and behaviour. The reformers of the nineteenth century, following the lead given by Moses Mendelssohn (1729-86) earlier, were anxious to free Judaism from slavery to the letter of the Law. In an era when 'higher criticism' was being applied by Christian scholars to the Old Testament, these reformers accepted the validity of such criticism and sought to apply it to their own situation. Soon they began to use the vernacular in their public services and to modify their synagogue ritual in many ways. In Germany the first Jewish Reform Temple, as distinct from synagogue, was built and prayers in German, as well as hymns and homilies, replaced those in Hebrew. Men and women were allowed to sit together and even the use of head-coverings was not insisted upon. Some reformers sought even to abolish circumcision, and to hold their weekly services on Sunday instead of on the Sabbath.

In these developments there was soon a criticism of the Mosaic Laws themselves and of many long-accepted Jewish doctrines. The Liberal Jews, as they became to be called, gave less attention to ritualistic laws and details, and more to the teachings of the Prophets. The test of many of the regulatory laws of the Torah was whether they, in fact, fitted into contemporary modes of life and behaviour. As a result, a large number of laws concerning dress and diet were rejected, and increasingly the prophetic message of ethical monotheism became the central feature of their belief and worship. Many liberal Jews began to see in the teaching of Jesus the thought of a Jewish teacher of great significance and importance in the development and reform of Judaism. In 1842 the West London Synagogue of British Jews was established. Here the prophets of the Old Testament were studied afresh and with new interest, once more leading to some reappraisal of the work of Jesus.

Orthodox Jewry at first sought to oppose all reforms and all modernity in Jewish life and practice. Many saw the retention of the ghetto as the only way in which to maintain Jewish identity with particular, traditional laws and actions. Others, however, began to accept that some form of accommodation was necessary if they were to live in a modern society. In England, for example, many Jews began to relax Sabbath laws, such as not using public transport in order to attend synagogue, not switching on lights or using the telephone. In general terms, there were those who emphasized Judaism as a religious belief and practice rather than as a separate ethnic or racial community. Others thought of Judaism as both a religion and a distinct group or society whose aim it was to have its own land and country, specifically in Palestine.

Thus, in broad terms, Judaism is represented by three main groups: the Orthodox, the Reform and the Liberal; and the Reform branch lies somewhere between the Orthodox and the Liberal elements. Usage obviously varies from country to country, and in the USA there are the Orthodox, the Conservative and the Reform, the latter being roughly equivalent to the Liberal movement in Britain.

(g) Sacraments and Rituals

Since the destruction of the Temple at Jerusalem in AD 70, there have been neither sacrifices nor sacrificial system in Judaism and no sacraments as such. The theory (however practice may differ) is basically that all life is sacred, and that all action should be performed with this in mind. Liberal Jews in particular do not accept that any ceremonies or ritual laws are God-given. Such rituals as exist are man-made and so are employed by man to evoke a greater awareness of God's permanent presence in life and of man's personal responsibility to him in all thought and action. Rituals are, in fact, our techniques for developing a firmer relationship with God.

Boys are circumcised at the age of eight days, although of course this ritual is by no means specific to Jews – it is also performed by Arabs, and also by large numbers of tribes throughout the world, and in a variety of ways. Among Orthodox Jews, boys are confirmed at the age of thirteen in a ceremony referred to as Bar-mitzvah, which means 'son of the commandment'. From here on the boy is regarded as fully responsible for his actions under the Law; and although he is obviously not yet an adult he must begin to develop adult attitudes and behaviour patterns. Liberal Jews delay this ceremony until the boy is fifteen or sixteen, whilst a girl is also included in the confirmation ceremonial by having a Bath-mitzvah, whereby she becomes a 'daughter of the commandment'.

(h) Services and Observances

The Jewish Sabbath is from sundown on Friday to sundown on

Saturday, and this time is chosen because in the Creation story[34] 'the evening and the morning' were the first day, second day etc up to the sixth day, and God rested on the seventh day. Two candles are lit to usher in the day and the *Kiddush* (or sanctification) is then performed, involving the recital of prayers followed by the drinking of wine as a symbol of joy, and the eating of bread as a symbol of plenty. This simple observance centres upon the family and its unity, since to the Jew the family is all-important and its relationships are cemented by this ceremony. During the Sabbath an Orthodox Jew must not perform any work – he may eat, read, walk, talk and sleep, but very little else. Nor must he cause other people to work. The Liberal Jew, however, is not surrounded by such detailed restrictions, but it is left to the conscience of each individual to decide upon what constitutes, in his current milieu, a breach of Sabbath observance.

Again, services in the synagogue vary between Orthodox and Liberal Jews. In an Orthodox synagogue the men sit in the main body of the building, whilst women sit separately in a gallery, or in a section divided from the main hall by a partition or grille. All must have their heads covered, and across the shoulders a shawl (*tallith*) is worn. The service is conducted in Hebrew. In the Liberal synagogue, however, there is no separation of sexes; in many of them even the covering of the head is optional. Prayers will be said in both Hebrew and in the indigenous language, and readings in Hebrew from the Bible will be translated.

In synagogues the worshippers will stand or sit, but not kneel. There are no altars, but at the east end there will be a large cupboard or recess covered by a curtain, and the whole is referred to as the Ark. The lamp which hangs in front of the Ark is kept perpetually alight. In the Ark itself are kept the scrolls of the Law which are carefully brought out, carried among the congregation, and returned to the reader's desk where they are unrolled to the appropriate lesson to be read on that particular Sabbath. There are no pictures or images in a synagogue, the only form of adornment being a seven-branched candlestick and a Star of David.

Today there are no priests as such because there are strictly no priestly functions; there are, however, some who claim descent from priests of the old Temple and who have the honorific title of *cohen*, which is the Hebrew word for priest. Normally a quorum of ten males is required before a service can begin. Whilst the chief officer of a synagogue is a rabbi, which simply means a teacher, the chief officiant in a service is the *chazzan* or reader, who usually reads the lesson and recites the prayers. A cantor, who may combine other offices as well, chants and sings as a leader of congregational worship.

In addition to the daily recital of the Shema, and the weekly Sabbath observances, including attendance at the synagogue, there are certain other home observances. These include the Passover or Feast of Unleavened Bread[35]; the Weeks Festival or Pentecost[36]; New Year[37]; the Festival of Tabernacles or Booths[38]; and the all-important Yom Kippur or Day of Atonement[39]. These festivals, held within the home, are an extension of the concept of the cohesion of the family, and every sincere religious Jew will try to be at home with his family to observe them.

(i) Jewish Literature

Apart from the section of the Bible which Christians refer to as 'The Old Testament', which was written in Hebrew (except for a few passages in Aramaic), there were many Jewish religious books written between circa 200 BC and AD 200, which are usually referred to as the Apocrypha. Apocrypha means 'hidden', and because they were written in Greek these works are not generally regarded as having the same inspirational value as the Hebrew books of the Old Testament. They include some 'historical' literature, such as the books of the Maccabees; books of wisdom, such as Ecclesiasticus or the Wisdom of Jesus, son of Sirach, and the Wisdom of Solomon; and historical fiction, such as Judith. Then there is a class of literature called, the Pseudepigrapha, that is, a collection of books written pseudonymously by 'Enoch', 'The Twelve Sons of Jacob', 'Solomon', 'Baruch', 'Moses' and 'Isaiah'. These works contain a strong apocalyptic element, in which there is warfare between Good and Evil, God and Satan, angels and demons. There is also a development of such ideas as that of the coming Messiah or Son of Man, the immortality of the soul, and heaven and hell. Attempts were made to discuss[40], and even to solve[41], the problem of evil; to describe the events of the millennium[42]; to predict the appearance of the Antichrist[43]; to appeal for a universalism in religion, including all Gentiles in God's divine purpose[44]; and even to describe the Resurrection[45].

The highly controversial Dead Sea Scrolls[46] are a set of scriptures written and collected, probably during the period 170 BC to AD 68, by a group of religious devotees such as the Essenes. Among the scrolls are copies of parts of the Old Testament as well as new scriptures relating to the discipline, rituals and beliefs of the Dead Sea Sect, and concerning a coming Messiah and Teacher of Righteousness or 'Right Teacher' (that is, a true exponent of the Law). These scrolls have helped to establish new readings in the Old Testament, to validate the old ones, and to provide invaluable material for developing ideas concerning the period from the Maccabees to the fall of Jerusalem.

The *Talmud* (a word derived from a Hebrew root meaning 'to learn', 'to teach') includes the 'Mishnah', which conveys the opinions of over one hundred teachers on the Jewish Law, and was probably collated circa AD 200. It also includes the 'Gemara', collated during the fifth century AD, which is a discussion by rabbis on the topics of religion, morals, conduct, rituals, etc. The following passage is one of the most famous of all the writings of the Talmud:

> Rejoice not when thine enemy faileth, and let not thine heart
> be glad when he stumbleth; who can deservedly be called
> a conqueror? He who conquers his rancorous passions and
> endeavours to turn his enemy into a friend. Thou shalt not say,
> 'I will love the wise, but the unwise I will hate'; but thou shalt
> love all mankind. Thou shalt love thy neighbour; even if he be a
> criminal and has forfeited his life, practise charity towards him
> in his last moments; what thou wouldst not like to be done to
> you, do not to others: this is the fundamental law.

Other Jewish literature included the *Midrash*, which was a collection of books which expounded the Old Testament, from about the second century BC to the tenth century AD. Another commentary on the Old Testament was written by the Rabbi Solomon ben-Isaac, during the eleventh century BC, and was referred to as the *Rashi*, from the initial letters of the rabbi's title and name. In 1168 the Jewish philosopher, Maimonides (1135-1204), attempted to reconcile the thought of Aristotle with Jewish teachings. He propounded some thirteen principles in the Jewish Authorized Book of Daily Prayer. These principles are:

   i.   The existence of and belief in a Creator
   ii.   Belief in His unity
   iii.   Belief in His incorporeality
   iv.   Belief in His eternity
   v.   All worship and adoration are due to Him alone
   vi.   Belief in prophecy
   vii.   Moses was the greatest of all the prophets
   viii.   The Torah was revealed on Mt Sinai
   ix.   The immutability of this revealed Torah, or Law
   x.   God knows all the actions of men
   xi.   He will reward or punish men according to their works
   xii.   The Coming of the Messiah
   xiii.   The Resurrection of the Dead

Another strain of Jewish literature, a mystical one, includes the *Kabbala* (meaning 'that which is received'), a book which is a collection of hidden and mysterious doctrines concerning God's nature and his dealings with the created world. A mixture of Neo-Platonism, Gnosticism and other esoteric philosophies, it discusses angelic beings, demiurges and emanations of God. All souls are pre-existent, are reincarnated, and eventually will return to God, their origin. The most outstanding of the Kabbalistic works was *Zohar, The Book of Splendour*, written in Aramaic and compiled over a long period of time. It was very much in vogue after Jews were expelled from Spain in 1492, and was read as an exposition and encyclopaedic summary of the Kabbalistic teaching.

(j) The Zionist Movement and the State of Israel

The Jews seem always to have suffered persecution wherever they have been, and from the fourteenth century onwards there has been virtually a permanent atmosphere of anti-Semitism in Europe somewhere or other. In 1897 there began a movement to bring back Jews, dispersed all over the world, to their ancient home of Israel. This has naturally presented vast problems, particularly since conquest, colonization and voluntary transfer movements have all made it very difficult to decide what land 'belongs' to whom. Zionism was founded in order to restore Jews to Palestine and to establish them as a nation. Between 1933 and 1945 about six million Jews were massacred in Hitler's Germany. Some Jews managed to escape and fled to Palestine, but soon Britain imposed an annual quota in order strictly to control their entry. Humanitarian considerations alone dictated that many more were somehow allowed to enter. After Britain gave up her mandate in 1947, the frontiers of the new State of Israel were determined by the United Nations Organization, and the State itself was officially brought into existence in 1948 by Ben Gurion.

Israel, as a nation state, has steadily accepted Jews, as well as sympathetic and cooperative Gentiles, into her society ever since. There are, however, many millions more Jews outside Israel than inside. Moreover, many Jews see it as no part of their ultimate aim or purpose to swell the ranks of the Israelis in Palestine. In terms of education there has been a determined effort, through the use of Hebrew as a modern (or modernized) language, to recreate a Jewish culture, but there are some grave difficulties both of identity and definition. For example, a Jew may be defined in religious, ethnic, racial or cultural terms. Some have suggested that a Jew is one born of a Jewish mother; but such a person may, in some way, have entirely rejected the Jewish culture or faith. As, however, J D Rayner[47] comments:

The Jewish religion, if fully practised, regulates the individual Jew's life so extensively that he seems almost to live within a culture-pattern of his own, a civilization within a civilization.

13 Christianity

1 Background

In general terms the background and context of Christianity were essentially Judaism and the land of the Jews. There is little doubt that Jesus was born during a period when there was an air of expectancy among the Jews. Their apocalyptic literature, though written mainly in Hellenistic Greek, must have been fairly widely known, and there was a sense of crisis which was further supported by such groups as the Zealots and the Essenes (however much they may have differed in belief and intention). These sects had an anticipation of some event, some 'divine' event, which would be calculated to change both their history and their condition. The nature of such an event and change seems to have been revealed in some of the books of the Old Testament Apocrypha, and in the scriptures of the Dead Sea Sect. Such documents referred to a coming Messiah, or 'Anointed One', who would be a unique teacher of righteousness, or a 'right Teacher', that is, one who would teach the truth and would lead his people into all truth.

Many of the ideas to be found in the inter-testamental literature were clearly current in the time of Jesus. The idea, for example, of physical resurrection was strongly supported by the Pharisees, who also accepted much of the sort of demonology to be found in both the Apocrypha and the Pseudepigrapha. Evil spirits were regarded as responsible for sickness, madness, epilepsy and a whole host of illnesses; but they were not, nevertheless, left in full control of the human situation, for there was a corresponding angelology which involved a whole army of good angels, ready to support those who wished to overcome evil and temptation, and who positively made the attempt to do so.

The Pharisees taught a belief in the resurrection of the body and in a significant future life, whereas the Sadducees accepted neither. Many Jews conceived of a coming Messiah who would be the King of Israel. In the *Psalms of Solomon*[1], for example, the Messiah was represented as an ideal future deliverer, the Son of David and the Lord Christ. He was to deliver the Jews from Roman supremacy as well as from Sadducean rule; he would shatter unrighteous rulers and cleanse Jerusalem from all its Gentile oppressors; he would bring back the Jews of the Diaspora (Dispersion), scattered throughout the Roman Empire; he would free his people from sin and make them holy, and he would win his victory 'by the word of his mouth'. Such a Messiah was definitely a human figure. In the *First Book of Enoch*[2], however, the Son of Man (the first mention of the title) appears as a transcendent figure descending with the clouds of heaven. In some books the term 'Antichrist' is used in reference to the Prince of Darkness, Belial, and much of this dualistic concept derives from Persian angelology.

In the *Testament of the Twelve Patriarchs*[3] there is the development of a universalistic outlook virtually unique at this time, for Gentiles were here associated with the Jewish salvation, and it was accepted that righteous men were to be found in every nation on earth. Moreover, at the great consummation of all things 'the twelve tribes shall be gathered together, and all the Gentiles, until the Most High shall send forth his salvation'. The Jewish synagogues, scattered throughout the whole of the Roman Empire, were to prove very fertile ground, not merely for the proselytizing of Gentiles to Judaism but also for the subsequent spread and development of Christianity itself.

2 The Historical Jesus

Today no really serious historian doubts that Jesus was a historical person, although undoubtedly many different interpretations are made concerning his nature, character, significance and teaching. There are several references to Jesus in the *Antiquities of the Jews*, written in Greek by the Jewish historian Josephus, who died in AD 100. He provided a detailed account of John the Baptist, and in reference to the life of Herod Antipas he mentioned the baptism offered by John, the latter's general popularity and his final destruction by Herod. The specific references to Jesus are to be found in Books 18 and 20 of the *Antiquities*, although they are couched in such a way that there must be some suspicion as to their origin. Would a non-Christian Jew, such as Josephus, use language such as the following?

> A man, Jesus, if it be lawful to call him so.
> A teacher of Truth.
> He was the Messiah.
> He rose again; for he appeared again to them on the third day alive.
> A doer of miracles, as the prophets had foretold these and ten thousand other wonderful things.
> Jesus, who was called the Christ.

Pliny the Younger, Roman Governor of Bithynia and a historian, in a letter to the Emperor Trajan which he wrote circa AD 112 concerning his examination of Christians, spoke of their 'obstinacy and unbending perversity'[4]. He went on to say that it was their custom 'on a fixed day to assemble before daylight and to sing by turn a hymn to Christ as (a) god'. Pliny regarded all this as a 'wicked and arrogant superstition'; although Trajan in his reply made it clear that Christians were not to be sought out. Tacitus, the Roman historian who wrote his *Annales* circa AD 115, gave an account of the Neronian persecution of AD 65, in which he said:

They called them Christian. Christ, from whom the name
was given, had been put to death in the reign of Tiberius by
the procurator Pontius Pilate, and the pestilent superstition
checked for a time[5].

When Suetonius wrote his *Life of Claudius* in circa AD 120, he said
that Claudius expelled from Rome those Jews 'who made a tumult
because of Chrestus'. It seems likely that we have here a reference by
a Roman historian, writing some seventy years after the events, to
the Christ, Messiah or Christus whom the Christians worshipped.

When one adds to the non-Christian historical material, the
first three gospels (known as the Synoptics) and the gospel of John
in the New Testament, and the many apocryphal gospels which
show considerable developments in legendary material, there seems
to be little doubt that it was all based upon the life of a historical
personage. Even the most early opponents of Jesus and Christianity
saw no reason to doubt his existence. And it would have been a very
odd conspiracy indeed that promoted an imaginary figure and his
teaching by producing, during a period of less than a century, the
letters of Paul, the various gospels, and the Acts of the Apostles.
Today there is an overwhelming consensus of historical judgement
that a man called Jesus existed and taught in the way that the gospels
of the New Testament suggested. The acceptance of his existence is
hardly open for discussion any longer; the acceptance of his divinity
and of his teaching is more a matter of faith.

Thus, Jesus was a Jew living in north Palestine in Galilee, although
tradition has it that he was born in Bethlehem in the province of
Judaea at the time of a census which the Roman legate of Syria,
Publius Sulpicius Quirinius, made circa 6 BC. It should be noted
that the Christian calendar was first formulated in the sixth century
AD by a Roman monk whose attempt to make it correspond with
the Roman calendar was not very successful, since he appears to have
been about six years out in his calculations. The birth of Jesus was
celebrated in December by at least the fourth century, but the precise
time of his birth is unknown. The writers of the gospels according

to Matthew and Luke recount the miraculous conception of Jesus without a human father – Mary, it was said, conceived through the agency of the Holy Spirit. There is no indication, however, of any belief in the Virgin Birth in the other canonical gospels, although the story is elaborated by apocryphal gospels which appeared considerably later than the first century AD[6]. Nor is there any mention of it in the various epistles of the New Testament. Although there is very little evidence that the Christians of the first century accepted the idea, the Early Church soon made it one of the dogmas of the creeds.

According to the gospel narratives Jesus was presented in the Temple for circumcision on the eighth day after his birth. He was then taken into Egypt by his parents in order to avoid the slaughter of the innocents by Herod the Great. After the latter's death (in 4 BC) the family returned to Palestine, and it would appear that Jesus grew up in Joseph's home in Nazareth. At the age of twelve Jesus was taken to the Temple by Joseph and Mary; and after searching for him high and low for three days they found him in discussion with some of the learned teachers of the Law in the Temple, asking them questions. We are informed that 'All his hearers were amazed at the intelligence of his own answers'[7]. When his mother slightly rebuked him, he replied: 'Why did you look for me? Did you not know that I had to be at my Father's house?'[8] – literally, 'in the things of my Father'. Luke's gospel goes on to tell us that Jesus increased in wisdom, in physical stature and in favour with God and with man[9]. Joseph seems to have died when Jesus was still quite young, and it is possible that Jesus was left to look after his mother and make his contribution with the rest of the family, who according to Mark[10] numbered at least four boys and two girls.

Jesus' public ministry began in circa AD 27 when he was in his early thirties. At this time the ascetic John the Baptist suddenly appeared on the scene out of the deserts in the area of the Dead Sea. He came as a prophet telling of the imminent judgement and of the need to prepare for the Messiah who would appear and who would free them from the Roman yoke. John baptized large numbers of people in the River Jordan, and Jesus himself was baptized by him.

During the baptism, Jesus had an experience in which, we are told by Matthew[11], 'he saw the Spirit of God coming down like a dove upon him'. Jesus then went into the desert for a period of fasting, prayer and meditation. It was during this time that he was tempted for forty days and forty nights and, although these temptations have been somewhat stylized in their presentation, their meaning seems fairly clear: men's spirits need to be nourished as well as their bodies; the Messiah should not use supernatural powers for personal or selfish purposes; he should not seek to conquer his enemies by force or use his powers in a political way as a military Messiah, for this would be in effect the worship of evil. We are told that, 'after exhausting every kind of temptation, the Devil left him till a fit opportunity arrived'[12], and the temptations undoubtedly recurred from time to time during the rest of his short life.

John the Baptist was in some doubt as to whether Jesus was in fact the Messiah that he himself expected, and after his own arrest and imprisonment by Herod Antipas, then the ruler of Galilee, John was put to death. Jesus began his own ministry in Galilee and in the surrounding districts. Here he taught in the synagogues and healed the sick, and eventually went with his twelve chosen disciples into the hill country where he instructed them in their missionary purpose. After further wanderings he went south to Jerusalem. There he rode into the capital city on a donkey, a beast of burden, not upon a horse of the military Messiah. After he had cleansed the Temple and healed openly in its courts, the Sadducees, who curried favour with the Roman authorities, regarded Jesus as a real threat to their authority. He was, therefore seized by night with the connivance of Judas, one of the twelve disciples and most likely a Zealot, hoping to force the issue of messiahship.

Jesus was tried for blasphemy before a Jewish court, which had been summoned with some haste, and he was subsequently accused of high treason before Pilate, the Roman governor. Jesus remained unmoved by the accusations and steadily refused to defend himself. Eventually Pilate acquiesced in the condemnation of Jesus, who was led outside the walls of Jerusalem and crucified with two common criminals on the hill called Golgotha or Calvary. The crucifixion occurred on a Friday in the Passover week, and the body of Jesus was removed before the onset of the Jewish Sabbath at sunset. It was then placed in a rock tomb provided by a rich man called Joseph of Arimathaea. Both Paul, in his letters, and the writers of the gospels refer to the appearances of Jesus after his resurrection. It was belief and faith in this resurrection from the grave that provided the disciples and others with a missionary zeal, and with a basis for the Christian Church. To the followers of Jesus the resurrection was the final proof and demonstration they needed that he was indeed the Messiah and the Son of God.

3 The Teaching of Jesus

(a) The Records and Their Subject

Jesus spoke and taught in Aramaic, the language spoken by the Jews from the time of the Exile in 596 BC to about AD 600, when it was finally superseded by Arabic. The Jewish Bible, referred to by Christians as the Old Testament, was read in the synagogues. In addition, a form of Greek was spoken in Palestine called Hellenistic (*koiné* or 'common') Greek. Before the teaching of Jesus was finally written down, it was undoubtedly repeated orally in Aramaic; and there would also have been a parallel oral tradition of his acts and signs. Gradually, in order to ensure accuracy and permanence, both teaching and acts were written down in Aramaic, as well as in Syriac and Hellenistic Greek.

Between about AD 65 and AD 110 the larger biographies or gospels, including both sayings and actions, were written. There would, of course, be varying traditions growing up around the life and teaching of Jesus, according to the group or area concerned. Hundreds of copies of the same gospels were made and copying errors inevitably crept in. Two of the oldest manuscripts surviving today are from the fourth century, namely, Codex B (Vaticanus), and Codex Sinaiticus. Perhaps the amazing thing about all the extant manuscripts is their large area of agreement. Before, however, an acceptable translation could be made, all the manuscripts, particularly in their groups or families, had to be studied analytically and critically, and a Received Text (Textus Receptus) arrived at.

The precise dating of the gospels is not our concern here, but they would seem to have been published in the order of Mark, Luke, Matthew and John. The first three gospels are referred to as 'synoptic' since they provide much the same view of Jesus, and in fact Luke and Matthew contain the whole of Mark with the exception of about thirty verses[13]. In addition, they reproduce a large amount of the same material which appears to have come from a common origin, referred to by scholars as 'Q' (that is, *Quelle* the German word for 'source'). When the Edict of Diocletian in AD 303 ordered the burning of all the sacred books of the Christians, it did much to establish the final canon of Scripture. Numberless manuscripts were ruthlessly destroyed, but the most valued books were hidden; and out of the many books which had been circulating since the second century the gospels of Mark, Luke, Matthew and John were held to be canonical, and were therefore closely guarded. Rejected gospels[14] were referred to as 'apocryphal' gospels, which probably originated later than AD 303, and some possibly as late as the fifth century.

Luke, in his introduction to his gospel[15], speaks of the many writers who had undertaken to write an account of Christian events, and insists that his own is reliable because he has had 'perfect understanding of all things from the beginning'. John, however, selected his material with the avowed propagandist and proselytizing purpose 'that you might believe that Jesus is the Christ, the Son of God; and that believing you might have life through his name'[16]. Thus, Luke looked for historical reliability, whilst John's main concern was to array the facts in such a way as to command faith. Interestingly enough, because John's gospel was so different from the three synoptic ones, it barely escaped being consigned to the non-canonical works during the second century.

Thus, Jesus is presented somewhat differently in the synoptic gospels; and even the synoptic writers, by their omissions, additions and arrangements, each presents individually a different aspect of Jesus. To Matthew he appears as the King Messiah; to Mark he is the Man; and to the physician Luke he is essentially the Healer. John presents a more mystical figure who is the Son of God and Saviour of the world. Selections only were made from Jesus' actions[17] as well as from his sayings because of the vastness of both the written and the unwritten material[18]. His words were so paradoxical at times that the meaning of much that he said must have been lost, even if the words were accurately remembered. Moreover, he taught at varying levels – for his inner circle of twelve disciples (the mysteries of the Kingdom of God), for the seventy sent forth to evangelize, and for the rest (parables). Many of the mysteries were unquestionably misapprehended; and many of the parables had to be explained even to his privileged, but uncomprehending disciples.

(b) The Teaching

Jesus taught the inwardness of religion, for the Kingdom of Heaven (or God) was within. This Kingdom comprised certain types of people, such as the humble or 'poor in spirit', the gentle, those who 'hunger and thirst after righteousness' the pure in heart, the persecuted and reviled, the merciful and the peacemakers. He said that, in order to enter such an inner Kingdom of values, we had to become 'as little children'. Jesus did not hesitate to contrast such types of people with those, like the Pharisees, who seemed mainly concerned with the externals of religious practice, and who 'strained at gnats' but succeeded in 'swallowing camels'.

The teaching of Jesus was a counsel of perfection[19]. Man needed to rethink his own inner nature, 'to repent', and to see himself whole and entire. He himself did not come to annul or to abolish the teaching of the Law and the Prophets, but rather to fulfil it by internalizing what had remained for so long mere external observances. It was the integration, or integrity, of the person that Jesus sought – making people 'whole' and not some addiction to ego-fulfilment. No doubt it was because of this that many of his speeches appear harsh, perhaps exaggerated, when directed at members of the establishment who held to the letter of the Law but rejected its spirit. 'You must be perfect as your heavenly Father is perfect'[20]. The Greek word for 'perfect' here is *teleios*, and it implies a completion, a tying-up of loose ends, an integration or wholeness.

Jesus was essentially concerned with the individual in a society in which the religion and nationhood emphasized 'corporate personality'. To most Jews it was the survival of their nation that was of vital importance; to Jesus it was the survival and salvation of the individual. The ninety-nine righteous could safely be left to look after themselves; it was the one who was lost who was of vital concern and importance. And it was at this very level of national interests that Jesus failed as a potential Messiah in the eyes of most of his contemporaries. His very universalism, his love of all men including his enemies[21], prevented any narrow nationalistic concept: he was the Son of Man first and a Jew second. He would accept no barriers of creed, class or caste; a Samaritan, a Syro-Phoenician woman, a Roman centurion, a prostitute – all were worthy of attention and consideration.

Jesus taught that whatever criterion of judgement we applied to others we must be prepared to apply also to ourselves. He gave the Golden Rule: 'Do unto others as you would that they should do unto you'; and it was only through the love which we showed to others that all men would recognize that we were his disciples. And inasmuch as we did anything to help anyone, even the least of Christ's brethren, we did it to Christ himself. He thus emphasized the right relationships with our fellows, our service of others and our face-to-face encounters with all people.

Forgiveness was of the essence in the teaching of Jesus. It is interesting to note that John's gospel can breathe the spirit of forgiveness throughout its record of the words and works of Jesus without actually mentioning the word itself. In fact, there are far fewer references to forgiveness in the synoptic gospels than one might perhaps imagine. Nevertheless, the actual array of statements concerning forgiveness is uncompromising. If we cannot forgive others we clearly cannot forgive ourselves: 'Forgive and you shall be forgiven'[22]; there is no limit to the extent to which we should forgive[23]; our loving of others brings with it forgiveness of our sins[24]. And this dynamic and uncompromising teaching of Jesus managed to antagonize scribes, lawyers, priests, Sadducees, and Pharisees alike – in fact, the whole establishment.

Part and parcel of the teaching of Jesus concerning 'wholeness' was his activity in healing. Disease was contrary to the will of God, and Jesus was strongly moved by man's personal sorrows and sufferings. Out of his great compassion he healed large numbers of people who followed him, or sought him out, that he might work his miraculous cures upon them.

4 The Early Church

The newly-born Christian faith spread rapidly after Pentecost when, according to the Acts of the Apostles, the Holy Spirit came upon the disciples of Jesus like a violent wind. Paul of Tarsus, a Roman citizen and former Pharisee, was one of the main agents in extending the gospel to the Gentiles. Wherever he travelled he founded churches, in particular in some of the chief centres of culture and trade in the Roman Empire, such as Corinth, Athens, Ephesus, Thessalonika and Philippi. The first Christians accepted Jesus as the Messiah and Son of God, and doctrines were soon developed in relation to such themes as the Incarnation, the Trinity and Salvation. Early converts, however, both to Judaism and to Christianity, had to submit themselves to the whole of the Jewish Law, including circumcision. Paul did much to relieve the burdens of converts by ensuring that they were subjected only to a minimum of food regulations and similar legal obligations, whilst greater emphasis was placed upon the moral law. Circumcision ceased to be a compulsory rite. Such greater freedom in terms of the minutiae of the Jewish Law ensured that increased numbers of Gentiles became members of the Christian Church. Paul insisted that in Christ there could be neither Jew nor Greek, bond nor free, male nor female[26].

Christianity gradually ceased to be regarded as a sect of Judaism and became a religion in its own right. Liberated from the confining legalism of Judaism, the Christian Church began to spread throughout the Mediterranean world. Jews, Greeks and Romans were all exercised in their minds by this new faith that rejected barriers of class and race, and which preached purity of heart at a time when the Roman Empire was declining both in power and in moral standards. Christians, however, soon became an object of severe persecution, particularly when they were no longer confused with Jews *per se*. Tradition has it that Peter was crucified upside-down and that Paul suffered decapitation at the instigation of Nero in AD 64. In the Colosseum at Rome Christians were burnt alive, crucified, tortured, thrown to lions, and made unwilling participants in duels with professional gladiators in the arena.

During the period between the destruction of Jerusalem in AD 70 and the reign of Trajan (98-117), there was considerable activity and expansion on the part of the Early Church. Trajan himself said that Christians were not deliberately to be sought out, but that if they were accused and convicted they had to be punished –

> yet on this condition, that whoso denies himself to be a Christian, and makes the fact plain by his action, that is, by worshipping our gods, shall obtain pardon on his repentance, however suspicious his past conduct may be[27].

Whilst the chief centres of Christian life and practice were the churches of Rome and Antioch, there were, nevertheless, Christian communities in Asia Minor, Greece, Italy, Gaul, Britain and North Africa. Christians came from all stations in life, including the army and the civil service, and some were even appointed to provincial governorships[28]. But the successors of the Emperor Trajan were by no means so indifferent to the activities of Christians; there seemed to be an alternating policy of active suppression and unobtrusive toleration. The Stoic emperor, Marcus Aurelius (161-180) reflected upon the 'sheer obstinacy'[29] of Christians, and he ordered them to be sent into the arena. He attempted to repress Christianity, not so much on theological or philosophical grounds as on the basis that Christians were a distinct menace to the moral well-being and unity of the Empire.

During the third century, Christianity was treated with a general tolerance, although persecution broke out from time to time under such emperors as Maximinus (235-238), Decius (249-251), Gallus (251-253) and Valerian (253-260). Decius, for example, saw himself as a religious and political reformer, and he considered that the State was thoroughly corrupt and that vice and wickedness were destroying the very roots of Roman society. In consequence, he argued that the Empire could be saved only if there were a wholesale return to the ancient worship of Roman deities. Christianity had, therefore, to be destroyed.

One of the longest persecutions in the history of the Early Church occurred during the reign of Diocletian (284-305). At first he showed almost a studied toleration of Christianity, but in 303 he issued edicts which enforced the destruction of Christian churches, the confiscation of their books and property, and the dismissal of all Christians from official positions. Clergy and teachers within the Church were arrested and, if they recanted, they were granted their freedom; if they refused to recant they were tortured. All individuals throughout the Roman Empire were required to offer sacrifice, on pain of death, to the Roman gods and to the Emperor[30]. Finally, however, in 313 Constantine, who had entered Rome in the previous year under the Christian banner, published the Edict of Milan. This granted full religious liberty to all subjects in the Roman Empire. All Christian property that had been confiscated had to be restored. Christianity itself very soon became the official religion of the Roman Empire.

5 Divisions in the Church

Towards the end of the second century most Christians recognized the rule of overseers or bishops (Greek *episkopoi*), and accepted a canon of scripture and a creed. With its recognition by the Roman Empire, in the fourth century, its increased authority and support made Christianity strong. Constantine transferred the centre of political power to Byzantium, which was then known as Constantinople. The head of the Christian Church in Rome, known as the Pope (*Papa*, or 'father'), became in 445 the primate of all Christians throughout the Empire. The Church remained as one institution until 1054, when it split into two main sections: the Eastern element was represented by what was called the Orthodox Church, the division of the Christian Church that provided what it considered was 'right teaching'; and the Western element was represented by the Roman Catholic Church, that is, the division of the Church that provided 'catholic' or universal application. The reasons for this Great Schism were concerned with theology, ritual and observances in religion; but they were also geographical, cultural, linguistic, political and organizational. Disputes involved dress, vestments, the tonsure, the dates of Christmas and Easter, and even the addition or subtraction of a Greek iota or a Latin word in articles of faith. During the eleventh century, Russia became converted to Christianity and its church became the largest representative of the Orthodox Church.

The West experienced ever-recurring contests between Popes and Emperors, Church and State, and these came to a peak during the sixteenth century. There was a schism within the Papacy itself, and rival popes set up at Avignon and Rome between the years 1378 and 1417. The power of the Papacy was considerably weakened as a result of this. The Renaissance of the fifteenth century provided a great revival of learning generally, and the influence of Islam was felt as a result of their conquest of Constantinople.

Abuses continued within the Church itself and there was considerable opposition to any attempt at reform. Individual reformers, such as John Hus in Bohemia and John Wyclif in England, were raising their voices in protest during the fourteenth century. In Germany, in 1517, Martin Luther condemned the sale and purchase of Indulgences, and the worldliness of the Church generally. He boldly nailed his Ninety-five Theses to the door of the church at Wittenberg, and claimed that the scriptures were open to all and could be interpreted by private judgement, guided by the Spirit of God. Salvation, he said, was by faith alone, and he based his arguments upon the writings of Paul, particularly the Letter to the Romans . The influence of Luther was felt in Switzerland where attempts at reform were taken up by Ulich Zwingli in Zurich and by John Calvin in Geneva. Zwingli's reform began in 1542, and a complete break was made from the faith and practice of the Catholic Church. Calvin supported Zwingli in his opposition to the Catholic doctrine of the transubstantiation of the elements of bread and wine into the body and blood of Christ in the Eucharist, and also in his opposition to the doctrine of consubstantiation (or the Real Presence) as maintained by Luther. Although Calvin accepted the doctrine of justification by faith, he asserted that God was absolute sovereign and that he had predestined some (the Elect) to salvation, and the rest to perdition. Despite their differing interpretations, most of these reformers regarded the scriptures as verbally inspired.

As a result of the Reformation and the various breaks with Rome, a great number of Protestant sects and denominations arose. John Knox (1505-1572) organized Prebyterianism in Scotland on the principles of the government and doctrine propounded and developed by Calvin. Also deriving from Geneva was Congregationalism, followed by the sect of the Baptists. During the seventeenth century the Quakers, or Society of Friends, were founded by George Fox, who based the movement not upon dogmas of belief, or upon forms of sacramental practice, but upon the personal spiritual experience of the individual through what was termed 'the Inner Light'. Another group, called the Unitarians, rejected the doctrine of the Trinity as well as that of the Divinity of Jesus as interpreted in orthodox Christology.

The Christian Church in England made a breach with Rome in 1532 as a result of a dispute between Henry VIII and the Pope on the issue of Henry's marriage with Catherine of Aragon. The Pope refused to annul the marriage, and so Henry made himself head of the Anglican Church. His title, 'Defender of the Faith' (*Fidei Defensor*) had been conferred upon him by Pope Leo X in 1521 because of his tract against Martin Luther, the Heresiarch, entitled:

'On the Seven Sacraments, against Martin Luther, by the Illustrious Prince Henry VIII'; and the title was retained by his successors. At first the Anglican Church kept most of the dogmas and practices of the Roman Church, but gradually other influences prevailed. In 1599 Queen Elizabeth I attempted, through her compromise (referred to as the *Via Media*), to present a middle road between extreme Catholicism and the developing Protestantism of the time. The apostolic ministry of bishops, priests and deacons was retained, the basic creeds of the historic faith were established, and the sacraments of baptism and the Eucharist were maintained, together with confirmation.

During the eighteenth century in England, John Wesley, an Anglican minister, and his supporters organized a crusade based upon the beliefs of a Dutch theologian named Arminius (1560-1609), who held that the doctrine of predestination was wrong and that salvation was open to all people through faith in Jesus Christ. Wesley called his movement 'Methodist' because of the method of prayer involved, and Christian practice and fellowship which they pursued. Wesley engaged in preaching in the open air and organized groups of 'Methodists' wherever he went on his journeys. The movement flourished and Wesley requested that ministers might be ordained for his developing societies in the USA. When the bishops refused his request he began to ordain his own ministers, and Methodism became one of the separate free churches. Within the Anglican Church itself there was an evangelical revival, missionary enterprise developed considerably, and through the work of such people as William Wilberforce the slave trade was abolished.

Within the Roman Catholic Church there were signs of self-criticism and a clear desire for some internal reforms. In 1545 a Council assembled in Northern Italy at Trent which discussed for eighteen years the cardinal doctrines of the Church, and sought to correct some of the abuses within it. Its final decisions laid down the main lines of Roman Catholic development in what has been termed 'the Counter-Reformation', and they were confirmed by Pope Pius IV in 1564. New religious orders were steadily being founded and organized, such as the Capuchins (1528), the Jesuits (1534) and the Oratorians (1556); and they in turn sought to develop the missionary side of the Church's activities. In general, as a result of the Council of Trent's deliberations, there was an emphasis upon the supremacy of the Pope and on the centralization at Rome of all the Church's activities.

6 The Christian Church Today

So numerous are the branches of the Christian Church today that it would be quite impossible in a general study of this nature to give an outline description of them all or, indeed, even to mention many of the sects and denominations that have arisen over time. For more detailed information the reader is referred to the Bibliographies. All that we can hope to do here is to mention some of the major divisions of Christianity and some of their more recent developments.

(a) The Roman Catholic Church

The Roman Catholic Church is the largest Christian organization in the world today, and it comprises about 60 per cent of all Christians. At the head of the Church is the Pope of Rome, who is assisted by the College of Cardinals and by the local archbishops and bishops throughout the world. In England, Roman Catholics suffered many disabilities, as did also Nonconformists generally, until in 1829 they were granted full citizen rights by the Act of Emancipation.

The Roman Catholic Church regards itself as the teaching authority of Christianity, and as the sole authoritative interpreter of the Scriptures. St Peter is considered to have been the first bishop or pope of Rome[32] ; and some of the later doctrines of the Roman Church are regarded as having been implicit even though not explicitly stated. Thus, the doctrine of the Immaculate Conception of the Blessed Virgin Mary (that is, that she herself was born without the taint of sin) was established as late as 1854. Papal Infallibilty did not finally become a doctrine of the Roman Church until

1870 at the First Vatican Council. Nor does it mean that the Pope is incapable of making mistakes in general terms but that, when he speaks *ex cathedra*, or officially, on matters of faith and morals, God stays him against the possibility of error. The doctrine of the Corporal Assumption into Heaven of the Blessed Virgin Mary was finally established in 1950[33], although the seeds of the doctrine are to be found as early as the fourth century in the book called 'The Assumption of Mary'. Here it was stated that, two years after the ascension of Jesus, Mary was warned that her end was approaching. All the apostles were miraculously borne on clouds from the ends of the earth to witness her departure; and, in the full sight of them all, Mary was carried up into heaven without dying.

The Catholic Church of Rome also regards itself as a 'sacramental agent', that is, it points the way in which its members should live and it mediates to them the power required to live in that particular way. Its seven sacraments correlate closely with the human cycle of life, and they are specifically: (i) baptism, (ii) confirmation, (iii) marriage, (iv) confession, (v) the Mass, (in which the elements are sacralized) and the Holy Eucharist (through which grace is conferred), (vi) extreme unction, and (vii) holy orders. Thus birth, adolescence, maturity, vocation and death are covered by the sacraments of the Church. The Mass probably derives its name from the Latin expression, 'Ite, missa est' ('Go, it is the dismissal') and it is believed that, in the Host (*hostia* is the Latin for sacrifice) and the Chalice, the consecrated bread and wine become Christ's human body and blood; that is, they are transubstantiated. The congregation partake of the bread only – usually in the form of a wafer – whilst the cup is reserved.

In 1962 Pope John XXIII called the Second Vatican Council and invited members of the Orthodox Church and of Protestant churches generally to be present as observers. Discussion of questions of authority and doctrine were freely encouraged. In recent years the service of the Mass has been conducted in the vernacular of each country concerned, as opposed to the Tridentine Mass in Latin; and there has been a liturgical revival which strives to involve the people more intimately in the service.

(b) The Eastern Orthodox Church

The Eastern Orthodox Church is to be found in such countries as Russia, Greece, Cyprus, Sinai, Albania and Bulgaria. The seven sacraments are interpreted as in the Roman Catholic Church, except that in the Holy Eucharist the cup is offered to communicants along with the bread. The Orthodox Church sees no need for 'innovations' such as the doctrines of the Immaculate Conception and the Bodily Assumption of the Blessed Virgin Mary. In terms of moral and ethical behaviour, far less guidance is given to individual members than is provided by the Roman Catholic Church. It obviously does not accept that truth in matters of faith and morals comes only through the Roman Catholic Pope; neither does it believe that truth comes through any infallible member of its own membership. Truth is elicited through the conscience of the Church as a whole and by means of the consensus of Christians. It is basically the collective judgement of the church bishops in Council which ultimately establishes God's Truth, in and through the Church itself which is the mystical body of Christ. Unlike the priests of the Roman Catholic Church, Orthodox priests need not be celibate, and the laity itself is referred to as the 'royal priesthood'. There is a sense of equality among all members of the Church, whilst the Patriarch of Istanbul himself is *primus inter pares* – first among equals.

The main act of worship in Orthodox churches is the Liturgy, or celebration of the Eucharist. At the end of the church is a screen, colourfully decorated, which conceals the altar. At certain stages in the Liturgy the doors of the screen are opened, and then the Gospel book is brought in with the Chalice (cup) and the Platen (plate) containing the consecrated wine and bread. The language of the Liturgy is usually that of the country in which it is being celebrated, and the services themselves may take on local colour and variation.

After considerable persecution in Russia, and in countries of the Eastern communist bloc in Europe, the Orthodox Church still remains very strong, influential and resolute in keeping faith with its fundamental convictions. Its total membership is possibly within the region of 200 million.

(c) The Church of England or Anglican Church

The Anglican communion has about seventy million members all over the world, including Africa, South America, and the USA where the Protestant Episcopal Church is Anglican. In England, the Anglican Church claims to be the 'catholic church' directly descended from the See of Canterbury, which was founded in the sixth century by St Augustine. It has a threefold order of bishops, priests and deacons who have recognition by the Eastern Orthodox churches but not by the Papacy of Rome. The Anglican Church is established by law in England and it is, therefore, the national church. Nevertheless, its missionary work has taken it to countries all over the world. Its articles of faith, the Thirty-Nine Articles, were drawn up in the sixteenth century after the break with Rome, and they are included in the standard Book of Common Prayer, which was revised in 1928.

The High Church, or Anglo-Catholicism, began as a movement within the Church of England which emphasized the Catholic rather than the Protestant tradition in forms of worship. It originated in the Oxford Movement of the nineteenth century which made an attempt to emphasize the continuity of Anglicanism with mediaeval Catholicism. High churchmen, such as John Henry Newman, J Keble and E B Pusey, wrote a series of *Tracts of the Times* (1833-1841) which sought to expose the dangers that threatened the Church from secular authority. In the last tract of the Tractarians (Tract No 90) Newman sought to demonstrate how the Thirty-Nine Articles could be equated with the doctrines of the Roman Catholic Church. Finally, after the tracts had been condemned in Oxford in 1841, Newman became a member of the Roman Catholic Church (in 1845), and it was left to Pusey and Keble to establish Catholic liturgy and doctrine in the High Church wing of Anglicanism. The Low Church section of Anglicanism is concerned to preserve the Anglican Prayer Book and to emphasize the missionary aspects of worship and religious activity.

(d) Lutheranism

Martin Luther (1483-1546) had recommended the formation of a

German national church, the abolition of all indulgences, and the end of the enforced celibacy of the clergy. Luther was excommunicated by the Roman Catholic Church, and Lutheran followers were outlawed by the Edict of Worms in 1521. In 1530 Melanchthon drew up the *Confession of Augsburg*, which provided Lutherans with a guide to belief and behaviour, and in 1580 a full collection of Luther's writings was made, called the *Book of Concord*. Lutherans in Europe retained the old churches and cathedrals, as well as the order of bishops, and they emphasized the importance of the frequent celebration of the Communion.

Today the Lutheran Church is to be found chiefly in Germany, Denmark, Norway, Sweden, Finland and the USA. Their services resemble those of the Presbyterians, and they still use the hymns which Luther composed and translations of the Bible based upon Luther's own translation. For Lutherans the Holy Scriptures contain the sole necessary guide for truth and they present the only rule of faith – all other creeds and confessions are subordinate to them.

Each individual has the right to reach God through the Scriptures, and he or she is answerable to God in matters of faith and belief. Salvation and justification are through faith, but there is a great deal of support for some form of the doctrine of predestination.

(e) Presbyterianism

Presbyterianism looks back to John Calvin as its Reformation leader, and it is a system of ecclesiastical government which is overseen by ministers and elders (that is, presbyters) who are equal in rank. The beliefs of Presbyterians are to be found in the *Westminster Confession of Faith* (formulated in 1647); and these beliefs have generally been accepted by Scottish and American Presbyterians, as well as English Presbyterians, as the most thorough statement of the Calvinist creed.

The Reformation in Scotland was concerned to reform the discipline, forms of worship and doctrine of the Church; and John Knox, who had worked with Calvin in Geneva, determined to change the religious system in Scotland. In 1560 the *Scots Confession* was drawn up and signed by Knox. Presbyterians regard the Word of God, that is, the Christian Bible, as the supreme and ultimate rule of life and faith. They have a hierarchy of courts, the lowest of which is the local kirk-session which comprises the minister and lay elders elected by popular vote. Next after the kirk-session is the court of the presbytery which has jurisdiction over a particular area; and above the court of the presbytery is the court of the synod, ruling over a number of presbyteries. The Supreme Court of the Presbyterian Church is the General Assembly, over which the Moderator presides, and which has both legislative and judicial functions. Different branches of the Presbyterian Church are to be found in Scotland, Wales and Ireland.

(f) The Free Churches

Whilst it is certainly true that there are well over 250 Free Church groups or sects, it is also true that something in the region of eighty-five per cent of the Free Church population belong to about a dozen denominations.

Congregationalists represent one of the oldest sects of Non-conformists, and they have always held that each church assembly should be quite separate as a local body of believers, and should rule itself democratically and independently of any external ecclesiastical authority. They originated in Elizabethan times when Robert Browne (1550-1633), who was an Anglican clergyman, rejected the rule of the bishops and fled with a group of followers to Holland. Later he took refuge in Scotland where he was imprisoned. His views were spread by Henry Barrow and John Greenwood, who were subsequently found guilty of dissension under an Act passed in 1592, and they were hanged at Tyburn for 'obstinately refusing to come to church'. Their views were that Jesus Christ was the sole head of the Christian Church, that the Church should have no political ties, and that it should remain unrelated in any way to the State. They considered that the only authoritative religious book was the Bible, and that each congregation was entirely independent.

Congregationalists were eventually granted full liberty under

William III (1609-1702), and in 1883 the Congregational Union of England and Wales was formed. Its Declaration of Faith was binding upon no individual, and its ministers were responsible to their own church only. In 1972 the Presbyterian Church of England and the Congregational Church in England and Wales joined forces to form the *United Reformed Church* (URC). In 1981 a further unification took place with the Reformed Association of Churches of Christ, which in turn became a part of the URC. A third union took place in 2000 with the Congregational Union of Scotland.

The *Baptists* considered that infant baptism as taught and practised by the Roman Catholic and Anglican Churches was unscriptural and therefore wrong, and that members should be baptized only upon confession of their faith and their sins. Because infants were incapable of such a confession, baptism was by total immersion of adults. The beginnings of the modern Baptist movement are traced to John Smyth, who in 1609 was a minister of the Anglican Church, and who came under the influence of the Mennonites and Arminians when he was in Amsterdam. The first Baptist Church in England was built at Newgate in 1612, the year in which Smyth died. The General Baptist Church rejected Calvinistic teaching and regarded redemption as open to all who believed. But the Particular Baptist Church refused to accept this Arminian doctrine, which it considered to be heresy, and accepted the Calvinistic doctrine of Election. In 1891 the Baptist Union was formed which united most members of these two groups, and the Baptist denomination spread, by its missionary efforts, throughout the world and particularly in the USA.

Methodism arose out of John Wesley's visit to Georgia in the USA, where he was deeply moved by a sect called the Moravians, a revival of the 'Bohemian Brethren' who had originated among the followers of John Hus in 1457. In 1738 John Wesley founded the Methodist movement, and his chief concern was the evangelical one of saving souls. He was supported by his brother Charles, who composed a large number of hymns, and at first by George Whitefield, who broke with the Wesleys because of his own Calvinistic views.

John Wesley established a conference of those ministers who were interested in his 'Methodism', and such conferences have met regularly since 1744. 'Circuits' were established under a minister, and the circuits in turn were formed into 'districts', all being brought together in the annual conference. Ministers were moved from circuit to circuit each year. At first Methodists did not divorce themselves from the Anglican Church, but worked within it, attending a local church on a Sunday morning and their newly-established chapel in the evening. Wesley began a Sunday school scheme, developed open-air meetings as one of the main methods of reaching the people, and reintroduced the Agapae, or Love Feasts, of the Early Church in order to deepen the fellowship among the members. He also introduced cheap books of educational value by way of encouraging the poor both to read and to become edified.

After Wesley's death in 1791 the Methodist movement began to develop schisms. In 1810 the Primitive Methodists gave more power to the laity and reintroduced what might be termed the 'camp-meeting' type of service, whilst in 1811 there was a break between Arminian and Calvinist supporters. Eventually, at a conference held at the Albert Hall in 1932, the Wesleyan Methodists became one Church, that is, the Methodist Church; and today it is one of the largest of the Free Churches, with over 60 million Methodists worldwide.

In very general terms, the members of most of the Free Churches believe that salvation is a personal phenomenon which does not necessarily require the mediation of the Church or the minister for it to occur. Apart from the most exclusive sects, for whom there is absolutely no alternative, the creeds or doctrines of any sect are open to challenge, criticism and change; and within the same church congregation there might be almost every variety of belief. Within most Protestant sects there is considerable room and freedom for personal belief and acceptance.

In 1948 the World Council of Churches was founded, and it meets from time to time for consultation and discussion of religious, social and political problems, and for positive action in social and world affairs. For example, in 1973 it sold all its holdings in companies that were trading with or investing in Southern Africa. The concept of *ecumenism* has developed, during recent decades, as a world movement springing from the belief that all men are brothers and all women sisters; and that, in some way, the Christian Church should be reconstituted in order that this belief might have the best and fullest expression.

But Christian *unity* is not necessarily seen as something to be expressed in Christian *uniformity*, and not all supporters of ecumenism want there to be just one Church with one form of organization, liturgy and worship. There have, however, been many successful attempts to reunite churches, such as, for example, the Uniat Churches in which the Eastern Churches of Hungary, Yugoslavia and Ukraine have become reunited with Rome; the Church of South India (founded in 1947), in which there has been the union of Anglican, Methodist, Presbyterian and Congregationalist Churches; and the Church in Canada in which Methodists, Congregationalists and Presbyterians have come together. The World Council of Churches itself unites in conference Lutheran, Anglican, Presbyterian, Congregational, Baptist, Eastern Orthodox, Calvinist Reformed, Salvation Army, United and Uniat Churches; whilst the Roman Catholic Church attends as an observer.

14 Islam

1   The Historical Background of Islam

> God, there is no god but he, the Living, the Everlasting....
> His throne comprises the heaven and the earth;
> He is the All-High, the All-Glorious. (*The Koran*, sura 22)

In order fully to understand and appreciate the tenets of the Muslim faith it is necessary to trace its origin in Arabia during the sixth century AD. Professor A Guillaume maintains that the ancient Habiru 'are almost certainly to be identified with the Arabs'[1], and that the Hebrews of the Old Testament were Arabs and part of the inhabitants of the Arabian peninsula. He also considers that the most likely meaning of the word 'Arab' is 'nomad' or 'wanderer', which is precisely what most of the Arabs were. They wandered perpetually throughout the peninsula and raided wherever they could.

At the time of Muhammad the Arabs worshipped a number of gods, including Al Ilah (Allah) or 'the God', Al Lat or the Sun, Al Uzza or Venus, and Manat or Fortune. Allah was regarded as the father of the other three who were female; and, whilst there were certainly many other deities worshipped both at Mecca and elsewhere in Arabia, these were at the head of the hierarchy. Al Lat was regarded as the great mother-goddess who had been represented in so many ancient religions and who has reappeared in a variety of different guises in more modern ones. In connection with the worship of the three daughters of Al Ilah there occurred a considerable amount of sacrifice, both human and animal, as well as fertility ritual. Coupled with this typical polytheism there were also various animistic beliefs, largely involving stones, trees and wells, and the spirits or *djinns*, which were believed to inhabit both natural objects and places and which were thought to need placating in a variety of ways.

There were, however, other currents of belief in Arabia including both Judaism and Christianity. How and when the Jews entered the peninsula is disputed by scholars, some of whom would argue for a date as early as the eighth century BC, and others for a date as late as the first and second centuries AD. It seems highly probable that from the time of the fall of Samaria in 721 BC there were fugitives from Palestine moving into Arabia under pressure from surrounding countries, down to the ruthless repression and persecution by the Romans in the first two centuries after the death of Jesus. The Jews who entered Arabia sought to proselytize wherever they settled. And they were not without success both in religion and in the realm of business.

It is clear that many of them became large landowners, traders, organizers of prosperous marts for the barter of iron goods, including arms and armaments, and woven articles. The general prosperity of the Jews presented a challenge to the Arab traders, in particular to the Quraysh at Mecca and certain tribes in Medina[2]. And it was a challenge which the Arabs, in the long run, resented very much and which finally led to some harsh treatment of the Jews when the Muslims eventually took up arms in order to establish their Islamic empire.

Christians in Arabia belonged, broadly speaking, to three different sects: the Greek Orthodox, the Nestorians and the Monophysites. Each of these groups was active in making converts among the Arabs, and both monasteries and churches were established close to the major caravan routes. Perhaps the most important link with Islam itself as it developed through the teaching of Muhammad was the doctrine of the Monophysite sect that there was only one nature in Christ, and that 'the Trinity is one Divinity, one Nature and one

Essence'. This belief led to a great deal of intolerance and persecution among the Christians themselves – orthodox and heretics against one another – for the Nestorians argued that Christ was truly man, but he was born as God of the Virgin Mary, uniting in himself two natures. Nevertheless, the Monophysite doctrine established a link with the unrelenting monotheism of Islam, and in consequence Christians found themselves, for some years at least, rather better treated than the Jews.

2   Muhammad (AD 570-632)

Mecca had for hundreds of years been a centre for trading in a great variety of requisites, from camels to ivory, and from silks and spices to precious stones. It had also been a place of pilgrimage for visitors from all over Arabia, and it contained a sanctuary, the Kaaba or 'Cube', which was the centre of polytheism, idolatry and superstition. There was a tradition that, in the time of Abraham, Al Ilah had thrown down a black stone (possibly an aerolite) as a sign among the Arab people. This stone was later embedded in the wall of the Kaaba in order that it might be touched or kissed by the visiting pilgrims. There were other holy objects and places in Mecca, such as Zamzam, traditionally the sacred well revealed by Yahweh to Hagar and Ishmael when they were dying of thirst in the hot and dusty desert.

Muhammad was born in Mecca in AD 570, the year in which, according to tradition, an expedition of an Ethiopian army against the Arabian city was miraculously routed. Apparently there were elephants in the ranks of the invading army and, according to sura 105 of the Koran[3], the strong attack was eventually stayed by the intervention of Allah who sent flocks of birds against the enemy. The birds dropped stones on them and killed them outright. Some scholars have suggested that the Christian King of Ethiopia, Abraha, and his army were in fact destroyed by a virulent attack of smallpox.

Muhammad's father had died before the prophet's birth, and his mother died when he was only six, so that he was brought up mainly by his grandfather and then a foster-mother. There are the usual late legends surrounding his birth but, as Guillaume[4] pointedly remarks:

> A prophet's personality should be able to stand on its merits. If it can, it needs no portent; if it cannot, a portent merely compromises the credibility of the whole narrative by importing the incredible.

Muhammad was a member of the Quraysh tribe, and as soon as he was old enough he began to travel with the caravans trading between Mecca and the capitals and marts of the Middle East. At the age of twenty-five he was employed by a rich widow of forty, named Khadija, who successfully ran a trading business. Khadija appears to have been impressed by Muhammad's trading acumen and by his personality and appearance, and it was not long before they decided to get married. They had seven children, but unfortunately no male heir survived. As long as Khadija lived Muhammad remained faithful to her. After her death he appears to have had at least eight more wives and a number of concubines. His great anxiety was to obtain a male heir, but this he eventually failed to do since all his sons died in infancy.

His many journeys must have brought Muhammad into contact with Jews, various sects of Christians, and Zoroastrians from Persia. Although it is usually claimed that Muhammad could neither read nor write, it seems reasonable to suppose that he had considerable conversation with members of a variety of religions; and that wherever he found an acceptance of monotheism and dualism (God-Devil) he discovered a response within himself. He was personally disgusted with the moral laxity of the city of Mecca, and was strongly opposed to its polytheistic and idolatrous practices. He saw the struggle between right and wrong, good and evil, as a dramatized battle between God and the Devil, that is, between Allah and Iblis (or Shaitan). And as he listened to the accounts of Yahweh and Ahura Mazda and of their struggles with the powers of darkness,

Muhammad must have felt his inner being responding to the truth as he saw it in other religions.

When he was about forty years old, Muhammad became increasingly contemplative, and he would repeatedly retire to the hills surrounding Mecca, particularly during the holy month of Ramadan, and there sit in meditation in a cave. It was during one of these periods of retirement and contemplation that, according to the prophet, he felt very strongly the presence of some strange supernatural power and eventually it materialized before him in the form of the Archangel Gabriel. The latter said to him, 'Thou art the apostle of God', held out a piece of silken brocade and asked him to read or recite what was written upon the silk. This, quite naturally, is the point of emphasizing Muhammad's illiteracy – he obviously could not read or recite what was written upon the silk if he had never been taught to read. But three times the voice demanded that he should cry out the words that he saw. Some eleven centuries before, a similar demand had been made of the Hebrew prophet usually referred to as Deutero-Isaiah:

> The voice said, Cry. And he said,
> What shall I cry?
> All flesh is grass...[5].

Now to Muhammad the voice comes back:

> Cry, in the name of the Lord!
> He who created man from clots of blood.
> Cry, the Lord is wondrous kind,
> Who, by the pen, has taught mankind
> Things they knew not (being blind)[6].

At first Muhammad was considerably disturbed, both mentally and spiritually. He felt that he must be possessed by a *djinn* which had transformed him into a *sha'ir* or soothsayer, and that the only solution for him was to hurl himself over a precipice. This was for

Muhammad a period of darkness and distress, but there was nothing novel about such an experience for a great religious leader and prophet. And just as, for example, Gautama formerly answered a similar situation, (there will always be some who will understand), so Muhammad found the immediate understanding that he required in his wife Khadija; she believed in her husband and in his visions, and encouraged him to go on seeking the truth.

Throughout his life the voice and the visions came repeatedly to the prophet, revealing to him Allah as the one and only God. All other gods were simply idols; and the struggle between good and evil, between Allah and Iblis, would soon result in the judgement of God and the supremacy of the Good. As he became convinced of the supernatural origin of these phenomena, of the things he saw and the words he heard, Muhammad began to preach amongst his relatives and friends. His wife was one of his first converts.

The immediate reaction generally was hostile; a hostility directed against Muhammad himself because of the presumption of his claim to be a prophet, or *nabi* – indeed, the chief of the prophets – and an apostle (*rasul*) sent by God. But it was also a hostility directed against his uncompromising message. Muhammad had attacked the worshippers because of their idolatry and polytheism. It was said that at this time there existed three hundred and sixty shrines in Mecca, one for each day of the lunar year, providing a considerable revenue for the Meccan traffickers in idols, images and prayers for pilgrims. In a period of moral laxity he taught that man must be responsible for his own sin and evil. And in a society in which there were the very rich and the indescribably poor, Muhammad, in typical prophetic fashion, attacked those who were grinding in the faces of the poor – just as the Hebrew prophet Amos had attacked oppressors in his society nearly fourteen hundred years before. Muhammad believed that in Allah's eyes all men were equal, and that in consequence there should be no distinction of class, whether on the basis of inheritance or of acquired wealth.

Ridicule, threats and open persecution could not prevail upon Muhammad to cease his teaching. He was repeatedly stoned, imprisoned, beaten and even on occasion left for dead; but during his first three years of proselytizing he made only forty or so converts. Muhammad was certainly not the first debunker of the gods to find himself suffering as a result of his temerity; Socrates had similarly been persecuted for seeking to drive the lower deities from the heavens.

Despite, however, all the attempts to undermine and destroy him Muhammad not only survived but began to receive increasing support. Gradually pilgrims began to come from a desert oasis about two hundred miles north of Mecca called Yathrib, later to be known as Al Medinat, 'the City', that is, the City of the Prophet. They listened to Muhammad and were so impressed that they returned to Yathrib full of his message and of his dynamic personality. Eventually, in AD 622, seventy-five leading citizens came as a delegation to Mecca to ask Muhammad to go to Yathrib as their leader and ruler. Muhammad agreed to go, and that year is regarded by Muslims as the beginning of the era of Islam. The word *hijra* (or hegira) is used to describe this great event and, although often translated as 'flight' or 'migration', it connotes rather the concept of 'separateness'[7], the breaking away from old ties as much in a spiritual sense as in a physical one. Muhammad developed into a powerful politician and statesman, and was appointed the supreme magistrate of the Arab courts in Medina. In doing all this, Muhammad accomplished a task that only the most competent and diplomatic could possibly achieve. In fact, during his rule at Medina he welded together five tribes, including two Jewish, into an orderly confederation agreeing to accept himself, the prophet of God, as the final arbiter in all their problems – social, legal and political.

After several battles and skirmishes between the Medinans and Meccans, and the subjugation of the Jews in the Hejaz, Muhammad descended upon Mecca in AD 630 with a force of his followers. He entered as a conqueror and performed a ritual 'cleansing' of the Kaaba by destroying all the images of the gods and all traces of idolatry. In victory he showed mercy, forgiving all of his enemies save only four who were put to death. He then returned to Medina from where he gradually succeeded in uniting all Arabia and its many different tribes and beliefs under the banner of Islam.

When he died in AD 632 Muhammad had established a new religion with a completely monotheist creed having universal application. The concept of the *jihad*, or holy war, was already impressed upon the minds of believers as a sacred duty in the battle against the heretics, amongst whom by now were classed both Jews and Christians who were regarded as *mushrik*, or polytheists. The justification for this view is undoubtedly derived from a passage in the Koran which virtually accuses the Jews of worshipping Ezra as the Son of God, and the Christians of similarly worshipping Jesus Christ[8]. The reference to Ezra does not seem to have any sort of basis in fact, but it is one of the many misconceptions in the Koran concerning both Old Testament and New Testament characters. Muhammad also left the framework of a social system which has remained virtually unchanged in Arabia during the intervening fourteen hundred years. And although Muhammad may certainly not have written or compiled the Koran, any more than Jesus wrote the Christian gospels, there seems little doubt that in the main the book represents a collection of the teachings of Muhammad as revealed – so he believed – by Gabriel, the Archangel of Allah.

3   The Koran (Qur'an)

'Islam' means submission, and Muslims (or Moslems) are those who have submitted to the will of Allah. The term 'Muhammadan' is objectionable to Muslims on the ground that they do not worship Muhammad, nor do they regard him as divine, nor indeed is he central in their religious beliefs. Allah, *the* God (Al Ilah), is first and last, and Muhammad is his prophet. It is, of course, inevitable that Muhammad should be regarded with considerable reverence, if on this side of idolatry; but he was and remains, for the great majority of Muslims, a man.

The Prophet Muhammad was but a man; of a purely human nature. He was neither a great God, nor a small God, nor a sub-God, nor even an auxiliary of God. ...The prophet led us into the light of truth, but however great our respect for him may be, he is not raised above the level of man... .he was God's Apostle and servant[9].

The Koran means, literally, a 'reading' or 'that which ought to be read'. Muhammad considered that this book was the only miracle that God had worked through him, although the later accounts of his life represent him as a wonder-worker. It is claimed that the original of the Koran was inscribed on pieces of bark, leaves, stones, scraps of parchment and bones, as Muhammad dictated to his followers. Allah himself had preserved the literal accuracy of everything written, and so the *general view* of Muslims towards their scriptures is a fundamentalist one: Allah had dictated it all to Muhammad over a period of about twenty-one years through the Archangel Gabriel, and its truth must be accepted by converts to Islam in a literal fashion. The Koran in its totality is about the length of the New Testament and comprises one hundred and fourteen suras, or chapters, arranged in a very artificial order of decreasing length. [Note that N J Dawood has rearranged the suras in his translation in order to begin with the more Biblical and poetical revelations, and to end with the much longer but often more topical suras.]

In the Koran, Allah is represented throughout as a single God, who is immaterial and invisible, and who enlightens the entire cosmos with his grace and power. This monotheism is quite uncompromising and it denies the Christian concept of the Trinity, which to the Muslim is at best a tritheism, at worst simply another form of polytheism. Allah is without equal and without division. He is omnipotent, creator of heaven and earth, life and death, and in his hands reside dominion and indomitable power. Being an absolutely just God he will wreak vengeance upon all heretics on the Day of Judgement; nevertheless, he is loving and compassionate towards all those who repent.

Between his God and himself nothing intervenes for the Muslim; nothing stands in the way of his communication with the divine. There is no need for a priest or intermediary, for Allah is omnipresent as well as transcendent. Indeed, Allah

> knows what is in the land and the sea; no leaf falleth but he knoweth it; nor is there a grain in the darkness under the earth, nor a thing, green or yellow, but it is recorded in his glorious book[10].

Allah created man as the crown of his creativity, and one of the impressive facts about the Koran is its emphasis upon the value of the individual. The individual soul is eternal, and the ultimate salvation or damnation of each person is finally his own responsibility.

> Whoever goes astray, he himself bears the whole responsibility of wandering... .whoever gets to himself a sin, gets it solely on his own responsibility[11].

And yet there is the same sort of adherence to predestination and divine election as one may find in the *Articles of Religion*, Numbers X and XVII, of the Anglican Church. For the Muslim the will of Allah is supreme, to the extent that one cannot even will to take the right path to his Lord except by the will of Allah[12]; no one takes heed to the message of Muhammad and the Koran except by God's will[13], 'but let him who will, take heed'. One must have faith in God, yet 'none can have faith except by the will of Allah'[14]. We cannot question God's choice or his will; it is supreme, and we can only accept, obey, and in the direst of our troubles shrug it all off and say, 'It is *quismat* (kismet, destiny, fate)' or 'it is Allah's will (*inshallah*)'.

The reconciliation of man's freedom with God's absolute will has always presented problems to monotheistic religions. In the Jewish Old Testament, Yahweh was regarded as responsible for evil as well as good[15]; and in the Christian New Testament, God has decreed from of old those whom he has predestined for salvation[16]. Individual freedom appears to have something of a vague unreality about it, even where it is affirmed.

Muhammad is regarded in the Koran as the servant, apostle and prophet of God, who was promised to Adam and foretold by Jesus. These ideas appear to be developed from references to the 'seed of the woman' who would 'bruise the head' of the serpent; and in John's gospel to the advent of 'another Comforter' whom Jesus promised to his disciples, 'that he may abide with you for ever'[17]. It is also stated that Muhammad was carried in a trance state into the presence of Allah, through seven heavens, and that there he received the revelation of God. St Paul seems to have had quite similar experiences[18]. Although Muhammad spoke by revelation, as many of the Old Testament prophets claimed for themselves[19], he at no time made greater claims than this. It is a fact that in the Koran the same reverence is accorded to Jesus as to Muhammad. The invocation, 'Peace be on him', is always afforded both of them when their names are mentioned.

Jesus is somewhat strangely regarded as the son of the Virgin Mary, and yet as no more than a prophet and apostle like Muhammad himself[20]. He was certainly not, in the Muslim view, the Son of God or divine, or more than a human being elevated to the position of a revealer of God's truth. It is clear that Muhammad at no time read any of the Jewish or Christian scriptures, but that he obtained his information through discourse with Jewish and Christian traders. We have already mentioned something of the variety of the sects of the latter, and there must have arisen a considerable amount of confusion in the minds of the Arabs concerning Christian theology. The Koran states that Jesus was not crucified, but that Judas took his place; and, therefore, any question of a supernatural resurrection in the case of Jesus is by-passed. But the prophetic position of Jesus is assured in Islam:

> After those prophets We sent forth Jesus, the son of Mary,
> confirming the Torah already revealed, and gave him the
> Gospel, in which there is guidance and light, corroborating

that which was revealed before it in the Torah, a guide and an admonition to the righteous[21].

There is, however, a belief in personal resurrection on the Day of Judgement, or Day of Separation, when the trumpet shall sound, and the dead will stand up upon the earth. On that day,

> when the sun shall be folded up, and the stars shall fall, and when the mountains shall be set in motion.... and the seas shall boil.... then shall every soul know what it has done[22].

Every individual will have to give an account of the way he has lived, and the good will go to Heaven, or Paradise, which abounds in delightful, deep rivers of cooling water with unendingly fruitful and fertile valleys, with lovely mansions, beautiful youths and maidens. The evil will go to Hell, a place of boiling liquids, molten metal, fire and torture where the individual will suffer eternal torment. It is possible, as with Christianity, to take these things literally; and some Muslims do. But the more sophisticated today would interpret these pictures of Heaven and Hell as allegorical, since the afterlife would for them involve a spiritual rather than a physical state. Heaven is, ultimately, the beatific vision of God, which is as inexpressible in Muslim terms as it is in Christian or Judaistic.

Every man has his own particular guardian spirit watching over him[23], such are the care and concern which Allah has for all mankind. Moreover, his grace is infinite and he bestows it upon whomsoever he will[24]; and the individual should seek forgiveness of the Lord, for he is ever ready to forgive[25]. Whilst in one context the Koran exhorts, 'Let evil be rewarded with like evil; but he that forgives and seeks reconcilement will be rewarded by Allah'[26], yet in another context there is a completely positive and unconditional approach to the individual's attitudes: 'Requite evil with good'[27]. The Koran makes a plea for unity in religion, and rejects any possibility of sectarianism: 'Do not split up your religion into sects, each exulting in its own beliefs'[28]; yet, at the same time, 'There shall be no compulsion in religion'[29], and 'You have your religion and I have mine'[30]. Such is the implicit tolerance in the teaching of the Koran; but there is no tolerance on the question of Allah's uniqueness and unity. One whole sura[31] is given to this affirmation:

> In the Name of Allah, the Compassionate, the Merciful, say, Allah is One, the Eternal God. He begot none, nor was He begotten. None is equal to Him.

4 The Five Pillars of Wisdom

The path of Islam is the 'straight path' – one that begins with the revelation of Allah to Abraham, then to Moses in the Ten Commandments, followed by the Golden Rule of Jesus and, finally, ends with the inspired suras of Muhammad in the Koran. Abraham, Moses, Jesus and Muhammad were all authentic prophets producing between them, directly through the revelation of God, the 'straight path' which reached completion in Muhammad himself.

The five pillars of Islam represent the essential supports of the Muslim belief and faith: they are the creed (*kalima*), prayer (*salat*), charity and almsgiving (*zakat*), fasting (*saum*) and pilgrimage (*hajj*). The creed of Islam is simple, straightforward and memorable – 'There is no god but Allah, and Muhammad is his prophet'. Compared with the intricacies and complexities of some of the formulated Christian creeds, such a simple statement of belief must inevitably prove attractive to societies which are themselves, for the most part, uncomplicated in thought and structure.

The Koran admonishes the faithful to 'be constant in prayer'[32], in order that they may submit themselves perpetually to Allah's will, and that they may keep the whole of their lives in proper perspective. The devout Muslim must pray five times a day – on rising, at noon, in the mid-afternoon, at sunset and before retiring. These acts of devotion and worship may take place anywhere, although the devotee is required, if possible, to wash first and then to kneel (usually on a small prayer-mat) facing Mecca, and with his forehead touching the ground. It is clear that these demands can create problems in a society which is foreign to the worshipper, upon whom there are other pressures of study or work in community with non-Muslims.

Prayer is certainly no isolated ritual, but a full participation in life's activity. The washing ceremony requires a specific order and application – thus, the devotee washes his face from the top of the forehead to the chin, and from ear to ear. This is followed by the cleansing of the feet up to the ankles, the arms up to the elbows, and the rubbing of a fourth part of the head with the wet hand. Then he must cleanse his teeth, rinse out his mouth and nostrils three times, rub the space between fingers and toes, and finally comb his beard with his fingers. Wherever possible noon prayers are held collectively in a mosque on the holy day of Islam, which is Friday; the Koran is also recited corporately by the congregation. A sermon is usually provided by an *imam*, who is the leader of the mosque and responsible for the organization of both worship and religious teaching, but who is in no sense regarded as a priest or intermediary between Allah and his disciples. Muslims are called to prayer by the *muezzin*, or proclaimer, who climbs the slender turret of the mosque, and cries out:

> God is most great! God is most great!
> God is most great! God is most great!
> I witness that there is no god but Allah.
> I witness that there is no god but Allah.
> I witness that Muhammad is the apostle of Allah.
> I witness that Muhammad is the apostle of Allah.
>
> Arise and pray; arise and pray.
> Come to the good; come to the good.
> God is great; God is great.
> There is no god but Allah!

During prayers the devotees utter the *takbir* (a statement of God's greatness) at specific intervals. Finally, the prayers close with a united affirmation concerning Allah's greatness, and a plea for his mercy upon Muhammad and his descendants, even as he had mercy upon Abraham and his descendants.

Charity and almsgiving are a very strong feature of the Muslim religion, and to some extent obligatory upon all believers. 'Give generously for the cause of Allah', says the Koran[33]; 'Be charitable; Allah loves the charitable'. The compulsory form of almsgiving is assessed by Islamic canon law as being 2.5 per cent of a man's annual income in money or in kind. Like everything else in religion, almsgiving is open to abuse. If it is more blessed to give than to receive there will always be those beggars and scroungers only too willing to assist others to be 'blessed' by the simple acceptance of their offerings. But the sometimes wearing and wearying cult of *baksheesh*, whereby the beggar seeks by persistent importuning and harassment to cajole others into giving him 'alms for the love of Allah', is a complete perversion of the Koranic desire to assist those in need; and certainly the Muslim pillar of *zakat* should not be judged by those who abuse it.

The fourth pillar of fasting is obligatory upon all Muslims throughout the holy month of Ramadan. This is the month, so it is said, during which the Koran was revealed to Muhammad. All devotees must, during the hours between sunrise and sunset every day of Ramadan, abstain from all forms of food, of drinking, and from smoking. The only exceptions to this are those Muslims who are ill or on a journey; they are excused but must still make up the time later on with fasting. Again, there will be those who will abuse a religious injunction; some will turn the night into day, and during the hours of darkness will feast and make merry and be unfit for work during the daytime. No one would suggest, however, that such people represent the norm; and when one reflects upon the incredible heat and aridity of most Muslim countries one can only marvel at the self-restraint displayed during the hours of light.

Once in a lifetime the devout Muslim is expected to perform a pilgrimage to Mecca. Some followers save up for this experience during the whole of their lives; others walk hundreds of miles in order to fulfil what is not merely a religious requirement but also a heart's desire. The richer Muslims, however, may travel by bus, car, plane or ship in order to get as close as possible to their final destination. Some of the poorer Muslims may sell themselves into slavery for the rest of their lives in order to see the birthplace of their prophet, and to touch and kiss the Black Stone in the wall of the Kaaba. As he reaches Mecca each pilgrim has to change into two simple robes so that all worshippers may appear equal before Allah. Many pilgrims also visit the tomb of Muhammad at Medina, and some go on to the Dome of the Rock on the site of the old Jewish temple in Jerusalem.

5   Some General Ideas and Developments in Islam

Before the time of Muhammad there was considerable inter-tribal warfare and violence; Muhammad brought unification and peace for a time to the Arab peoples. It is true to say that, before Muhammad became the founder and leader of the Islamic faith, women were regarded as mere chattels, and baby girls were frequently buried alive as sacrifices to the djinns that terrified the superstitious Arabs. The reforms which Muhammad introduced considerably improved the general social and legal status of women, and the sacrifice of baby girls was forbidden. There has been some misunderstanding about the Muslim attitude to women, and it has to be emphasized that Muhammad sought to protect both the institution of marriage and also the position of women. Anyone who is in doubt about this *official* attitude, at least, should carefully read sura 4 of the Koran, entitled 'Women'.

Muhammad lived in the midst of a polygamous society, and the reforms that he introduced were not calculated to transform that society completely, but rather to stabilize it and to mitigate its worst evils. The rich sheiks bought up as many women as they could for wives, concubines and slaves, and as a result many poor men were unable to find a wife. Certainly there was considerable anxiety among men to produce a male heir, for male children were delicate and frequently died in infancy, leaving a surplus of women. Muhammad accepted polygamy, but he prescribed a limitation to it; a man might have up to four wives at any one time, but no more[34]. He himself was an exception to this rule[35], and eventually he had nine wives before he died, but no male heir survived him. He gave, however, a certain dignity to marriage and a regulation to divorce and female inheritance. In a time of considerable moral laxity he made adultery an offence punishable by death. The state of *purdah* (separation) was introduced into the Muslim homes in order, not to demean the position of women, but rather to elevate it and to protect them from the lecherous advances of men and the widespread promiscuity of his day. Similarly, the yashmak, or veil warn by many Muslim women in public, was conceived largely as a protection for women from the lustful eyes of men. Today, where eastern societies have had the full impact of culture-contact with the West, both purdah and the veil are increasingly regarded as male instruments of domination and subjugation, and some Muslim societies are slowly emancipating themselves from these customs.

Muhammad, who must have acquired considerable wealth during his lifetime, felt that acquisitiveness should be balanced by compassion for the failure and poverty of others. He had been brought up in a world of extremes – extreme wealth and extreme poverty. He taught that every Muslim was a brother to every other Muslim, and that one should help another within the Faith in every way possible. Where there was obvious need, any required capital should be loaned to a brother Muslim, whilst any interest taken should be reasonable and on business loans only.

It is noteworthy that each of the hundred and fourteen suras of the Koran (save only the ninth, which may in fact be a continuation of the eighth sura) begins with the statement, 'In the Name of Allah, the Compassionate, the Merciful'. Even the ninth, which is preoccupied with repentance, making war on unbelievers, and the punishments of hell-fire, states that 'Allah is the Forgiving One, The Merciful'. It is this compassion and mercy that the Muslim is enjoined to show towards all members of the Islamic brotherhood.

Much has been made of the concept of the *jihad*, or holy war, in Islam, particularly by its enemies. Certainly a holy war is enjoined by the Koran, which says:

> Fight for the sake of Allah those that fight against you, but do not attack them first. Allah does not love the aggressor[36].

This would seem to regard the jihad as a purely defensive measure, and to some extent this view is supported by other passages which seem to suggest that there should be no compulsion in religion[37], and even that there may be room for more than one religion[38]. Other passages, however, appear to support a more aggressive opposition[39]. Muslim scholars, however, deny that their record of intolerance is in any degree greater than that of any other major world religions, and it is certainly not a very profitable exercise to attempt to weigh the atrocities of one religion against those of another. We would certainly not care to elaborate on such things as the 'Christian' pogroms against the Jews, or the activities of the Spanish Inquisition against heretics of all religions, including sects of Christianity itself. The jihad was undoubtedly originally conceived as a means of self-defence against those who would destroy the disciples of revealed truth; that it has since been used for territorial conquest or as a political weapon in no way nullifies the original truths of the religion defended or propagated by such means. And if it should be used in the future in such a way, it could no more claim the sanction of Muhammad than the thumbscrew, rack or Crusader's sword could claim the imprimatur of Jesus.

There are some general teachings of interest which require mention here. Muslims are, where it is possible, buried in an upright position. There is a strong belief that the resurrection is a physical event which will take place at some preordained time in the future, and that each individual will literally rise up and stand upon the earth[40]. The belief in the resurrection of the body was not accepted by the early Hebrews, but it seems to have been a somewhat late development during the Diaspora or Jewish Dispersion. Certainly the influence of Persian Zoroastrian belief can be detected here, and it was a tenet of the Pharisaic belief in the time of Jesus, although the Sadducees strongly rejected it. Muhammad's own acceptance of it was originally ridiculed.

The doctrine of the Holy Spirit in Islam is somewhat difficult to delineate. The Koran implies that the Spirit of God was breathed into Mary in order that the Virgin might conceive Jesus[41]. This was an inbreathing of God similar to that whereby Adam was produced[42]. Indeed, the Hebrew word used in the Old Testament for the Spirit of God is *ruach*, which means breath or wind. There is certainly no belief among the Muslims of a separate 'person' or being involved in the concept of God's Spirit or the Holy Spirit (although in some verses of the Koran the 'Holy Spirit' is taken to mean Gabriel). It would appear to mean a dynamic emanation of God in his act of creation, for Allah is always and only One God. Professor Guillaume[43] argues that the Muslim doctrine of God in philosophical theology is not so far removed from the Christian system until the crucial dogma of the Trinity is broached. He says:

> The day may come when Muslims and Christians will realize that they have so much in common that they need no longer regard one another with suspicion and dislike.

No doubt if one looks for common ground there is much in the basic principles of Islam and Christianity that can form the foundation of both agreement and further dialogue – if only the spirit is willing.

6 The Spread of Islam

After his death, in AD 632, Muhammad was succeeded by his faithful friend and father-in-law, Abu Bakr, who had also been one of his first converts. Abu Bakr was elected *khalifa* (caliph), which means a lieutenant, deputy or successor. He immediately made his position felt by participating in punitive campaigns against those tribes which refused to pay their taxes. Once Arabia had been firmly reunited under the flag of Islam, the trained and drilled Muslim troops looked further afield, and gradually Persia, Babylonia, Syria, Palestine and Byzantium became subject to the Arab peoples. Then when Egypt and North Africa fell into Muslim hands, many more converts to Islam were made, although it is important to emphasize here that no great intolerance was expressed towards those who were members of Judaism or Christianity.

Despite their own internal rifts and religious divisions, the Arab armies very soon crossed into Spain in AD 711, and then entered France where, in AD 732, they were driven back from Tours by Charles Martel who defeated them at Poitiers. This has always been regarded as one of the most decisive battles of history in that the proselytizing powers of Islam, which some have argued might well have converted the whole of Europe, were frustrated. This, however, seems a somewhat unlikely possibility when one views in perspective the actual attitude of the Arabs to the Jews and Christians they had conquered elsewhere. In the event, the Arab armies retired into Spain where they had a considerable influence upon culture until the fifteenth century. Scholars from all over Europe migrated to Spain in order to study, under Muslims, such subjects as philosophy, medicine, mathematics and astronomy.

At the time when the Muslims were being driven back by Martel in France, other Muslim armies were successfully moving eastwards into India and even as far as China. Later, during the sixteenth century, the Moguls drove south into the subcontinent of India through the Afghan passes, and were successful in subjugating the Indian population in some of the most fertile land of the peninsula. There was some strife between the Muslim and Hindu religions from this time, but the Emperor Akbar (who ruled from 1556 to 1605) made a personal study of all the great religions and, although a Muslim himself, he declared an open policy of toleration. To some extent what Kabir (1440-1518) and Nanak (1469-1539) had sought to accomplish at the purely religious level, Akbar attempted to do at the more political level. After the reign of Akbar there was some degeneration in the Mogul court, and what began very reasonably as religious tolerance ended in a toleration of incredibly loose moral behaviour. During the later reign of the Emperor Aurangzeb (1658-1707) manpower and wealth were wantonly wasted on grandiose schemes for the conquest of the whole of southern India.

Eventually India was taken over by the British, who first obtained a foothold there through the activities of the East India Company which was formed in 1600. From the year 1784 the British Government supervised all the political activities which the East India Company undertook, and men who had been selected from outside the company's service were appointed as governors-general. After the Indian Mutiny, which broke out in 1857, and after order had been restored by the middle of 1858, British rule was at last accepted by the population. In 1879 Queen Victoria was proclaimed Empress of India.

It was in the 1930s in the midst of considerable argument, aggravated by mutual Muslim and Hindu jealousy, and mildly accompanied by the sweet reasonableness of Mahatma Gandhi's principle of *satyagraha*, the force of spiritual love or 'passive resistance', that Jinnah, Leader of the Muslims, first proposed a scheme to protect those provinces which were predominantly Muslim. This was the concept of Pakistan, 'the Land of the Pure'. When the partition of India was eventually effected in 1947, Pakistan was established – a country then bound together by a common acceptance of the monotheistic Islamic faith.

7 Some Aspects of Islam

One of the outstanding features of the Koran is its continual insistence upon not only the unity of Allah but also the essential unity of true religion.

> Therefore stand firm in your devotion to the true faith, which Allah Himself has made, and for which He has made man.

> Allah's creation cannot be changed; this is surely the true
> religion, although most men do not know it. Turn to Allah and
> fear Him. Be steadfast in prayer and serve no other god besides
> Him. Do not split up your religion into sects; each exulting
> in its own beliefs... .We sent before you other apostles to their
> peoples and they showed them veritable signs[44].

But it is unrealistic to expect any religion to have absolute unity, for
it is not in man's nature to accept everything of a spiritual character
without criticism or personal interpretation. Islam is no exception.
We cannot describe here all the sects that have developed in Islam;
but the main division is that between the Sunnis, who represent
something like 80 per cent of the Muslims, and the Shias.

The *Sunnis* are the orthodox who follow the path or tradition
recording the practice of the prophet Muhammad. These followers
accept the first four caliphs as rightly guided, and Ali is regarded
by them as the last of their legitimate caliphs. On the other hand,
the *Shias* are the partisans of Ali and regard him as the first of the
imams, or leaders. From Ali to Al Mahdi, who was born in Samarra
in AD 880, there were altogether twelve imams. Al Mahdi, the
twelfth, is said to have disappeared in his youth but did not die, and
he remains as the 'hidden imam' who will return at the appointed
time to establish a reign of purity and righteousness. These Shias
are known as the 'Twelvers' because of their belief in twelve imams.
There are also, however, the 'Seveners' who believe that seven imams
have existed and that the last was named Ismail. The latter is also
believed to have disappeared, but he will eventually return and
rule over the earth. The Twelvers are today a strong group in Iran,
Yemen, Iraq, Syria and Pakistan. The Seveners, or *Ismailis*, are to be
found in parts of Africa, Asia and the subcontinent of India where
they are referred to as *Khojas*. The latter subgroup of the Ismailis, in
particular, pay tithes to the Aga Khan who is their spiritual head,
and who makes good use of the money in providing his people
with schools and other social amenities. The disappearing, 'hidden'
imams and their ultimate self-revelation or return underline the

fundamental yearning of man for some supernatural or extra-natural means of redemption from his present unhappy or unfulfilled state. There is hardly any major religion which does not, in one of its forms or sects, anticipate the return of a messiah, imam, avatar, bodhisattva or buddha.

The *Assassins* (*Hashishis*) were an offshoot of the Ismailis, and some are still to be found in small numbers in East Africa, India and Pakistan. At the time of the Crusades they used to drug themselves with hashish and then, in a completely abandoned manner, would set upon their enemies and destroy them. Their leader was referred to as the 'Old Man of the Mountains'. Another subsect are the *Druzes*, who derived their name from their leader, Darazi, who lived during the eleventh century. Darazi supported the claims of a certain Al Hakim to divinity, and when the latter mysteriously disappeared it was held that he would eventually return in some future age. Today the Druzes are virtually a minor secret society with an esoteric teaching, which makes their connection with Islam somewhat nominal[45]. Druze population today is estimated at about a million, and they live mainly in Lebanon, Syria, Jordan and Israel. They were the first among the Muslims to declare polygamy as illegal. Like all Muslim sects, they have a strong belief in the unity of Allah. One of their most important beliefs, however, is that all individuals are immediately reincarnated after death.

The most recently formed sect of Muslims is that represented by the *Ahmadiyya movement*. In 1890 a Punjabi called Ghulam Ahmad made a claim to be the Islamic Mahdi, the Christian Messiah, and the Hindu Avatar, Krishna. Not surprisingly the Ahmadiyyans are not regarded as orthodox Muslims. When Ghulam Ahmad died in 1908 the sect split into two groups, one with its headquarters at Qadian in India, and the other at Lahore in Pakistan. They are thus today represented by the Qadians, who regard Ahmad as a prophet, and who have founded a mosque in England at Southfields in London; and by the Seceders, to whom Ahmad is merely a reformer, and who have established a mosque at Woking in Surrey.

It is interesting to note that out of Islam, one of the most transcendent of religions, there has arisen one of the most profound forms of mysticism that the world has ever produced – namely, *Sufism*. The devotees of this mysticism derived their name from the cloak or habit of white wool (*suf*) which they usually wore:

> Because of their clothes and manner of life they are called Sufis, for they did not put on raiment soft to touch or beautiful to behold; they only clothed themselves in order to hide their nakedness, contenting themselves with rough haircloth and coarse wool[46].

The Sufis lived an ascetic life of meditation, prayer and poverty. They believed in the unity of Allah, but Allah comprised all beings, all existence. At least one of their members, Al Hallaj, was put to death for blasphemy when, in AD 922, he was crucified for saying, 'I am the Truth'. The Sufis, however, always claimed that their view of God and of his immanence and omnipresence is well represented in the Koran, in which Allah reveals that:

> *We* created man. We know the promptings of his soul, and are closer to him than the vein of his neck[47].

Man has already a union with God in which his immortality is assured, and in which all the souls, emanations and incarnations from God are finally one. And although his origin may be found in Islam, the Sufi himself is at home in all religions where the individual is permitted to develop a personal relationship with God. That personal relationship has been expressed through such mystics as Farid al-din 'Attar (born 1119), Muhammad al-Ghazali (1059-1111), Jalalud-din Rumi (1207-73), and Muhammad Iqbal of Lahore (1876-1938). 'Attar concluded his great poem entitled 'The Conference of the Birds' with an expression of the ultimate unification of the individual soul and Allah:

Come you lost atoms, to your Centre draw,
And *be* the Eternal Mirror that you saw;
Rays that have wandered into darkness wide,
Return, and back into your Sun subside.[48]

SECTION THREE:
SOME SECTS AND
IDEOLOGIES

15 Some Millenarian Sects

Those readers who are interested in some of the earlier millenarian movements of the period from the eleventh to the sixteenth centuries are recommended to read the brilliant work of N Cohn[1]. Here we shall concern ourselves with those movements which are of relatively recent origin, evolving in the nineteenth and twentieth centuries, and some persisting quite strongly at the present time. Cohn[2], however, pointed out that millenarian sects or movements seemed almost invariably to picture their salvation as collective (the faithful formed a redeemed collectivity), terrestrial (it would be realized on this earth), imminent (it would all happen suddenly and soon), total (it would completely transform life upon earth), miraculous (involving supernatural agencies), and it would inaugurate a new dispensation of perfection. Beyond these relatively common elements there was a considerable variety of presentation and of activity. Some movements were violent, aggressive and militarist, whilst others were pacifist, or at least passivist, and looked for redemption from outside. The leaders of such movements were invariably strange, striking and charismatic personalities who bore the marks of the prophet, going into trances, predicting the future usually in terms of crisis and cataclysm, to be followed by a period of unalloyed bliss. Frequently, too, their words were accompanied by strange signs and healing.

Most of these cults have evolved in countries conquered, colonized, dominated and missionized by the whites of European countries. All forms of tribal worship and custom have been suppressed and categorized as pagan and evil, and the indigenous populations have taken on the mores and ethics, as well as the ritual religious forms of the colonizing country. Thus in the unequal clash of cultures, age-long social habits have been virtually destroyed and tribal identity has been eliminated. A bewildered, frustrated and resentful group of people have felt unequal to the task of combating the superimposed culture of a more advanced people, with their inexplicable technologies, their abundance of 'goods', and their frequently (though not invariably) sophisticated beliefs.

Many have had their lands invaded by a succession of peoples from other societies, seeking political and economic advantage and imperial domination – white European groups, English, French, Dutch and German, have been followed by Japanese and then by white and coloured Americans. The traumatic experience involved in these invasions has rarely been given consideration, except by expert anthropologists and sociologists researching a particular field of study. Few people who have grown up in the West, without the sudden domination of their whole culture by another race, can really appreciate the individual and social confusion and perplexity that must inevitably be aroused by such culture clash.

That there are certain common features about millenarian and messianic cults is inevitable since that is the basis of their classification, but it is equally inevitable that there should be many differences since they arise in, and develop in, countries with vastly different traditions and backgrounds, which are not to be eroded by such portmanteau words as 'primitive', 'backward', 'simple', 'pagan' or 'animistic'. Each area has its own specific history and development, and these are sufficiently different as to make the culture clash, in each case, of a different nature and presenting its own problems. That comparative studies[3] of such groups will help to elicit types and patterns there can be no doubt, but in the main we are concerned here with a descriptive analysis of these movements within each major continent and among certain island groups.

1 North America

The Indians of North America are a people who have felt increasingly the insecurity of those who have rejected the so-called 'civilization' of their conquerors, with their 'goods' and their technology, as well as their religion; and yet who, because of the limitations placed upon them, are unable to pursue freely their own traditional culture. Peyote (or peyotl) was a drug used in Mexico by the Aztecs in the sixteenth century (if not before) to heighten their general awareness, and to develop trance states. Peyote has been used increasingly by the Indian population. Life in the reservations, deprived of their old hunting habits, prevented from pursuing their own trials of manhood through intertribal warfare, has caused a large number of Indian tribes to seek for a new religion which would provide them with a sense of independence from the white man, yet a culture which was both old and at the same time developing out of their changed situation.

The peyote is a small cactus, having the shape of a carrot, found in the Rio Grande valley and further south. It is the round top, or button, which is eaten sacramentally and which produces a general sense of wellbeing. The eater (or drinker, since it is sometimes made into an infusion) increases considerably his sense of perception in relation to colour, shape, weight, size and sound. He has hallucinations of levitating and of being in some other place, or in some other time. Analysis shows that peyote contains a large number of alkaloids, including mescaline, lophophorine, anhaline etc. Despite its strange physiological effects, it is claimed by many who have examined it that it is not a narcotic and is harmless. Moreover, it does not appear to be habit-forming.

Thus, peyote is used by North American Indians in a ritualistic manner to produce supernatural states in which they have visions, to lessen their fatigue or hunger, and to heal sickness. The peyote is to them a form of protection from the evils of the society in which they are forced to live. Their dreams are fulfilled in the drugged state which peyote produces, and the kingdom of their God is realized upon earth through its ministrations. Not surprisingly, there is a good deal of Christianity in the content of their beliefs. The eating of the peyote is itself the equivalent of the Eucharist and, in fact, it has been identified with the Comforter that should come[4]. It is a cure for all their ills.

Peyotism has become a sort of religious pan-Indianism, and has spread throughout most of the tribes in the USA as well as South Canada. It accepts that there is no point in seeking to oppose the whites, or in attempting a complete recrudescence of their ancient worship. They must go on to a new dispensation in which much of Indian culture will be renewed, but at the same time there will be a march forward into new experiences and new rituals. Peyote will bring collective protection to the tribes and prevent that total disintegration which has for so long threatened them. Their sacramental meal is usually taken at night in a tepee specially prepared for the purpose. There is a moon-shaped altar, and the sick are brought into the centre in order to be cured. There are prayers, singing and a baptismal rite which takes the form of sprinkling the head with peyote tea.

Peyotism has received a great deal of abuse and opposition from the white man, but it has seemed a somewhat shortsighted policy and prejudiced attack for, as Lanternari has pointed out:

> The peyote cult was the fruit of the Ghost Dance in the same sense that peace is the fruit of war and that reconstruction follows upon revolution or defeat. Peyotism contains elements of Western culture selected to meet certain new conditions[5].

The cult seeks to preserve the essentials of ancient Indian culture, myth and ritual, with particular worship of the sun and moon, as well as of Peyote woman. Jesus himself is identified with the Peyote Spirit, and with this identification there is coupled a belief in salvation and the road to Good into which the Peyote Spirit leads. The white man brought with him many diseases to which the Indians had no immunity, and they have therefore sought it in the healing powers of peyote. The repression to which the white man subjected the Indian led to a general sense of fatality and the impossibility of survival. They have, therefore, resorted to a religion that provides a pacific unification of all members of Indian tribes in what is a mystical opposition to Western culture, as distinct from an aggressive and overt violence. They all firmly believe that, when all members of all the Indian tribes have shared in the peyote sacrament, the Kingdom of God will come upon earth and the millennium will have arrived.

Another movement among the Indians, with a real messianic element, was the Ghost Dance movement, to which was linked two essential features of Indian belief, namely, the religion of Mother Earth and the cult of the ancestors (or ghosts). The Indians lived by fishing, hunting and harvesting – these were the products of Mother Earth. But the earth was sacred, and not to be harmed or destroyed, so that they had never farmed their land. The soil was the home of the dead, from which they would rise again, and it was a form of sacrilege to attempt to till it. The Ghost Dance cult developed as a religious opposition to the white man, with a rejection of his tools and agricultural implements, his arms and his possessions. The Ghost Dance itself was a ritual performed to herald the coming of the Old Man Coyote who, after a series of floods and earthquakes, would bring back the dead and all animal life as soon as the grass was high in the fields. Thus the Old Man Coyote has a messianic reference.

2   Central America

A people who have been freed after many decades of slavery will seek, as soon as they are able, to establish some form of identity as a group. The only real link the Jamaicans (for example) had was with their ancestors in Africa, the land of their origin. In the 1860s there spread through Jamaica a movement which sought to restore and revitalize their natural spiritual inheritance. This movement was called 'The Great Revival' and 'The Great Awakening', and it developed into what must, at times, have been a frightening return to mass trance states, abandoned dancing, sexual orgies, public confessions, and masochistic forms of self-punishment and flagellation. This sort of 'revivalist' movement was sporadic and spontaneous; it lacked organization, direction and self-criticism; and it depended very much upon the persuasion and eloquence of the few. A people who have recently acquired freedom after a long period of cruel repression often look for some temporary messiah who might afford them some spiritual solace and redemption.

Alexander Bedward (born 1859) was such a man, and in 1894 he established the Jamaican Baptist Free Church in August Town, St Andrew, and became its leader. He claimed that he received visions from God himself, and that he was a reincarnation of Moses, Jonah and John the Baptist. He believed that God's Spirit had revealed to him that the waters of the Hope River would cleanse all sins and cure all diseases. Many hundreds of 'cures' were claimed as a result of such baptism in this river. There were, however, many other Jamaicans who were not impressed by Bedward's achievements, and a mocking song was composed about his activities:

> Dip dem, Bedward, dip dem;
> Dip dem in de healing stream;
> Some come from de Eas'.
> Dem favour wil' beas'.
> Dip dem in de healing stream;
> Dip dem, Bedward, dip dem;
> Dip dem in de healing stream.

In 1920 Bedward went a stage further than he had done before and called himself the Messiah, or Christ, the Son of God. This was no mean claim for a man who was virtually illiterate and a labourer; though no doubt many followers felt that he compared quite favourably with one who, making similar claims, was in fact the son of a carpenter's wife. Bedward possessed just that element of eloquence and persuasion which impressed an inarticulate group who were frustrated and desperate. Many of them were, in any case, used to missionaries who preached of Christ's Second Coming at almost any moment in time, and anyone who had the promise of being or becoming a 'saviour' or a spiritual 'shepherd' was welcome.

No doubt Bedward received considerable support from certain elements in his society who were looking for a leader and a prophet. Soon he was prophesying that he would, like Elijah, be taken up into heaven, after which he would return in power to earth and would gather together his Elect. After his 'Second Coming' the earth would be destroyed in some cataclysmic and apocalyptic convulsion, involving hurricanes, fires, earthquakes and general devastation. But Bedward went too far. In one unguarded moment he stated that his 'Ascension' would take place on the 31st of December 1920. Sadly, however, when the day approached and then was past, Bedward failed to fulfil this, the ultimate in prophecies. Then, like most prophets who have overreached themselves by being rather too precise, Bedward attempted to quieten his followers by further predictions. Eventually, after a whole series of failures in fulfilment, Bedward was arrested and confined in a mental home.

There is always something very tragic about the charismatic leader who lacks the power to fulfil his promises, and the history of messianism and millenarianism is replete with sorrowful stories of leaders retiring to homes for the mentally unbalanced or (perhaps more cynically) to their own mansions where they may practise a comfortable and divinely sanctioned polygamy; or who like the Mahdi or the Bab may end their days in violence or ignominy. Perhaps even more sad is the fact that thousands of followers who came from all over the island of Jamaica, having sold their few possessions, had waited with Bedward to ascend with him into heaven as God's Elect. Thus his failure was essentially theirs as well. Yet this was by no means the end of Bedwardism, for his church in August Town still exists to commemorate his life and memory; and Bedwardites are still in the list of official religious sects.

More important than Bedwardism is the flourishing movement in Jamaica of the 'Rastas' or *Rastafarianism*[6]. This is as much a politico-religious movement as a cult and, whilst its forms are religious, its purposes appear to be mainly political. Individual Rastafarians or small cells of followers may be found throughout Jamaica. It arises frequently among unemployed people who are themselves dissatisfied with their social position and economic conditions. In general terms, the movement emphasizes a cultural and spiritual identification with Africa, and it is basically a reaction against domination by the West. Whilst it has always centred mainly upon Kingston, it now has many adherents outside the Corporate Urban area and in other parts of the world.

The beginnings of the movement appear to be connected with Marcus Garvey's 'Back to Africa' campaign which began in the early Thirties. He attempted, with a great deal of drive and revivalist oratory, to instil into the black people a pride in their race, colour and country of origin; he was a messiah preaching the possibilities of a new identity from archaic beginnings to a people who lacked purpose, unity and self-esteem. In 1918 he had established the United Negro Improvement Association with the avowed purpose of bettering the lot of the negroes in Africa, the Americas and elsewhere. He hoped also to provide eventually complete independence for the black man from white society with the ability to create his own culture and institutions. As a result of his enthusiastic endeavours a scheme was developed to encourage emigration to Liberia, on the West Coast of Africa. Gradually the black Jamaicans developed an awareness of their identity and also the beginnings of a political consciousness. After a term of imprisonment in America, and later deportation to Jamaica, Garvey renewed his former activities against all forms of opposition, but eventually decided to go to England where he died in 1940.

The years between 1930 and 1939 were a period of desperation as a result of economic depression and a series of hurricanes which caused considerable devastation. It was during this period that the Rastafarian movement was born and developed, and it is clear that Garvey's programme, which certainly appealed to thousands of negroes in the West Indies, America and Africa, proved to be an inspiration to the movement. In 1930 Haile Selassie was crowned Emperor of Ethiopia; and his full title was 'Ras Tafari, son of Ras Makonem of Harar, King of Ethiopia, Haile Selassie, King of Kings, Lord of Lords, Conquering Lion of the Tribe of Judah'. The title Ras means 'Prince', and the name Haile Selassie means 'the Power of the Trinity'; and to the Rastafarians he was the Living God, 225th in the line of Ethiopian kings in unbroken succession from the Queen of Sheba, who (so it has been asserted) bore King Solomon's son.

A Jamaican, Archibald Dunkley, found confirmation that Haile Selassie was the messiah, concerning whom Garvey had so often spoken, in I Timothy 6, verses 13-16. This was further supported by passages in the Book of Revelation, chapters 17 and 19, referring to the Lamb as 'Lord of lords' and 'King of kings', and to the Word of God, who has 'on his vesture and on his thigh a name written, King of kings and Lord of lords'. This belief in Ras Tafari as their messiah inspired them in their early evangelistic work, and militancy came later on as a result only of the conflict which some of their leaders had with the law. It was during the Italian invasion of Ethiopia that the Rastafarians discovered in Revelation 19, v 16 a further confirmation of the battle of their messiah against the powers of evil.

Under the Jamaican Leonard Howell, the movement came into strong conflict with the law of the country. In 1940 he became the leader of a community at 'Pinnacle' in the parish of St Catherine. About five hundred members of the Society lived at Pinnacle, although they paid no rent but cultivated the large property there. The main crops of the plantation were yam and ganja (or marijuana). In 1941 the police systematically raided Pinnacle and many, including Howell, were sent to prison. In 1953 Howell intensified safety precautions at Pinnacle, and from then on many of the Rastafarian Brethren took on a fierce appearance of 'locksmen', with beards and long hair ('dreadlocks'), and were referred to as 'Ethiopians'. Howell himself, after making claims of divinity, was committed in 1960 to Kingston Mental Hospital.

After the destruction of Pinnacle in 1954, the residue of the community returned to Kingston to Back-O-Wall or Shanty-Town.

Gradually new groups developed in and around Kingston, and there followed a period of reorganization. Wherever they went their somewhat wild and fanatical appearance attracted an audience; they defied society, shouted profanities and disturbed the peace. Many were arrested. In 1958 the Rastafarians held a convention, and the press devoted considerable space to its activities. They congregated at their Back-O-Wall headquarters, and there followed nightly rituals of singing and drumming, abuse directed at passing policemen, and many physical clashes with the police. Many were arrested under the Jamaican Dangerous Drug Law for using ganja, and there was considerable search and harassment. In 1959 many of their camps were burnt down; but after their trial those who had been arrested were set free. Both social scientists and the more socially aware politicians realized that they were dealing here with a problem that went beyond the fanaticism of a small group of people, and that their aspirations, however expressed, could no longer be ignored.

Rastafarians were promised a great Exodus from bondage by one of their leaders, Claudius Henry, who would lead them into the Promised Land of Ethiopia. Henry, however, never fulfilled his promises, and he was eventually sentenced to a long term of imprisonment, and his son and four of his followers were later sentenced to death. As a result of the 'Henry affair', and of the general disturbances and unrest that followed, the Government decided to have a full investigation into the problems faced by the various Rastafarian communities. The appointed committee made their report in 1960 and made some very positive proposals. These included the acceleration in the construction of low-rent houses, and much more encouragement to people generally to develop self-help and cooperative building schemes. There was some attempt to provide and develop water, lighting and sewerage systems in the areas in which the Rastafarians had squatted and established living quarters. There was an attempt also to provide youth clubs, child clinics and classes in technical subjects. 'Repatriation' to Africa was also mooted.

Today, the Rastafarians are a heterogeneous group of people, and it is not easy to summarize their beliefs. There are, however, a number of common features which are held by most Rastafarians whatever their sectarian allegiances. Haile Selassie was for all of them originally the Living Black God, despite any setbacks they may have experienced. Black is beautiful, good and holy – 'So we hail our God, Selassie I, Eternal God, Ras Tafari: hear us and help us, and cause thy face to shine upon us thy children'. Ethiopia is heaven, the Promised Land, whilst Jamaica and any other country outside of Ethiopia are a part of Babylon, a living hell. In this living hell the Rastafarians represent the lowest element in Jamaican society, and some of the Brethren avoid society and its complexities as much as possible; they have become separatist. Others accept the total situation since they feel that there is nothing that they can do about it. Still others become aggressive towards society and seek in some positive way to disrupt it and bring about its final demise.

The black man, they assert, is the reincarnation of the Ancient Israelites, and he has been in exile in Jamaica for many years through the cruelty and rapacity of the white man, who is evil, ugly and inferior. We are now in the age of theocracy – the rule of God on earth, originally heralded by Haile Selassie I. This rule will eventually be centred in Ethiopia, and sometime in the future the black man will govern the world, whilst the white man will become his servant.

The Rastafarian groups have their own organization and hierarchical structure. At the head is a leading brother or priest who is responsible for convening meetings, and he is assisted by a chaplain who opens meetings with a religious service and closes them with songs, chants and benedictions. The recording secretary, who very occasionally may be a woman, takes the minutes of the meeting, presides over roll-calls and makes a note of members' subscriptions. The treasurer is in charge of all the funds of the group; and the sergeant-at-arms is there to guard the gate at all the meetings in order to prevent the intrusion of police or unauthorized snoopers, particularly when ganja is being smoked. Ganja is the 'herb' or 'wisdom weed', which they believe was found growing on the grave of King Solomon.

A considerable proportion of Rastafarians were brought up in a 'Christian' home, which means that they have been taught to read or recite passages from the Bible, particularly the Old Testament. To them the Bible is a book of symbols to which the Rastafarians alone have the key. All the Old Testament prophecies and the eschatological visions of the book of Revelation are interpreted in terms of Rastafarian beliefs and expectations. In general, they oppose the Christian faith as practised in Jamaica; white ministers, as well as white educators, remain as the last remnant, but ever-present reminder of British imperialism in Jamaica.

Rastafarianism is predominantly a male cult, and women are not only held in a subordinate position, but they are also regarded as inferior in some way to the male. To some extent the movement is not only political and religious but also psychological; it represents a male protest against the matriarchal structure and function of a great deal of Jamaican family life, which is founded and rooted in slavery itself. It is strongly felt that the 'Christian' form of marriage is not really a part of the black man's world and, to the Rastafarian, woman is basically evil, and man's failure is essentially hers and her doing. She is changed and cleansed by association with her mate; and this is not a loving relationship, merely a sexual one.

Thus, in Rastafarianism there are elements of messianism, escapism, and nativism in the recrudescence of 'African culture', organized by its members in such a way as to elicit specific elements in their cultural past for resurrection and artificial promotion. Deprivation, with the despair that accompanies it, has helped to make this movement at least a pseudo-political one. There is a 'cause' of a political nature, however inadequate or irrelevant the Rastafarian movement may be for its support and final resolution. It is, in consequence, dysfunctional in that although it opposes social ills and deprivation it does not, as a total movement, seek to rectify those ills since this would destroy its very *raison d'être*. It acts, therefore, as an irritant, socially and politically looking for its own millennium, not in active reconstruction but in a dream paradise materialized by an Ethiopian messiah.

In factual terms, of course, Haile Selassie died in 1975 and one might, perhaps, be forgiven for thinking that this was the end of the Rastafarian hopes and beliefs. But human beings with strong religious hopes and expectations are very resilient. The tomb was not the end of Christ for his followers, nor was his ascension after resurrection. He would come again to reign in majesty and have dominion over the earth. During the first century AD there was current a myth about Nero Caesar – he was not dead, but was hiding somewhere in the East, whence he would most certainly return riding at the head of Parthian hordes, conquering and eventually taking dominion over the whole world. *Nero redivivus* was a hope nourished in almost the same way as in the present era many fanatical Nazis were quite unable to accept the death of their 'divine' leader, Adolf Hitler, but believed that he would one day surprise the world with his return. The myth of the death and return of the hero-god is perennial in human cultures, and it requires no further detailed exemplification here.

There were ambivalent attitudes towards the 'reported death' of Haile Selassie among the Rastafarians. There were those who believed that he was still alive, and who regarded the whole episode as a trick or a plot designed to destroy their hopes of ever being released from 'Babylon', and to reduce in consequence their political and anti-social activities to a minimum. But whilst they do recognize that certain changes have taken place in Ethiopia, they also believe that their beloved Ras Tafari is still somewhere in command.

There are those, however, who are quite logical in their approach to the theological problem. Man can destroy the physical body of the 'Divine', but not the Divine Spirit itself. Negus will return in power to redeem his faithful followers from the slavery of 'Babylon', and he will rule over the conquered earth in majesty. Indeed, nothing has really changed except that their god is no longer physically present. But he is omnipresent in spirit and will come in the clouds with the hosts of heaven. Just as the death of Christ was little more than a temporary setback, so the death of Haile Selassie has been absorbed into the Rastafarian eschatology. Their eternal and spiritual hopes remain alive. They boldly affirm that 'Jah Live'.

3   South America

There have been a number of Messianic cults among the peoples of South America, notably among the Tukunas living in the jungles along the banks of the Amazon, and among the Tupi-Guarani tribes – the Tupis dwelling in the basin of the Sao Francisco River in East Brazil and the Guaranis on the border between Brazil and Paraguay. Their movements were directed mainly against whites, and they predicted universal catastrophes including a great deluge and the rising of the dead. After these events their cultural heroes would return to liberate them, and the evils brought by the white man would be eliminated.

In recent years the most striking messianic movements have been of the Macumba-Umbanda variety[7]. There has been organized spiritualism in Brazil since 1873 when the 'Society for Spiritualistic Studies of Confucius' Group was founded. Today, the Umbanda movement numbers several million, although one cannot be very accurate since *umbandistas* are found in almost every sort of congregation. Like Spiritualism, and many other spiritist or ecstatic sects, Umbanda believes that supernatural spirits or beings suddenly take possession of living devotees. There follow obsessive states in which the possessed believers become ecstatic, have strange and often beguiling visions, heal with extraordinary power, and often become completely unconscious. There are strong similarities between the voodoo of Haiti and the Umbanda of Brazil, and both stem from African origins. The South American tradition has variously been referred to as *macumba, Xango* (or Shango) and *candomblé*. In the Umbanda sect there is a considerable identification between the old African gods and Catholic saints: thus, Shango, the old god of war, is identified with St Jerome; Orisha Yansam becomes St Barbara; whilst Yemanjá, goddess of the sea, becomes the Virgin Mary; and Oshala, a hero figure, becomes Jesus Christ.

Negroes, mulattoes and whites all join together in a vigorous movement in which mass ecstasy provides a unity amongst the differing social levels which no political movement *per se* has been able to evoke. Macumba was originally a movement pursued by poor blacks during the 1920s, but it was forced to go underground and to work in secret with the advent of the Vargas government. In more recent times, however, it has operated more openly, and through its 'folk psychiatry' and therapeutic work it has done more to break down the existing social order than any political movement might have done. It is, however, not by any means a simple situation:

> As a matter of fact the position of the Umbanda is very difficult, and this difficulty includes contradictions which seem to be understandable only within the complex, ethnically differentiated, cultural context of Brazilian society. The transition from Macumba to Umbanda was characterized mainly by giving up African cult elements which were denounced by public opinion as signs of ignorance and backwardness of the largely coloured lower classes. Such cult elements were replaced by certain Spiritualistic principles granting the Umbanda an intellectual respectability and attraction which the Macumba lacked... .Thus, one can speak of a social rise of the Umbanda, expressing itself not only by an avalanche-like increase in the number of its followers, but, above all, by the growing self-respect of its coloured members as well as by an active participation of many persons belonging to the upper classes[8].

This is a movement in which women have a great role to play as mediums, healers and teachers. They assist in the training and development of new mediums, and are particularly involved in the cult of Yemanja, the Sea Goddess, in which there is considerable preparation effecting trance states and healings, and this is all followed by a night procession to the sea. Images of Yemanja, or the Virgin Mary, are carried aloft and the whole procession eventually walks into the sea. Some worshippers have to be held carefully otherwise, in their trance state, they would drown. In their mass meetings *caboclos*, the ghosts of American Indians, frequently appear and are identified (eg Red Feather), and proceed to give advice on all sorts of matters, including financial and marriage difficulties. Similarly, 'Old Blacks' or *Negros velhos* appear, and in this way both the Indian and African elements among the *umbandistas* find a revived link with their ancestors.

There is an acceptance that in their trance states the devotees may sometimes be invaded by evil spirits, and therefore there must be some attempt to come to terms with them in order to neutralize the evil that they might otherwise do. Whilst on the right-hand side there are *caboclos*, Old Blacks and *orishas*, so on the left-hand side there are *eshus* and *bombashira*. One is reminded of the myalism and obeah which occur in Jamaica[9] and which represent, in broad terms, white and black magic. But, whatever magic is performed in Umbanda, it is the solace and relief from stress of the individual that is sought. Their millenarian hopes are expressed through the ever-increasing number who find the solution to their problems in mass trance and ecstasy, and in a communal hope of the future redemption assured. In an attempt to obtain freedom from every form of oppression, religious movements in South America express a great variety of movements, sects and cults – prophetic, mystical and social[10]. They all in turn express the desires of a people who are looking for ways out of intolerable situations.

4 Africa

It would be impossible to discuss the many and varied movements of a cultic and religious nature that have developed over the years in Africa as a sort of bulwark against white domination. J W Fernandez[11] has provided an analysis of these movements in the following diagram:

```
                         acculturated
              separatist    |    messianic
instrumental ───────────────┼─────────────── expressive
              reformative   |    nativist
                         traditional
```

Many of the nativist movements have had overtones of messianism, such as the Maji Maji in South Tanzania and Mau Mau in Kenya. But, as Fernandez has pointed out, messianic movements have been those which have arisen out of 'intense xenophobia'. This xenophobia has taken the particular form of opposition to all colonial domination and hatred of whites in particular. There are, and have been, pure messianic movements in Africa although many others have had a messianic element or have passed through a messianic stage.

Some of these African cults have derived much of their thought and drive from Christian religious sects, and the *ngunzi*, or prophet, movement found its material for revolt or change wherever Christianity itself had been promulgated. For example, the very simplicity of the Salvation Army appealed strongly to the Congolese when the sect arrived in 1935, and their very insignia and dress, particularly the letter 'S' on their uniform, seemed to them to imply some relationship between the salvation offered by the Army and their own contemporary prophet and saviour, Simon Kimbangu. The Kimbangu messianic movement eventually became, in 1956, L'Eglise de Jésus-Christ sur La Terre par le Prophete Simon Kimbangu.

Similarly, the Jehovah's Witnesses or Watchtower Movement gave rise to an indigenous imitation in 1925, founded by Romo Niyirenda, a native of Nyassa, who called his cult Kitawala or Kitower. He proclaimed that he was Muana Lesa, the Son of God, and that after Armageddon (that is, a final battle between God and the Devil) the millennium would come and all true believers would be saved. This salvation was the redemption of individuals and society from all current ills, particularly foreign oppression and rule. In positive terms it would involve the healing of illnesses, the return to native culture and mores, including such things as polygamy, the eradication of witchcraft, and the establishment of their own social order. Whatever Christian missions may, or may not, have done to help the indigenous population, and whatever millennial and messianic element the latter may have adopted from them, such missions were seen in the main as disruptive of native culture and therefore something to be eradicated. They sought, in fact, a return to their own ancient myths and traditional forms of belief and ritual. The removal of colonial governments has given most of these African societies the freedom to develop entirely along their own lines. Although many messianic beliefs and cults persist they no longer relate immediately to xenophobia or white oppression.

5   Melanesia and Polynesia

In the development of millenarian cults in Melanesia and Polynesia we have the expression of the sometimes violent clash and encounter between two vastly different cultures. In what follows we shall concentrate upon Melanesia, but similar movements have been encountered in Polynesia. The Vailala Madness of the Gulf Division of Papua New Guinea was first reported in 1919, and then by F E Williams in 1923[12]. This 'madness' was in fact a form of ecstatic possession, followed by strange convulsive movements, and finally by inspiration in which leadership and action were expressed. During some of these moments of possession, certain revelations prophesied the coming of a ship which carried the spirits of their dead ancestors on board as well as large quantities of 'Cargo'. Such Cargo included rice, tobacco, flour and even rifles, and all belonged to the native peoples themselves and not to the whites, who had to be driven out.

The idea of cargo was soon linked with concepts of Heaven, from which God or Christ descended to give the cult leaders messages; and many of the cult followers referred to themselves as 'Jesus Christ men'. The spirits of the dead, their ancestors, would return, the millennium would follow and there would be Cargo in abundance for all.

The movement spread rapidly in New Guinea, and it was obvious, from the hostility expressed towards the whites, that it was something that had to be taken seriously. People began to believe that the things which had been prophesied in the initial stages had really taken place. But shortage of food and lack of material exemplification of the millennium led, by about 1935, to a sense of disillusionment. During the years 1940 to 1942, the Mekeo tribes at Cape Possession on the Gulf of Papua began to experience similar psychical states to the Vailala Madness. They went into trances, had convulsions and collective seizures. Once more there were visions and revelations of Cargo, and it was predicted that all the Europeans would be driven out. Missionaries and police would be attacked and killed because they were all stealing goods which had been sent to the Mekeo by their spirit ancestors. As time went on the natives came to accept that, in fact, the sacred cargo from Heaven had been dropped – books, money, tobacco, guns etc – but that these had quickly been snapped up by the white men. Thus their 'miracles' had happened, but only for the whites. Indeed, they had seen with their own eyes the many packages which were parachuted down from Douglas Transport planes for members of the Allied Forces fighting the Japanese in the jungle.

The Cargo cult continued to develop in other islands such as Tanna, Ambryn, Pentecost, Epi and so on. On the island of Tanna, in the New Hebrides, there was a great deal of dissatisfaction expressed with the mission teaching, and this gave the natives a predisposition to radical change.

> One native told a District agent that he had been so
> disappointed with prayers and hymns all the time, and the
> 'little practical gain' of missionary activities, that he had joined
> another Church. Here also he found 'pray, pray, pray and
> sing, sing, sing, all the time'. Except for one missionary, no
> European could communicate with the natives in anything but
> pidgin and none had the confidence of the natives or lived with
> them[13].

In early 1940 the natives began to hold meetings to receive messages from John Frum (or Jonfrum), who began to encourage cooperative movements among the natives, advocated kava-drinking and dancing, and denounced laziness.

John Frum predicted that there would be a great cataclysmic

occurrence flattening Tanna, and that he would then reveal himself and usher in a millennial age of bliss. The whites would be driven out and they would rule themselves once more. Eventually, after many disturbances, John Frum – a native of about thirty-five – was arrested in 1941. It is not easy, however, to break up a messianic cult, and it received a fillip when American troops, many of them black, arrived in Tanna. The John Frum cult, despite many arrests and fines, continued to prosper until 1948. From then until 1952 there was calm on Tanna, but when prices of copra suddenly began to fluctuate John Frumism reared its head once more.

The Melanesians have felt a personal right to the Cargo which the white man has greedily prevented him from possessing. Their sense of want and deprivation led to hysterical phenomena in terms of trance, convulsions, visions and often glossolalia. They received revelations concerning the ways in which they could appropriate what rightfully belonged to them, and this in turn led to a rejection of missionary teaching and white dominance. After WW2 they turned abandoned US Army camps and aeroplane runways into store-houses to receive the Cargo that never came. Their new totems became model aeroplanes and images of John Frum. The cults have become, at least temporarily, somewhat passively absorbed into a new form of acculturation. High world prices for local products and plentiful employment have resulted in a slackening of enthusiasm for millennial expectations[14].

Lanternari[15] has analyzed a survey of religious movements in Polynesia as revealing three chief stages of development. The first is based on a belief in total regeneration of the world, the resurrection of the dead, and a strong resistance to the incursions of the West. The second stage, which invents new gods which are partly Biblical and partly pagan, organizes resistance on a military basis, and eventually becomes involved in total war against Western governments, churches and missions. This stage has been found chiefly in Polynesia, which has a military class and a well-developed economy that provides security for the entire year[16]. The third stage is one in which the native societies tend to identify themselves with the Israelites, and Christ usually becomes one member of the divine hierarchy. In general terms, however, Polynesia has demonstrated the extreme difficulties in establishing Judaeo-Christian monotheism within their religious format, and their millenarianism is an attempt to free themselves from any Western influence and domination.

6 Vietnam

Vietnam was formerly known as French Indochina until 1954 when the 17th parallel was used by the Geneva agreement to establish Vietminh in the Communist northern area and Vietnam in the south. It was understood that eventually the states would become one country as they are today. From hereon we shall refer to the country as Vietnam throughout. In 1925 there began a religious movement called Cao Dai, meaning the 'High Place' or 'Reigning God'. In a sense it seemed to present a sort of Lowest Common Multiple of all religions, having elements of Spiritualism, Buddhism, Taoism and Christianity as well as many others. It was consciously syncretistic, looking for any element in any religion or philosophy that might give status to itself. Thus, among its prophets and saints were Moses, Lao-Tzu, the Buddha, Jesus and many other historical figures such as Confucius and various literary giants. In trance states and visions, the members of the Cao Dai believed that they were in communication with these personalities.

Their church was based chiefly on the pattern of Roman Catholicism with quite elaborate ritual in churches, chapels and even a cathedral. All religions were found acceptable, and Cao Dai was a deliberate attempt to unify them under the banner of 'love, life, truth and salvation'. The main symbol of religion was the Eye of God, which represented his omniscience, omnipresence and universality. Their churches were decorated everywhere with these eyes, projecting rays in all directions, and their statuary included not only the great religious leaders but also prominent historical personages. Cao Dai, whilst international and universalistic in religious intention, was strongly nationalistic in political terms seeking total emancipation from French colonialism. And when Vietnam gained its independence in 1949, under the Emperor Bao Dai, it was undoubtedly the Church of Cao Dai that promoted its forward development in the New World – away from subjection and feudalism towards the benefits or otherwise of civilization. During its history it experienced moments of strong messianism and millenarian hope as, for example, when a group called Tian Thien emphasized the return from Japan of their national hero, Prince Cuong De, who would lead them all to victory, peace and prosperity.

In 1939 another religious movement, called Hoa Hao, was initiated by Huynh Phy So, a youth of twenty years who had been born in the village of Hoa Hao, after which the movement was named. It was said that as a child he was sickly and weak, but later was sent into the mountains where a medicine man cared for him and initiated him into the skills of healing. One day, whilst worshipping, he himself felt completely healed and was filled with an urge to teach the doctrine of Phat Thay, a prophet who in 1830 had predicted that the people from the West would destroy the Vietnamese Empire. Huynh Phy taught simplicity in religious, that is Buddhist, worship without costly temples and pagodas. Prayer was the one essential. He opposed all excesses as well as the use of drugs and liquor, the sale of child brides, and gambling. The messianic element in his religion related to the Kingdom of the Enlightened Lord in which there would be peace and harmony under the auspices of the final Buddha to come on earth. After several terms of imprisonment and exile, on charges of inciting rebellion, he was finally liberated by the invading Japanese in 1942. Three years later, when the Japanese surrendered, Hoa Hao was controlling the areas west and south of Saigon. Eventually Huynh Phy So was killed by Vietnam Communist agents, and his death spelt the gradual decline of the movement[17].

These two movements, the Cao Dai and the Hoa Hao, began as strictly religious sects but finished as political causes. They both found links with ancient traditions, Cao Dai being highly syncretistic and the Hoa Hao being Buddhist in the Mahayana mainstream.

Both were involved in some form of healing, magical practices and spiritualistic trances in which messages and prophecies were revealed by departed spirits. Their reaction to European rule was the same, and both movements quickly became political in intent arising out of a messianism and millenarianism which saw freedom and redemption through the leadership of charismatic personalities. At first universalist in approach they finally became very nationalistic and developed military groups which had all foreigners as their legitimate targets, but particularly white Europeans. They were sufficiently opportunist to link up with the Japanese invaders in their attempt to eradicate French colonialism.

*   *   *

If there really is any common denominator among the many millenarian and messianic sects that have arisen, among colonized peoples in particular, it is their desire to be free from foreign domination and to restore their former identity. The clash of culture has so often meant the final destruction of ancient holy traditions, religious rites linked with life and the land, and the complete breakup of tribal and social systems. Their salvation from foreign overlordship has been seen in terms, often culled from the religions of the foreigners, of some superhuman or human messiah, a ghostly ancestor reborn, or a god incarnate, who will lead them in a sort of Armageddon against the enemy. Once the latter has been destroyed, the millennial period of peace and tranquillity, and of abundance of goods or Cargo, and of restored identity would ensue. The Kingdom of Heaven, so often referred to by the missionaries of the conquering nations, would at last be fulfilled upon earth, on the land at last returned to its rightful owners.

On the road to the Kingdom there are, sadly but inevitably, many martyrs – leaders and empathic personalities – who are found to be amateur politicians so problematic that, eventually, they are adjudged insane and confined in mental homes, or regarded as traitors and imprisoned or killed, or as misguided native messiahs and sent into exile in the hope that they will be forgotten. From here they often return in order to set up their messianic kingdoms. But their return is usually shortlived and, even when the battle has been won and the foreigner leaves their soil, they are soon forgotten or abused and deposed. Others may subsequently take their place. But the millennium itself turns out to be something very different from what their 'voices' had indicated.

16 Modern Cults and Religions

There are clearly many reasons why new cults and religions develop from time to time, not the least being the internal dissensions within major religions, denominations and sects, and the resultant establishment of 'heretical' schisms, which in turn claim to hold the whole truth. An encyclopaedia of religions makes sometimes amusing, sometimes sad, but invariably interesting reading. There have always been speculations as to how or why certain cults have arisen in a particular place or at a specific time, and why certain charismatic figures have given birth to new ideas and fresh hopes. But such analyses are often either too simple or too complex, or they may completely fail to explain how someone quite illiterate manages to affect a whole group and sometimes eventually to produce a new religious literature.

In the present chapter we obviously have to be selective, and we shall consider firstly some quite substantial religious groups that evolved during the nineteenth century, and then proceed to the rash of cults and pseudo-religions which in the main have arisen in the twentieth century. Some of these, referred to as 'cults of unreason' by Dr Christopher Evans[1], are on the fringe of religion, mysticism, science fiction and mystical philosophy, but they attract all kinds of people for a great variety of reasons and cannot be ignored by any serious treatment of modern belief. Most of us – if not all of us some of the time – are gullible, and accept quite uncritically things that we *want* to believe. But it is equally true that most thinking people long for certainties in a world which seems to have very little to offer in that direction. Every new invention, every new discovery, makes us even less and less certain of the validity of ancient beliefs, so that almost every week some new panacea, or some fresh revelation is offered to the hungry sheep. The latter may become enthusiastic and satisfied for a time until, eventually, their new-found salvation proves as empty as Joanna Southcott's womb[2].

1   Christian Science

Mary Baker Eddy (1821-1910) founded the religious sect called 'Christian Science' in an attempt to restore what she regarded as primitive Christianity, in particular its acceptance of healing as a completely natural phenomenon according to the so-called laws of Nature. In 1875 she first published her textbook entitled *Science and Health*, which was subsequently revised and produced in 1891 as *Science and Health with Key to the Scriptures*. This book held that nothing was real except God and his spiritual creation, which included man made in his image and likeness. Man's essential nature was spiritual and wholly good, whilst matter, evil, disease and sickness were held to be unreal; they were illusions which existed only through ignorance of God. Christian Scientists renounce for themselves all forms of medicine, drugs and surgery and rely entirely upon healing through prayer.

The 'Science' element derived not from some new scientific discovery or technique, but from the acceptance that the teaching and acts of Jesus were grounded in the immutable, 'scientific' laws of God. Mrs Eddy claimed that she herself had been divinely healed through the help of a healer named Phineas Parkhurst Quimby, who was a great believer in the effects of mind-over-matter. Christian Scientists believe that all disease would be revealed as illusion and would disappear if only one had perfect faith in the healing power of Christ. But such perfect faith may be rare even among Christian Scientists themselves, although the writer has known some who seemed literally bursting with health and vitality and freedom from more common ills.

In the eighteenth century, Hume reiterated the three questions of Epicurus concerning God: 'Is he willing to prevent evil, but not able? Then he is impotent. Is he able, but not willing? Then he is malevolent. Is he both able and willing? Whence then is evil?' Mrs Eddy was quite uncompromising in her answers to these questions – evil is both literally and demonstrably nothing, non-existent, illusory. Disease, sin and death are not to be found in God, and therefore they are unreal. If our minds are but manifestations of the Infinite Mind of God then we cannot accept illusion as reality. If we but yield to the Divine Mind we must inevitably be healed. It was out of this apparently unassailable logic that the First Church of Christ Scientist was born in 1879, with the symbol of the cross and crown, and the surrounding motto: 'Heal the sick, raise the dead, cleanse the lepers, cast out demons.'

Mrs Eddy's starting-point in her religion was the command of Christ, 'Ye must be born again'. And to be reborn signified the discovery of one's pre-existent spiritual identity, fashioned not by material history but by Spirit. If, as she claimed, man's soul was immortal 'because it is Spirit, which has no element of self-destruction'[3], then it had no beginning in Time either. Man had always existed in God as the object of His thought and the very witness of His nature. Human consciousness, then, was:

> a transitional state of 'becoming', and the progressive
> appearance of the divine in it brought out all those transitional
> qualities that are rightly called *humane* – the courage and
> compassion and patience which reach out to a sick, scared,
> hungry world with the promise of something better[4].

Mrs Baker Eddy's religious philosophy was basically a method of therapy, of instantaneous healing, or at least of its possibility[5]; and in many respects she anticipated concepts of psychosomatic illness and healing in her insistence that all our illnesses had a mental origin, and that it was ultimately in the realm of Mind only that wholeness was attainable. Thus she says:

> Science [ie Christan Science] reveals the origin of all diseases as mental, but it also declares that all disease is cured by divine Mind. There can be no healing except by this Mind, however much we trust a drug or any other means towards which human faith or endeavour is directed. It is mortal mind, not matter, which brings to the sick whatever good they may seem to receive from materiality. But the sick are never really healed except by means of the divine power. Only the action of Truth, Life, and Love can give harmony[6].

Mrs Eddy emphasized throughout all her writing that *love* was of paramount importance in all healing activity, and that the true believer must exclude from himself all hatred, malice and uncharitableness. Even Dr Leslie Weatherhead[7], who was somewhat scathing in his criticism of Christian Science, had to admit that Christian Scientists themselves seemed generally to enjoy good health, and that they seemed also to have found a way of loving others, and in so doing promoted their health and healing as well. One might argue that there is nothing really novel in this, and that it is (or can be) the loving care of nurses and relatives, for example, rather than surgery or medication that finally heals.

Christian Science arose in the USA at a time when people seemed somewhat spiritually bankrupt and when the Platonic philosophy of Transcendentalism provided both rationality and mysticism, and was presented as an alternative to the barren orthodoxy. Even so-called 'miracles' were acceptable to individuals such as W H Furness and Ralph Waldo Emerson, if only because one had to allow that there was a whole realm of knowledge and natural laws as yet undiscovered; and one could not with any certainty claim that any recorded event was a violation of the 'natural' order. Mrs Eddy felt in no way alien to this general thesis, and she defines 'miracle' in her glossary as 'that which is divinely natural, but must be learned humanly; a phenomenon of Science'[8].

The 'religion' of Christian Science provided new realms of possibility in the human endeavour to become whole, and it emphasized healing and wholeness in a religion that had become so theologized that many were seeking freedom from the old dogmas as well as freedom from sickness. Some found a solution in Unitarianism which attracted many intellectuals; but perhaps many more found hope in the Science of Health which proclaimed that Mind, the only Spirit or divine Principle, found its full and perfect expression in man[9], whose sole purpose was to let that Mind be in them that was also in Jesus Christ.

2   Jehovah's Witnesses

When Abel offered to God a sacrifice which was more acceptable than that of Cain, and by which he obtained witness that he was righteous, he began (so say Jehovah's Witnesses) a religious movement which is still alive. Abel was the 'first witness'[10] and he was followed by others such as Enoch, Noah, Abraham, Moses and many more. Jesus Christ was himself 'the faithful and true witness' as described in the Book of Revelation[11]. Jehovah's Witnesses are the only organization (in their view) that has preserved unsullied the original teaching and worship of Jehovah God. In more sober historical terms, the movement was founded in 1881 by Pastor Charles Taze Russell of Pittsburg, Pennsylvania, under the name of the Watch Tower Bible and Tract Society. Later on the movement was taken over by Judge J F Rutherford, who became president in 1917. It has a strong and vigorous organization, and members continuously canvas from house to house selling their 'Watch Tower Magazine' and witnessing to the truth as they know it. They are very persistent and not easily dissuaded from discussing their very settled convictions.

Their main teaching concerns the establishment of God's new kingdom, preceded by the Second Coming of Jesus Christ, which the Witnesses believe has already occurred. The great Armageddon, or 'the war of the great day of God the Almighty'[12], will occur as soon as the Witness is complete. This war is not a mere 'world war' but one in which the invisible armies of God will take part[13]. The period of the millennium will provide for those who have not become 'Witnesses' a second chance of salvation. Those who are dead will progressively be raised until the full complement of places left after Armageddon has been fulfilled. The Witnesses have worked out the possibilities of some 20,000,000,000 being resurrected on the earth, and of being fed and instructed before five hundred years of Christ's thousand-year reign have elapsed. None of this will disrupt the harmony and order upon the earth.

> Thus God, with his almighty power and wisdom, is able to bring his purpose to a glorious conclusion fully within the framework of the laws and arrangements he has made for mankind from the beginning, with the added undeserved kindness of the resurrection. – Rom 11, vv 33-36[14].

The Witnesses support every belief that they hold by reference to the Scriptures, their view of which is fundamentalist – all the Biblical writings are fully inspired by God without the possibility of any error. Their *Aid to Bible Understanding* is a massive piece of cross-referencing and harmonization; it boasts a usage of a large critical apparatus[15], although a detailed examination of the articles reveals that its chief source is its own Bible translation, entitled *The New World Translation of the Holy Scriptures* (1961). Its use of other versions and translations is restricted almost entirely to those occasions where they can find support for any particular view or doctrine. Its most interesting and perhaps best documented article is that on 'Jehovah', where it concludes that their spelling and pronunciation of the Divine Name are preferable (in usage at any rate) to 'Yahweh' (favoured by most modern Hebrew scholars) because:

> The purpose of words is to transmit thoughts; in English the name 'Jehovah' identifies the true God, transmitting this

thought more satisfactorily today than any of the suggested substitutes[16].

Jehovah's Witnesses strongly oppose the use of blood transfusions in medical practice, since in Biblical terms your blood is your life. And the Witnesses have been persecuted, attacked and imprisoned all over the world for their opposition to war and their refusal to participate in it in any way. In Germany, during WW2, six thousand of them suffered in concentration camps. They are a very courageous people whose sole aim is to witness to what they believe is the truth. In their production of literature they are indefatigable; for example, by 1968 the 'Watchtower' magazine had been printed in 72 languages; in 1969 they produced '*The Kingdom Interlinear Translation of the Greek Scriptures*'; between 1969 and 1971 they had printed over one million copies of their *Aid to Bible Understanding* ; whilst their '*New World Translation of the Holy Scriptures*', which appeared in 1961 as a first revision of previous translations, and which was revised a second time in 1970, had at that date been printed in sixteen million copies – it also appeared in German, Italian, Dutch, Spanish and Portuguese. They have branch offices in about ninety countries in the world from Alaska to Zambia, and they seek to witness wherever there are people to be converted.

They have no priests and no sacraments. Most people would probably regard their lives as drab and world-rejecting, for they do not celebrate the 'Christian' festivals, and Christmas is just another day to them, without presents, decorations or cards, which are all regarded as pagan. They attract a very wide spectrum of the various social strata, and it is not always easy to see precisely what their appeal is. Certainly there is no room for doubt or variation in their dogma: it is a closed system with a very precise interpretation supported to the letter by scriptural references. There are many people who seek total authority in their religious beliefs. The literature of the Watch Tower leaves the adherent in no doubt as to what exactly each passage of any importance in Scripture really means.

3 The Church of Jesus Christ of Latter-Day Saints, or The Mormons

One of the great enigmas of the world of religion has deen the development and spread of the Mormons. Its founder, Joseph Smith, was the son of a Vermont farmer, and he had a religious upbringing, being involved very much in local religious revivals. He found himself very disturbed by the many denominations of Christianity and their often conflicting dogmas, until one day, as he prayed earnestly for guidance, he claims that two heavenly beings confronted him. They strictly charged him not to join any of the existing churches or denominations, but to prepare himself in meditation and prayer to become the leader of a new movement.

In a series of visions it was revealed to him that in a nearby hillside there were some golden plates inscribed with 'reformed Egyptian' characters. In 1827, therefore, at the age of twenty-two, Joseph Smith unearthed the plates, and with the help of 'Urim and Thummim' he translated them into English. The existence of the plates was attested to first by three witnesses, and then by a further eight. Five of the witnesses bear the surname Whitner, and three of them Smith, one of whom was Joseph Smith's father[17].

If this was a conspiracy involving members of three families at most, its immediate purpose is certainly not obvious. We are told that the *Book of Mormon* plates were 'about six inches wide, eight inches long and about the thickness of common tin'[18] but apart from Joseph Smith and the eleven witnesses, no one else ever saw them. Many people tried to get them from him, but they were unsuccessful. The heavenly messenger, Moroni by name, had warned Smith that he must not use the gold plates to get rich, but that his sole purpose in using them and in translating them was to glorify God. After the plates had been translated, with the magical use of the two stones, the Urim and the Thummim, they were delivered to the messenger, Moroni, and never again seen.

The Book of Mormon was published in English in 1830, and at the same time a small church was founded by Smith in Fayette, New

York, where he carried out his first miracle by casting out a devil. *The Book of Mormon* purports to be an account of the early history of the American Indians, from circa 600 BC to circa AD 421. They are identified with the Lost Ten Tribes of Israel who were deported by King Sargon of Assyria in 721 BC. The Mormons also hold that Jesus Christ appeared in America after his resurrection[19], and that he called and commissioned twelve servants or disciples to minister to these Lost Tribes, who were the 'Other sheep I have which are not of this fold'[20].

Smith insisted upon calling all converts to this new faith 'the Chosen People', and the remainder were Gentiles. He participated in local politics and commanded that all the Chosen Ones should vote and think as he did. Much trouble resulted, and the Mormons found themselves persecuted almost from their inception. They were repeatedly driven from one city to another, their homes and their possessions being destroyed. For a time they settled happily in Illinois, at Nauvoo on the Mississippi; but persecution was never very far away, and when in 1844 Joseph Smith was murdered at the early age of thirty-nine, a new and vigorous leader appeared.

Brigham Young, an extraordinary man by any standards, one day proclaimed that he had received a revelation indicating that he must lead the faithful members of the Mormon Church to the Salt Lake, involving a trek of something over one thousand miles, and to a land which was still outside the jurisdiction of the United States. Any who wished to remain could do so or could go their own way elsewhere; and some did, eventually to form in 1852 the Reorganized Church of Jesus Christ of Latter-Day Saints. Meanwhile Brigham Young led the faithful through the desert until, on the 24th of July 1847, they reached the valley of the Great Salt Lake. Within another four years some 30,000 Mormons had reached what to them was none other than the Promised Land.

Whatever one may think about the authenticity of their religion, there could be no doubt about their sincerity and energetic pioneering. They developed a vast irrigation system, and the desert literally blossomed as the rose. They built Salt Lake City which still remains the headquarters of the Mormons. In 1850 there arose the Territory of Utah, a Mormon settlement, and in 1896 it was incorporated into the Union. Brigham Young continued as their strict and autocratic leader until he died in 1877.

It is a perhaps somewhat sad reflection upon people's desire really to understand what others believe when one realizes that most people, if asked what they know about the Mormons, would reply that they are polygamists. The same people might conveniently forget that polygamy was practised among the Ancient Israelites, and that the wise old king Solomon himself supported seven hundred wives and three hundred concubines[21]. Polygamy was certainly sanctioned by Brigham Young after the building of Salt Lake City, and it had the utilitarian basis of developing more quickly the Mormon population. But it undoubtedly fostered a great deal of antagonism towards the movement. Polygamy was officially renounced in 1890, although the memory of the doctrine has lingered on. Moreover, there still exist small and isolated groups of Mormons (as in S E British Columbia, Canada) who practise polygamy.

Like Jehovah's Witnesses, the Mormons are millenarians and they await the return of Jesus Christ who will reign for a thousand years. They say that, when Jesus showed himself to the people of Nephi after his resurrection, he chose three who would 'never taste of death'[22] but would remain upon the earth until Christ came in his glory. They would suffer neither pain nor sorrow.

Among the Mormons are two orders of leaders or priests. There are the Melchizedeks, or higher order, who include the ruling elders or apostles and the high priest; and there are the members of the Aaronic priesthood, or lower order, whose role it is to attend to the temporal affairs of the church. All members are expected to engage in missionary work, which is unpaid and to fulfil which young Mormons usually give up one year of their working life to engage fully in this duty. All members must abstain from drugs, including tea, coffee, tobacco and alcohol. Revelation comes to them direct through visions; and they have a strong educational programme for all their members.

The Book of Mormon itself claims to be a translation of three classes of Record Plates, namely, the Plates of Nephi, the Plates of Mormon and the Plates of Ether. Another set of plates frequently mentioned in *The Book of Mormon* are the Brass Plates of Laban, supposedly brought by the people of Lehi from Jerusalem, and containing Hebrew scriptures and genealogies, many abstracts from which appear in the Nephite records. Mormon himself delivered up the record he had made to his son Moroni, circa AD 385[23], and others he hid in the hill Cumorah[24]. Moroni completed the record after the death of his father and of his people, between AD 400 and 421[25]. Moroni records[26]:

> And now, behold, we have written this record according to our knowledge, in the characters which are called among us the reformed Egyptian, being handed down and altered by us, according to our manner of speech. And if our plates had been sufficiently large we should have written in Hebrew; but the Hebrew hath been altered by us also; and if we could have written in Hebrew, behold, ye would have had no imperfection in our record. But the Lord knoweth the things which we have written, and also that none other people knoweth our language therefore he hath prepared means for the interpretation thereof.

Moroni finally sealed up the records circa AD 21, and hid them 'to be brought forth in the latter days, as predicted by the voice of God through his ancient prophets'. In AD 1827 Moroni, a resurrected being, delivered the engraved plates to Joseph Smith.

It is difficult to make a critical estimate of a religion which has spread all over the world, whose members are sincere and healthy, who have a sense of divine message and mission, and who never for one moment appear to question the origins of their scriptures. *The Book of Mormon* is a combination of what appears to be fictional history, a considerable usage of Old Testament names and material, and a great deal of the teaching of Jesus, much of it *verbatim* from the New Testament[27]. The testimony of the three original witnesses to the existence of the plates was something demanded by Moroni himself of the future translator of his writings[28]. At this point in time it is virtually impossible to evaluate the character of the founders of the religion, or the nature of the testimony of those who claimed to have seen the golden Record Plates neatly hidden by Mormon and Moroni. One can only say that, in the acceptance of and belief in the accounts of the finding, translation and disappearance of the plates, both faith and credulity are stretched to the utmost. And apart from giving a 'history' of the Lost Ten Tribes of Israel from 600 BC to AD 421, and filling in some gaps in the history of a continent virtually without recorded history, *The Book of Mormon* itself adds nothing of any importance either to the teaching of the Old Testament or to that of the New Testament.

4 The Baha'i Religion

There were certain Eastern religious developments in the nineteenth century which promised to have a more universal application, and which spread eventually to the West, particularly amongst intellectuals who were dissatisfied with orthodox Christianity. The Baha'i faith sprang out of the divisions of Islam. It was common belief among Iranian Muslims that their twelfth leader disappeared in the 260th year of their era and would reappear after a period of a millennium (that is, in 1260 AH or AD 1844). It was in that year of 1844 that Mizra Ali Muhammad, a young prophet of twenty-four, claimed that he was the Bab, or Gate, to ultimate Truth, and was the leader that they were looking for. He spoke of a wonderful paradise upon earth, the Kingdom of Allah, that he was about to inaugurate – and he was put to death in 1850.

At Ali Muhammad's death, many of his followers fled to Cyprus and Turkey and continued his teachings in Babi groups. His principal disciple, Mirza Husain Ali (1817-92), referred to himself as Baha'u'llah or the 'Glory of God', and maintained that he was the Revelator of God – that is, he was the very manifestation or emanation of God who was, in essence, unknowable. Baha'u'llah provided a way through which God could be known. This claim was not accepted with any great alacrity, and many regarded it as highly blasphemous. In consequence he was exiled to Baghdad, and later to Akka, in Morocco, where he died in 1892, after having written dozens of books and pamphlets.

The Baha'i faith lays great emphasis upon science in its current developments, upon service to others, and it regards itself as a world religion which seeks to unite all of mankind in a religious brotherhood. It considers that it has superseded Islam and is a religion for modern times. It does not deny the value of other faiths and revelators of the past – Krishna, Moses, Zoroaster, the Buddha, Jesus Christ and Muhammad have all had their place and have served their purpose in their time.

Its main teachings are the oneness of all mankind; the progressive revelation of God providing a common foundation for all religions; the independent and individual investigation of Truth; the equality of all men and women; the elimination of prejudices of every kind; universal compulsory education; a spiritual solution to all economic problems; a universal peace upheld by a world government; the essential and ultimate harmony of science and religion; and the value of a universal auxiliary language of some sort.

After its founder's death in 1992, many Baha'i centres were founded in Europe and in the USA, and today it is claimed that followers may be found in more than two hundred and fifty countries, and there are fifty-six National and Regional Assemblies representing major countries. Its great strength is that it is another movement of peace and unity that transcends national and narrowly conceived dogmatic beliefs.

5 Theosophy

In 1875 Madame Helena Blavatsky, with Colonel Olcott, founded the Theosophical Society in USA. This was an extremely eclectic movement, combining elements and scriptures of all religions, but emphasizing in particular the Hindu heritage and the *Upanishads* and their teaching in chief. The very name 'Theosophy' was the equivalent of the Sanskrit *Brahma Vidya*, or divine wisdom. Since its thinking was mainly Indian in origin its headquarters were established in Madras in 1878. Madame Blavatsky made claims that she was in contact with the Great White Brotherhood and its Masters in the Himalayas, outstanding among whom was Koot Humi, usually referred to as K H. When Madame Blavatsky died in 1891 an Englishwoman, Mrs Annie Besant, became the president and leading light of the Society.

The new cult attracted a large number of intellectuals, psychics, occultists and others who were genuinely seeking ultimate truth and the essential basis of all religions. One outstanding supporter was Rudolf Steiner, who left the movement in 1912 to form his own cult of Anthroposophy. He wrote in 1911, a very interesting book entitled *Atlantis and Lemuria*, in which he claimed to give an account of the prehistoric Lemurians and Atlanteans, which he had (he said) personally elicited from the Cosmic Akashic Records. Wrangles within the Theosophical Society led to many others leaving it. Soon after becoming its leader, Mrs Besant 'discovered' the new Messiah in the form of one young Brahmin child named Jiddu Krishnamurti. There was great opposition to her declaration that little Jiddu was destined to save the world, but she nevertheless took him around the globe proclaiming to all that he was the Christ in the flesh. Eventually, in 1929, Krishnamurti made a public disclaimer and left Mrs Besant without a Messianic protégé. She died in 1933 at the advanced age of ninety-five.

The teachings of the Society have always been a mixture of occult and scientific learning, mingled with extracts from various scriptures and the revelations of the great Masters, or Mahatmas, residing in Tibet, the Himalayas, and more recently in Western mountain areas such as the Rockies and the Andes. There is a firm acceptance of the brotherhood of all mankind and man's gradual and individual evolution towards perfection, via reincarnation. Behind the latter is the doctrine of *karma*, by which (as in Hinduism proper) we become what we make ourselves by our thoughts and our actions; and in this Law of Causation, or of Cause and Effect, motive is far more important than the action itself[29].

There is a unity underlying all religions which may be summed up in five main principles[30]:

i. There is one eternal,infinite, incognizable, real Existent.

ii. From THAT there appears the manifested God, unfolding from unity to duality, from duality to trinity.

iii. From the manifested trinity there develop many spiritual Intelligences who guide the Cosmic Order.

iv. Man is a reflection of the manifested God, and therefore a trinity fundamentally, his inner and real Self being eternal, one with the Self of the Universe.

v. Man's evolution is by repeated incarnations, into which he is drawn by desire, and from which he is set free by knowledge and sacrifice, becoming divine in potency as he has ever been divine in latency.

6 Vedantism

Vedantism has attracted such names as Aldous Huxley, Christopher Isherwood, Gerald Heard and Frederick Manchester[31]. Basically it is the philosophy of the Indian scriptures called the *Vedas*, which are generally regarded as some of the most ancient religious writings. Other writings, such as the *Bhagavad-Gita*, or 'The Song of God', and the commentaries of Shankara, belong to the corpus of works known as Vedanta. The philosophy of Vedanta is really the basis of all Hindu sects, and there are three fundamental propositions at the back of them all[32]:

i. Man's real nature is divine.

ii. The aim of human existence is to realize the Atman,

our essential nature, and hence identity with the one, underlying Reality, Brahman.

iii. All religions are *essentially* in agreement, although they may differ in external rituals and requirements, and in the statement of their dogmatic theologies.

The development of Vedantism in the West really began with the unorthodox behaviour and ideas of Ramakrishna, who as a youth took up priestly duties at the temple of Kali at Dakshineswar, near Calcutta. He came to regard Kali as his Mother; he became ecstatic, went into long periods of trance, and gave consecrated food to cats, because Mother was in everything. Of Ramakrishna, Christopher Isherwood has said[33]:

> Perhaps the nature of Ramakrishna's achievement can best be hinted at if we compare it with that of Shakespeare or Tolstoy in the sphere of art. Beside these masters, the intuition of lesser writers seems partial and restricted; it can only function along certain lines. The essence of spiritual, as of artistic greatness is in its universality. The minor saint knows one way of worship only, Ramakrishna's genius embraced the whole of mystical realization.

Around Ramakrishna there developed a group of disciples who were later known as the Ramakrishna Order. Chief amongst these were Swami Vivekananda and Swami Brahmananda, both twenty-three years old when Ramakrishna died in 1886. In 1893 Vivekananda attended a Parliament of Religions, which was held at the World's Columbian Exhibition in Chicago, and he became one of its most interesting and exciting personalities. In an ambiance of Christian fundamentalism, his main message was the universality of religious truth. In 1897 he visited England and then returned to India for the official founding of the Ramakrishna Order, with several monasteries and a headquarters at Calcutta. After one more visit to America in 1899 he sought peace, quiet and meditation and died in

1902. Brahmananda then became head of the Order and remained so until he died twenty years later.

Vivekananda had established the Ramakrishna Mission in India as an institution of social service and activity. In New York City he founded the first American Vedanta Society, and this has developed into a large number of centres, units and ashrams which have their own swami in charge whose duty it is to lecture and lead groups for the examination of Vedanta literature.

Aldous Huxley[34] has summed up the teachings of Vedantism in an article entitled 'The Minimum Working Hypothesis'. It is a statement of belief for those who cannot find a place in an organized church, and yet who find also that the various forms of humanism or nature-worship are insufficient to meet their spiritual needs:

i. There is a Godhead, Ground, Brahman, Clear Light of the Void, which is the unmanifested principle of all manifestations.

ii. The Ground is at once transcendent and immanent.

iii. It is possible for human beings to love, know and, from virtually, to become actually identified with the divine Ground.

iv. To achieve this unitive knowledge of the Godhead is the final end and purpose of human existence.

v. There is a Law or Dharma which must be obeyed, a Tao or Way which must be followed, if men are to achieve their final end.

vi. The more there is of self, the less there is of the Godhead; and the Tao is therefore a way of humility and love, the Dharma a living Law of mortification and self-transcending awareness.

7 Some Twentieth-Century Cults

All that one can do in this section is to suggest some of the reasons why so many cults and sects have developed during the twentieth century, and to give some idea of the range of their interests and coverage. Two World Wars and a continuance of warfare, revolution and change in every part of the world have made people uncertain, cynical and in many cases afraid. There is no even tenor of life suggestive of some divine and omnipotent Designer providing order and security. Even within the confines of religion itself there have been such drastic changes that many are no longer sure of what to believe, or even whether there remains anything to believe. The 'demythologizing movement' leaves many people with the feeling that somehow the baby has been thrown out with the bathwater. The numerous well-intentioned 'honest to God' approaches have provided many with a means of relief that there is no longer any need to accept all dogmas in a literal way; whilst they have left others with a sense of bewilderment and an inability to grasp what they are 'expected' to believe.

The 'God is Dead' theology[35] has left still others without a concept of God which is in any way meaningful to them; and the many divagations and subtleties of existentialist philosophy and theology are to some quite incomprehensible, although to others, of course, quite attractive. One of the best and clearest expositions of *Existentialism* is that of John Macquarrie[36], and in his discussion of man's search for reality he says[37]:

> Metaphysics is the search for ultimate reality, and in religion ultimate reality has been called God. Sometimes metaphysicians have tried to prove God's existence, and sometimes they have constructed atheistic metaphysics. Of course, it has often been said that the God of the philosophers is not the same as the God of religion, and this is a statement very congenial to the spirit of existentialism. For if the existentialist speaks of God, it is not on the basis of a rational argument establishing God's existence but as a result of reflection on the meaning of human existence, when this is explored to its farthest boundaries.

The philosophers, such as Kierkegaard (1813-55), who put away any hope of a unified field of knowledge, gave birth to modern man's despair at ever finding any unity or meaning in life itself. Out of this *Angst*, or vague feeling of dread, many (mostly intellectuals) have found some consolation – one can hardly call it security or salvation – in some philosophy of the existential. But many more have looked for hope and security elsewhere, particularly in what Dr Christopher Evans[38] has referred to as 'Cults of Unreason'. Associated with existentialism and hippy Zen has been much of the drug scene on the university and college campuses in America, particularly in California. The 'Beat Generation' was a term used by the author Jack Kerouac (died 1969), who wrote *On The Road*, which he employed to epitomize the variety of groups of young people of the post-war generation. Such groups held a pastiche of attitudes, such as: rejection of the traditional institutions of society and of the generally accepted values of those institutions; an acceptance of the immediate present, the 'now moment' only, in terms of the experience and sensations which it provides – hence the world of 'happenings' and absorption of the absurd; revolt against all stratified and organized society or authority – chiefly because authority represented an attempt to control people, their behaviour, nature and events. Such people were 'with it' as opposed to conventional 'squares'.

Eventually the more abrasive attitudes of rebellion backfired and the 'Beat Generation' transformed itself into the lovely 'Flower People' overflowing with love, flowers and beads. Little had, in fact, changed. Their superficiality was represented by a so-called 'existential' philosophy which meant living in and for the present. Drugs became, in the 1950s and 1960s, an essential part of the Love scene, and an assist in dissociating from the rejected 'rat race' of the society in which they were living. They wanted above all a new, reformed society, based upon love, community, peace and sharing, in which there were neither poor nor rich, high nor low. They became very interested in Eastern religions which they felt really held the key to inner peace and happiness. Thus there developed a considerable following of the *Transcendental Meditation* of the Maharishi

Mahesh Yogi, both in the practice of meditation itself through the use of a key word provided by the Maharishi, and in the pursuance of various forms of Yoga with Hatha Yoga and its many *asanas*, or positions, taking pride of place. Mantra Yoga, in which a word or phrase is repeated ad nauseam, found an outlet in the Hare Krishna cult which had a certain passing appeal in the streets of London – ecstasy, trance, self-hypnosis all being induced by the repetition of the words 'Hare Krishna'.

Some have pursued the drug interest in a hope and belief that it would heighten their powers of awareness and deepen their intuitions and inspiration. This has been termed *Psychedelism*, which for some is in itself a religion since they feel 'at one' with the universe, which in turn is identified with God. Among the psychedelics are such drugs as mescalin, LSD or lysergic acid, peyote, marijuana, psylocybin and hashish; and those who take them claim that their consciousness is expanded. In 1954 Aldous Huxley[39] discussed some of his experiences with mescalin, one of the more powerful hallucinogens derived from the Mexican cactus plant peyote. Huxley argued that the heightened perception he experienced could be invaluable to creative people such as poets, artists and writers. In a later sequel, which he published in 1956, Huxley[40] pointed out that whilst this psychedelic world might be full of colour, music and unexplored experiences redolent of the Paradise or Fairyland of folklore and religion, there were negative aspects of the experience involving dread, hatred, anger and suddenly unleashed malice, which would very quickly turn the experimenter's Heaven into Hell. And many have certainly had this experience.

In his last novel, Aldous Huxley[41] envisaged man at his sanest on the island of Pala, filled with compassion (*karuna*) for others, and seeking to live only in peace and contentment. A great assist in all of this was a *moksha* medicine, that is a medicine, or drug, that helped to produce a sense of liberation as well as of illumination and pure receptivity[42]:

A century of research on the *moksha*-medicine has clearly shown that quite ordinary people are perfectly capable of

having visionary or even fully liberating experiences. In
this respect the men and women who make and enjoy high
culture are no better off than the low-brows. High experience
is perfectly compatible with low symbolic expression....
Palanese culture is not to be judged as (for lack of any better
criterion) we judge other cultures. It is not to be judged by
the accomplishments of a few gifted manipulators of artistic
or philosophical symbols. No, it is to be judged by what all
the members of the community, the ordinary as well as the
extraordinary, can and do experience in every contingency and
at each successive intersection of time with eternity.

And this is what psychedelism (with certain other cultic elements)
offers – a world in which all are equal, all are brought to the same
levels of experience, at every point in time.

It was Dr Carl Jung who was one of the first to argue for a greater
link between the clergy and psychotherapists[43]. He suggested that
neuroses grew noticeably more frequent as the religious life declined.
By this statement he was not specifying any particular religion or
any particular sect of a religion – quite the contrary. There were
many people for whom the Catholic Church was the only possible
haven; there were primitive people to whom primitive religion
was better suited than Christianity; and there must be protestants
against the Catholic Church just as there must be protestants against
Protestantism.

In recent years there has been considerable protestation against
the Christian Church's failure to heal, and earnest people have
sought healing outside the Church in a hundred and one friendly
groups, societies, cults and religions. For a highly critical, as well
as interesting account of one such development, namely *Dianetics/
Scientology*, the reader is referred to the book by Dr C Evans already
mentioned[45]. Dr Evans deals with the cult, now a registered religion,
with a great deal of acuity as well as humour. One cannot deny, and
Dr Evans doesn't, that Scientology has its successes and certainly its
adherents, however costly the process of being 'cleared' may be. Dr

Evans suggests two major reasons for much success, both of which are relevant to the present discussion. There is, firstly, a considerable emphasis placed upon the importance of improving the effectiveness of interpersonal communication. This aids the individual who is shy and introverted to be outgoing. And, secondly, there is an equally strong emphasis upon prolonged and undivided personal attention[46]. In a mass technocratic age, people long to be noticed and to be regarded as something more than a National Health or Social Security number. Even if they had the time, many doctors have forgotten how to talk to and treat individual people as persons; they now examine, diagnose and pass 'the patient' on. In becoming a 'religion', Scientology may have had purely pragmatic considerations of survival – the unqualified psychotherapist or 'auditor' now became an official of the 'Church' of Scientology hearing a 'confession'; but in real terms this seems precisely what large numbers of people want – just someone who will listen with a sympathetic ear. And in many instances this is the only therapy that they need.

Healing, not merely in the sense of eradicating disease or sickness, but in the sense of providing wholeness, integrity or integration of personality, has become very important to people undergoing a variety of mental and physical stress, to say nothing of 'spiritual dryness'. Many have turned to the various Spiritualistic agencies that claim to be able to heal; others have resorted to occult and so-called 'magical' practices. Some have found a solution in the faith, divine or mental healing attached to a variety of small, esoteric groups and secret societies. People will, in fact, make a religion of anything. As Werner and Lotte Pelz have said[47]:

> We are always tempted to turn our provisional insights into a religion, because we hate above everything else insecurity.

This sense of insecurity has led people to follow astrology, paranormal phenomena which today seem to be all around us, pyramidology, the continuing search for the Holy Grail or the Ark of the Covenant, magic and witchcraft (both white and black) and Ufology or the pursuit of 'flying saucers'; or combinations or permutations of any of these. The Aetherius Society provides a link between orthodoxy and belief in Cosmic Masters by the messages it has received from Jesus who is, apparently, alive and well and living on the planet Venus. A variety of Atlantean and Aquarian societies look forward to the inauguration of a New Age, when Atlantis will arise again, the glories and paradises of the past will be revived, and the principles of love, tolerance and understanding will flood over the earth.

All these cults are not to be dismissed as the product of cranks, or the bizarre inventions of individuals who would prefer anything new to the dull pursuance of the traditional or orthodox. Of course, many of such cults have few adherents, many are short-lived, but some are positively antisocial, pursuing black and deleterious arts. In the main, however, they represent the deep yearnings of people seeking Truth, Reality, God – whatever connotations one gives to these concepts. They are mostly concerned with the fullest possible development of the individual in harmony with the total community of mankind – in peace, love and fellowship. In themselves these are laudable aims, and many individuals find some form of fulfillment – at least for a time – in their pursuit if not in their perfect attainment.

17 Some Current Ideologies

There are many people who think that, to seek the conquest of evil, disease or insecurity through religion or through some attempt to find 'God', is as about effectual as Don Quixote's tilting at windmills which, in his fertile imagination had been transmuted into giants. Of course, evil, disease and insecurity are always with us, but they are forever changing in nature and direction according to the wind that blows and according to the age and place in which we live. But the world is rapidly becoming one, and national boundaries are beginning to become less of an obstruction to the evildoer. We no longer tend to build up cosmic dramas of heavenly warfare between Good and Evil, but rather tend to increase our levels of 'Intelligence' and physical security.

In any serious consideration of religion we have to allow for the fact that there are people – perhaps an ever-increasing number – who regard religion (especially formalized religion) as effete, or just simply as an opiate of the people. Man, according to Werner and Lotte Pelz[1], desires an idol, ideal or ideology – 'something that justifies his desire to justify himself before it'. And usually he finds it convenient to bestow upon that something the name of whatever god is available. If one god is demoted, another has to take its place in one form or another, because this god is in a sense a projection of ourselves, individually or collectively. Werner and Lotte Pelz have put it in the following way[2]:

The pharisaical god bears a close resemblance to the Jungian
archetype, the 'wise old man', the 'shadow'. He is the
communal super-ego, the hypostasized 'archetype of meaning'.
He epitomizes man's struggle to integrate the multitude of
communal impressions and aspirations into a comprehensible
whole where he can find a justified and justifiable place. As
such he is performing a restraining and civilizing function.
But he is not a 'he', but an 'it', an emanation of the social life,
an 'epiphenomenon' of the economic process etc. It can give no
further meaning to our life. When a man realizes this, he turns
atheist or fundamentalist, communist or nihilist, 'Roman
Catholic', 'Anglican' or 'Methodist'. He gives a new name to
the shadow from which he cannot escape since it is his own.

There are undoubtedly many beliefs that people have cultivated
which either reject entirely the concept of God, or modify such a
concept so that eventually it has no significant meaning beyond
some aspect of the Self. Some of them would certainly not refer to
themselves as 'religious', and would repudiate entirely the idea that
they could be categorized as such. It is the purpose of this chapter
briefly to review a number of such 'isms', 'ologies', surrogate religions,
or whatever one decides to call them.

(a) **Atheism**, for example, states clearly and boldly that 'there is no
God'. But such a statement has, in itself, no meaning (even though
we may agree that we understand it) unless the atheist himself is
prepared to give some description of the Thing or Being in which
he does *not* believe. If, for example, I say that I do not believe that
Unicorns have ever existed, this has meaning since there is at least
some consensus as to what that animal – mythical or otherwise –
looked like, and the way in which it behaved. If, on the other hand, I
say that I do not believe in the existence of 'umbaboolanas', there can
be no possibility of agreement, disagreement, or even meaning, for
the word *per se* has no connotation. Somewhat similarly, there is no
consensus concerning a definition of God or his nature – except, of

course, in specific religious sects. So each atheist must define clearly what it is that he does not believe in when he says, 'I do not believe in the existence of God, or a god'. He may well find that many theists do not believe in the sort of God he defines either. To some theists God is a personal giant, autarchic and authoritarian; to others he is Spirit (whatever that is) 'blowing where It listeth', healing, inspiring and giving freedom; to others he is the windmill of our own minds, for ever changing in mood, force and direction, and being ever created and recreated by our own imaginations; to yet others he is Mind or Mind-Stuff itself. To some He, or It, is impersonal – Beingness Itself; to others He, She, or He/She, is highly personal and approachable through prayer. An atheist may well disbelieve in a personal Creator-God, and yet accept that there is some Cosmic Force or Mind-Stuff which holds the universe together. He may still, however, see no reason to worship it or to organize any body of belief about it.

There are probably very few today who accept that there are any intellectual 'proofs' for the existence of God, and one hears less and less of the ontological, cosmological, teleological and moral arguments. Yet, as arguments rather than proofs, they may present together some cumulative force which individuals might find convincing. If, however, there is no positive proof of God's existence, it is equally certain that there can be no positive disproof either. Perhaps the most that can be done in response to the atheist is to suggest that there seems to be some proof, in psychological terms, of *the need of the idea of God* – at least for a very large number of people. Carl Jung[3], for example, found the Divine Archetype as one of the images of the Unconscious. Man has a deep need for healing, for wholeness and for integration, and this need is met in some people by an image of Divinity within the innermost self. Jung[4] once said that among all of his patients in the second half of life – that is to say, over thirty-five-

> There has not been one whose problem in the last resort was not that of finding a religious outlook on life. It is safe to say that every one of them fell ill because he had lost what the

living religions of every age have given to their followers, and none of them has really been healed who did not regain his religious outlook.

This does not suggest, of course, that the image of God is the same for everyone; it is simply suggesting that some image was there, and it then somehow became lost. Nor was Jung suggesting that any of this was proof of God's objective reality; indeed he comments very clearly that it would be a 'regrettable mistake if anybody should take my observations as a kind of proof of the existence of God'[5]. The *need* which so many have for such an image of God does not, therefore in itself prove the existence of a God behind the image; but it may well go some way towards establishing a collectively held archetype of God in the Unconscious of all people. There is, of course, another very important point arising out of Jung's observations. He was concerned with people who were mentally sick or disoriented. His comments cannot be held immediately to refer to the rest of mankind. We cannot extrapolate evidence from the abnormal to establish the normal.

(b) Agnosticism is a collective term which covers a variety of attitudes, since one can be generally 'agnostic' in an approach to life's puzzles and problems without necessarily being *an* agnostic in religious terms. Some would equate agnosticism with a Pyrrhonistic scepticism which, on principle, doubts everything – even the existence of others, if not one's own existence – and suggests that we cannot really know anything about anything for certain. This tends to become a somewhat blasé, blatant and rather pointless philosophy of solipsism. In relation to the more specific question of God's existence there is the agnostic who might say, 'I don't know whether there is a god or not, and what is more I don't *want* to know'. One cannot profitably argue with that position, since it is clearly not based upon any serious consideration of the subject. There is, however, a more thoughtful as well as more humble position which suggests that, 'It is, in the very nature of things, impossible for the creature Man to have knowledge of this order'. This implies that the gulf between an

Omnipotent Creator, of whatever nature, and the animal 'man' is so wide that any possibility of enquiry into the existence of such a being is quite inconceivable. We just do not know where to start. God, by definition, would be unknowable – so there's no point in any further discussion. There are also deistic agnostics or agnostic deists, who would say that the acceptance of the existence of *some sort* of God is required, not through revelation, but as a hypothesis necessitated by reason; but we cannot *know* any more about him. There is, however, a 'scientific' agnosticism even within the realm of religious thought and discovery which says that 'I do not know, but I shall certainly try to find out'. And there then begins a search for God along every possible line of experimental and experiential enquiry. Such an agnostic approach can at least begin to establish certain known and accepted data in such universes of discourse as archaeology, history, psychology, psycho-analysis, anthropology, sociology and so on.

(c) **Humanism** has sometimes been referred to as 'the religion of Man', although no doubt most humanists would prefer to regard their ideas and beliefs as having no real 'religious' connotation. R L Shinn[6] states that

> Humanism is the appreciation of man and of the values, real and potential, in human life. It esteems man – not as an animal, a machine, or an angel, but as man.

Shinn[7] goes on to say that what was regarded as impossible only yesterday has today become virtually commonplace in the life of man; 'what men once begged the gods to do, they now do for themselves.' With the failure of much orthodox religion to appeal to the masses there has developed an increasing pursuit of the concept of man's own adequacy to deal with his personal and social problems. Man, so it is averred, has at last come of age, and he must take on full responsibility for his individual and collective activity. Man is in a position to improve his own conditions and environment, and he no longer needs to wait for a *deus ex machina* to do his dirty, or just difficult, work for him. Man has himself become the measure, or the measurer, of all things, and the limits of his knowledge, understanding and discovery are simply the limits which he places upon himself. He can equally well solve his moral problems if only he will put his mind to the task and consider the welfare, not of the few, but of the many. Man must respect all, without regard to class, colour or creed; and he must pursue with dignity the happiness and welfare of all with tolerance, freedom and justice.

Humanism, strangely enough, has had a great appeal in our own time. Strangely, because during the last hundred years we have seen more deliberate and calculated destruction of man by man than in the whole of recorded history[8]. Yet there are some fundamental questions which one has to ask about the nature and scale of 'man's inhumanity to man'. Is it, for example, essentially more evil to destroy six million Jews than to kill or torture *one* Jew? And just because it happens to be a Jew and for no other reason. Was the West Indian and American slavery of black Africans in the past really any more devilish or inhuman than the patent and remorseless exploitation of coloured labour in white-occupied territory in Africa and elsewhere? Has man become, or is man becoming, more human or humane or less so, or is he essentially and basically the same as he has always been? One thing seems certain, and that is that his power of devilish invention has kept pace with – if not outstripped – his power to invent the means of alleviating man's multifarious diseases. And the destruction which he might formerly have hesitated to participate in he now, without compunction, assigns to computer-operated missiles and destructive machinery.

Amongst some Christians there has evolved a belief that Humanism – like Christianity – means essentially that a man should fulfil his own nature; it means 'to be a man'. As long ago as circa AD 200, Tertullian[9] spoke of the testimony of the soul, by nature Christian; whilst in the fourth century AD Augustine[10] claimed:

> That which is called the Christian religion existed among
> the ancients and never did not exist, from the beginning of

the human race until Christ came in the flesh, at which time the true religion which already existed began to be called Christianity.

For Dietrich Bonhoeffer[11] Jesus did not call men to a new religion but to life itself, and the Christian was not a special form of *homo religiosus*, but 'a man, pure and simple', just as Jesus was man. This is all somewhat redolent of Spinoza's concept that in order to preserve our being we must become what we *potentially are*.

In an age marked more by alienation than commitment[12] this does not mean that men should be encouraged to join religious groups or societies, to become 'Christians' or 'Anglicans', or whatever; or indeed anything that is classified or categorized by historical incident or accident. It means 'having the courage to be' what we already are. The apparent meaninglessness of modern life has left man not merely with doubt or agnosticism, but with *Angst* or despair. Tillich, for example, believed that the theistic objectification of a God who is a being must be transcended. The 'courage to be', he says[13], 'is rooted in the God who appears when God has disappeared in the anxiety of doubt'. Thus, the final and ultimate source of our courage will be found in the 'God above God'[14].

In a letter which he wrote from Peiping in 1941, Teilhard de Chardin[15] spoke of his own optimism in relation to man, and considered that once more we must take up, although on a more scientific and philosophical basis, the idea or 'myth' of progress. This, he said, was the essential setting in which he saw 'the simultaneous rebirth of humanism and Christianity'[16]. This did not mean for him *more* of what was currently regarded as Christianity, but rather a transformation of it. Man was inexorably and inevitably moving towards 'hominization'[17], that is, he was becoming human, and the cosmic meaning of such 'humanism' was that the Christ element or Christ force was pervading the whole future domain of mankind.

The so-called 'uncommitted' and 'alienated' are still able to find room in some form of humanism, without feeling that they are personally labelled. Thus, *Existentialism*, or perhaps better 'the philosophy of the Existential', is a philosophy which has so little in the way of precise dogma that it has given rise to a whole catena of beliefs and ideas. One of the main themes of existentialist philosophy is that of personal freedom – although that cannot always be claimed to be a comfort since it brings with it its own dread and dreadful responsibilities. Jean-Paul Sartre[18] has said that man:

> is what he wills, and as he conceives himself after already existing – as he wills to be after that leap towards existence. Man is nothing else but that which he makes of himself.

For Sartre that was the first principle of Existentialism. We are the masters of our fate: we are in control of our own destiny, and the enemy is anything that would seek to destroy our own personal will and sense of fulfilment. Indeed, 'Hell is other people'[19]. One's sole commitment is to oneself (or one's Self) and its fulfilment. Teilhard de Chardin saw man becoming what he really *is*; Sartre saw man becoming what he *wants to make* himself to be. For Teilhard de Chardin man is essentially spiritual and moving towards the Point Omega, some far-off divine event towards which the whole of mankind is ineluctably moving. For Sartre man is precisely what he wants to be, no more and no less.

(d) Fascism. Those who reject outright any form of religion usually manage to find some political surrogate for it. Fascism, for example, developed between the two World Wars partly as a disillusionment with the outcome and peace settlements of WW1, and partly as a result of the general inadequacy of Christianity *per se* to solve economic, social and political problems. As early as 1922 the Fascist party was the only political party in Italy. Fascism is basically a belief in the right of a self-appointed and self-constituted élite to rule, with an absolute authority in the form of a dictator at the head. No opposing opinions are permitted, and it is accepted that certain inequalities in life are beneficial to the total system – such as social inequality and racial inequality. The Marxist view is that Fascism, in whatever form it may appear, is the last fling, as it were, of the ruling class and the bourgeoisie to hold down the proletariat, or the workers. In the form of *Nazism*, or the National Socialist Party, Fascism expressed itself in Germany as a sort of worship. In *Mein Kampf* Hitler referred to himself as the Holy Ghost, and he was accorded the worship of a demi-god, with some of the most formalized collective ritual the world has ever produced. Under Nazism, both alien races and all forms of religion were persecuted, except where religious groups and individuals deliberately made a point of cooperating with the new divinity. But a religion is no better than its god, and the 'religions' of Fascism and Nazism failed largely through the ineffectiveness of their leaders or very human, or inhuman, gods – depending upon how one views it all.

(e) **Communism.** To the philosopher Hegel, in the nineteenth century, ideas were themselves the motivating force behind beliefs and activities. On the other hand, to the proponents of Dialectical Materialism, Karl Marx (1818-1883) and Friedrich Engels (1820-1895), ideas themselves were determined by the social and economic changes effected as a result of materialistic forces. In the Marxian dialectic, thesis was followed by antithesis, and this in turn by synthesis. Historically, the thesis was represented by the feudalism of the Middle Ages, with its ruling class and the mass of the population as serfs. The antithesis was represented by capitalism and the creation of the bourgeoisie and the proletariat. Finally, the synthesis was epitomized in the classless society, in which ultimately the State, as a tool of the dominant class, would wither away.

Communism believes in the type of society in which all property belongs to the community, and social life is based upon the principle of 'from each according to his ability, to each according to his need', or perhaps 'his work'. It accepts as inevitable a class struggle between the oppressed and the oppressing classes, and between oppressed and oppressing nations. Communism has also had its gods (such as Lenin), who have in turn been demoted and replaced by others. And whilst there is undoubtedly oppression under such systems, it is always held to be for the benefit and security ultimately of the greatest number.

For many people the energies, hopes and ideals that were formerly expressed in religious belief and practice have found a substitute in the ideology of Communism, which can be as fanatical – and as ruthless – as many forms of religion have been, and still are. In his discussion of the collective issue, Teilhard de Chardin[20] painted a somewhat dark picture of such ideologies, and yet he himself was still optimistic and hopeful:

> At no previous period of history has mankind been so well equipped nor made such efforts to reduce its multitudes to order. We have 'mass movements' – no longer the hordes streaming down from the forests of the north or the steppes of Asia, but the 'Million' scientifically assembled. The Million in rank and file on the parade ground; the Million standardized in the factory; the Million motorized – and all this only ending up with Communism and National-Socialism and the most ghastly fetters. So we get the crystal instead of the cell; the ant-hill instead of brotherhood. Instead of the upsurge of consciousness which we expected, it is mechanization that seems to emerge inevitably from totalization.

The surrogates of religion are many, and the new gods become the State, the leaders, the bureaucrats, the system, or the ideology itself. Man must find something as an objectification of his innermost need, which is a *real* inner need, but to which he feels he must give some substance in the external world. Where orthodox religions and political systems have failed, he will create new systems – some of vast dimensions and social implications, and some small, personal and individual. Or, again, man may even make a religion of his atheism, agnosticism or humanism; or, by some strange, transmuting alchemy he may make an atheism[21] or humanism[22] of his religion. Teilhard de Chardin[23] despaired of what he referred to as 'the old stuff'. For him Fascism, Communism and even 'democracy' itself had ceased to have any meaning. He wanted to see the best of humanity recognized on a *spiritual* basis, determined by the three aims of Universalism, Futurism and Personalism, and 'cooperating in whatever political and economic movement should prove technically most able to safeguard those three aims'[24].

And so in some sense the wheel has come full circle. Almost everything that has been said in this chapter is little more than an extension of the perceptions of Werner and Lotte Pelz[25] when they say that:

> Religion gives us the feeling of ultimate security, offers us something definite to believe in, persuades us that we know what we believe and convinces us that we really believe what we think we believe.

So also do the many substitutes for religious belief in the form of the various ideologies that we have mentioned. And, of course, there are many more.

18 Mysticism

The Greek *mystae* were those who had been initiated into the 'mysteries' of their religion, which were closed to everyone outside the particular religion concerned but were revealed to those whose eyes were opened by the ceremonies performed. In addition, as members of such mysteries or mystic cults they were sworn to secrecy and were not permitted to reveal anything to the uninitiated. R C Zaehner[1] remarks that

> Religion, for them, is not so much something to be professed as something to be experienced; and such experience, in its higher form, is usually called mystical experience.

As such, it is an experience which is, in its essence, incommunicable to others. It is an individual and direct experience of God, and those who would seek to acquire such experience must first put themselves 'in the Way' to attain it by undergoing similar disciplines and techniques to those practised by the mystics themselves. There are no creeds or formularies to be learnt or accepted as embodying the Truth for, as Browning[2] insisted, 'Truth is within ourselves'. The Light comes from the innermost part of the Self, as Augustine claimed in his *Confessions*[3].

> I entered into my inward self, Thou being my guide... .And I beheld with the eye of my soul above the same eye of my soul,

> above my mind, the Light unchangeable.... .Nor was it above
> my soul, as oil is above water, nor yet as heaven is above earth,
> but above my soul because It made me; and I below It, because
> I was made by It. He who knows the Truth, knows what that
> Light is; and he who knows It, knows Eternity.

Thus the mystic looks inward in order to release the Truth that already abides there, according to his belief, in fulness. In his discovery of this Truth, and in his experience of the numinous, he finds that he is a passive recipient rather than an active cogitator. His direct and immediate experience so envelops and involves him that he feels that he is completely out of Time and out of Space and that, when he returns to what we are pleased to call normality, there are no words whereby he can fully express what he has experienced. Others will believe only when they have experienced something of a similar nature.

There are certain elements common to most mystical beliefs; and the 'perennial philosophy'[4], already referred to briefly in relation to Vedantism, is of a similar nature in all forms of mysticism. Behind the everyday world, the phenomenal world of matter and of the Individual awareness or consciousness, there lies the Universal or Divine Ground. Our daily experiences are partial even though they are, in their variety, manifestations of this Divine Ground. Indeed, the whole of human experience has its reality and beingness in the Divine Ground, and it is the purpose of man so to maximize this experience (or rather to put himself in the Way of so maximizing it) that as a result he may *find identity with* the Divine Ground.

Man is ever trying to find out God, by intellectual search and argument, by cogitation and by discursive reason and logic. But, as Dylan Thomas implied, 'when logics die' then it is possible for 'the secret of the soil' – and also of the soul – to grow 'through the eye'. When the agitation of the mind has ceased, it becomes possible for the individual to discover God by some form of direct intuition, and the seeker becomes united with the Sought. In all of this process man becomes aware that he has two 'selves'; that he has, in fact, a dual nature. There is his ego, the partial and phenomenal self, which in his ignorance he tends to regard as his real and true Self. He is, therefore, conscious of this ego most of the time. But, as we saw in Buddhism, the mystic holds that there is also a non-phenomenal self. This is what the Buddhist refers to as the *atman*, the eternal Self, the divine spark within which is essentially and potentially the same as Brahman, the Divine Ground. Man is able thus to identify with God, and in so doing he becomes what he already is.

Since man is ultimately spiritual, and so linked with the Divine, ultimate Truth is discoverable for him through the intuitive awareness which is already accessible to him. Man's chief aim in life, then, is of a double nature – first it is to discover *himself,* that is, his true identity beyond the known and partial ego; and secondly, through this full knowledge of the Self to know God.

> And he who dwells
> United with Brahman,
> Calm in mind,
> Not grieving, not craving,
> Regarding all men
> With equal acceptance:
> He loves me most dearly.
>
> To love is to know me,
> My innermost nature,
> The truth that I am:
> Through this knowledge he enters
> At once to my Being[5].

Such entry into God's Being is variously known as *samadhi, satori* or cosmic consciousness.

In all this we are obviously faced with the problem of the nature of knowledge. Current philosophical and sociological theories on the subject seem to have lent a great deal of support to the mystic's position, if not quite in the same terms. Reality, as we know it through the senses, is today regarded by many as no more than a logical or social construct, built up from our sense-data and (perhaps even more importantly) from our interpretation of them[6]. The hard, solid 'things' of the past no longer exist as such; they affect us all in very different ways, and our resultant descriptions will vary from one person to another. Even the postulation of their existence is at times capricious, depending very much upon general agreement and consensus[7].

One cannot pretend that all 'mystical' experience is sweetness and light, or that it is not attended by certain dangers not to be taken without deep consideration and judgement. St Paul's admonition to 'try (or test) the spirits whether they be of God or not' is certainly relevant here. John Custance[8], a highly intelligent manic-depressive, emphasized some of the analogies between insanity and mystical religious experience of various kinds – for example, the feeling of the certainty of knowledge; the belief in the unity of all things; the reconciliation of opposites in connection with anaesthetic revelation; the tendency to deny the reality of Time and even Space; and the inclination to believe that all evil is mere appearance, and that there is an ultimate reconciliation of good and evil. Without attempting to press these analogies too far, the warning which Custance[9] gives is, in the light of the history of religion, a very serious one indeed – both to the 'enlightened' individual and to the would-be followers:

> The sense of being intimately in tune with the ultimate stuff of the universe can become so overwhelming that those affected naturally proclaim themselves to be Jesus Christ, or Almighty God, or whatever deity they have been taught to look on as the source of all power.

But, although there are palpable dangers for anyone pursuing a mystic path, one might well ask whether they are really any greater than those which face the individual in a modern world which shows signs of mass neurosis, dread and disorientation. The mystic insists that all things are in some way linked in and through the Divine, and that if there is to be any sense of harmony or unity in the world we must first find such unity within ourselves. The poet Francis Thompson[10] has put it thus:

> When to the new heart of thee
> All things by immortal power
> Near or far,
> Hiddenly
> To each other linked are,
> That thou canst not stir a flower
> Without troubling of a star.

To the mystic the secret of becoming others, or recognizing ourselves in others (that 'empathy' so much on people's lips these days), is to become the Being who unites us all in his Being. This is well expressed in that wonderful poem by the Sufi poet, Attar of Nishapur, who lived during the twelfth century:

> Come, you lost atoms, to your Centre draw,
> And *be* the Eternal Mirror that you saw;
> Rays that have wandered into darkness wide,
> Return, and back into your Sun subside[11].

Once merged with God they become unified with one another – the birds in Attar's poem were no longer thirty separate, desperate and bedraggled things, but one great Sun shining in all its splendour.

Distinctions are sometimes made between Nature-mysticism, Soul-mysticism and God-mysticism, although all forms of mysticism, by their very nature, overlap. With *God-mysticism* it is union with the Ground of all being that is sought, and this is achieved through the return of the individual spirit, suddenly or gradually, to this Infinite Ground. *Nature-mysticism* involves a strong awareness of the presence or immanence of God (or of the One Soul) in the whole of Nature. This is expressed by Tennyson[12] in his poem concerning the Flower:

Flower in the crannied wall,
I pluck you out of the crannies,
I hold you, root and all, in my hand,
Little flower – but *if* I could understand
What you are, root and all, and all in all,
I should know what God and man is.

In *Soul-mysticism* it is man's own true Self that is being sought, for the existence of God is not found in any expressed form. Man seeks himself, and when he has really found himself, he has found all that it is necessary to know. The starting-point here is the Self, but it is not so different from the God-mysticism which, in finding the individual Self, discovers all selves and God. Our union with others comes through knowledge and understanding, and our knowledge and understanding come through love. At the highest level of knowledge, love and understanding, the individual – such as Jesus or Al-Hallaj – may say in the mystical sense, 'I *am* the Truth'. Those who are bold enough to make this identification may suffer persecution, ignominy and crucifixion; some may be confined in asylums for the mentally unbalanced. But the *real* to them is the *actual*[13] which they experience and confidently 'know'.

Mysticism is to be found in all levels and in all sorts of religion, whether it be in a simple, primitive religion, or in sophisticated forms such as Zen and Tao, in Judaism and Christianity, or in Islam. One outstanding group of mystics are the *Sufis*[14] who derive from Islamic religion. Their origins are somewhat obscure, but according to Idries Shah[15] the word *Sufi* itself suddenly became current about a thousand years ago. Of the many origins provided for the word itself, the one which has great appeal in terms of mysticism is that which suggests that the sounds SSS-UUU-FFF have a peculiar effect upon human mentation[16].

More important than the origin of their name is the variety of expression and experience of the Sufi. As Shah[17] points out, there is a certain 'timelessness' and 'placelessness' about the Sufi, and in consequence there is a sense in which he is at home in any age and at any era, bringing his 'experience into operation within the culture, the country, the climate in which he is living'. The inwardness of the Sufi mystical experience is perfectly expressed in the writings of Jalaludin Rumi (1207-73), perhaps no better than in the extract entitled, 'He was in No Other Place'[18]:

> Cross and Christians, end to end, I examined. He was not on the Cross. I went to the Hindu temple, to the ancient pagoda. In none of them was there any sign. To the uplands of Herat I went, and to Kandahar. I looked. He was not on the heights or in the lowlands. Resolutely, I went to the summit of the [fabulous] mountain of Kaf. There only was the dwelling of the [legendary] Anqa bird. I went to the Kaaba of Mecca. He was not there. I asked about him from Avicenna.... I looked into my own heart. In that, his place, I saw him. He was in no other place.

The sayings of the Sufi are so quotable that restraint is obviously needed to prevent oneself producing an anthology of Sufism instead of a general guide to mysticism. The Sufi professes no particular dogma or theology – for him, Truth is where you find it; if you meditate sufficiently and look deeply within yourself, you will find Truth there.

Because his beliefs have never hardened into doctrines, or formularies for acceptance by followers, the Sufi is able to find a message for every society in every age. He does not regard any society as complete: it is developing as all things in the universe are developing. But the needs of each society differ from every other. And because of all this, there is no serious attempt to set up institutions, mosques and so forth which it is hoped will persist in time and space. Moreover, the Sufi feels very strongly that his own very words are ephemeral and inadequate to express permanently, for all places and all time, his own religious experiences. There is a transiency about the format of expression and the connotation of the words which the mystic uses to encapsulate his 'ineffable' experiences. Yet despite this disclaimer that here is something which, when expressed, becomes an eternal embodiment of Truth, there is nevertheless a similarity of expression among mystics of very different backgrounds. Thus we find in the Gospel of Thomas[19]:

> Jesus said:
>   I am the light
>   which is over everything.
>   I am the All;
>   (from me) the All has gone forth,
>   and to me the All has returned.
>   Split wood: I am there.
>   Lift the stone, and you will find me there.

The Gospel of Thomas was an early Gnostic and apocryphal gospel rejected by the Christian Church as an authentic record of the teaching of Jesus. The Sufi, Hakim Jami (1414-1492), wrote a piece called 'Follow the Path'[20] which reflects the main theme of the above passage:

> Do not speak of your heartache – for He is speaking.
> Do not seek Him – for He is seeking.
>
> He feels even the touch of the ant's foot;
> If a stone moves under water – He knows it.
>
> If there is a worm in a rock
> He knows its body, smaller than an atom.
>
> The sound of its praise, and its hidden perception,
> He knows by His divine knowledge.
>
> He has given the worm its sustenance;
> He has shown you the Path of the Teaching.

In recent years there has been a steady movement of the physical sciences towards an almost mystical expression of their current descriptions of the universe; whilst the writings of the palaeontologist,

Pierre Teilhard de Chardin, are both scientific and mystical. Here is just one of the latter's writings, on 'the Nature of the Omega'[21], in which something of the God-mysticism already referred to is observable:

> The very centre of our consciousness, deeper than all its radii; that is the essence which Omega, if it is to be truly Omega, must reclaim. And this essence is obviously not something of which we can dispossess ourselves for the benefit of others as we might give away a coat or pass on a torch. To communicate itself, my ego must subsist through abandoning itself or the gift will fade away. The conclusion is inevitable that the concentration of a conscious universe would be unthinkable if it did not reassemble in itself *all consciousnesses* as well as all *the conscious;* each particular consciousness remaining conscious of itself at the end of the operation, and even (this must absolutely be understood) each particular consciousness becoming still more itself, and thus more clearly distinct from others the closer it gets to them in Omega.

Thus, it is held that Man is striving and evolving towards the Omega Point, the Cosmic Christ or God. And his final absorption into God does not mean the loss of individual consciousness; on the contrary, for Teilhard de Chardin, each individual remains self-conscious at the end of the process.

The intuitive leaps made by our imaginative physicists, their intuitive guesses, their 'crazy' ideas and hypotheses, are all very close to a mystical approach to life. The very language they use suggests an awareness of the immensity and the boundless variety of the universe. They are moved to use such words as strangeness, charm, singularity, 'truth', 'beauty' and so on[22]. Whilst he may not in any way claim to be a mystic, nor wish in any way to be associated with Eastern or religious mysticism, the physicist *grows into* a mystical approach to the whole of the workings of the Cosmos. He has a great respect for it, and he finds an identity with it which is more than just intellectual or mathematical. He appreciates its symmetry and its asymmetry. He empathizes with its aestheticism, its sheer beauty. And his speculative and imaginative theories become the 'scientific' constructs of Reality for tomorrow. But here he resembles very closely the Sufi, however much his language and his methods may differ. The Sufi's expressions of truth, beauty and goodness are beyond place and time, and yet they are geared to each particular era and society. The physicist's descriptions of his universe are culled from the tree of eternity, but they are the expression of a mere decade, often adapted to meet the needs of a specific situation in a selected society. Indeed, his descriptions are themselves no more the Reality than are the Sufi's intuitions. For their discoveries of the secrets that the universe holds need the sort of humility that was expressed by Saadi of Shiraz[23], a Sufi who lived in the thirteenth century:

> A raindrop, dripping from a cloud,
> Was ashamed when it saw the sea.
> 'Who am I where there is a sea?' it said.
> When it saw itself with the eye of humility,
> A shell nurtured it in its embrace.

19 Conclusion

No single study of religion can adequately deal with every aspect and development of it, and on reflection one can see whole areas that have received scant treatment or inadequate recognition within this work. Such a subject demands our serious attention to the smallest movements and groups, for they all encapsulate man's yearnings for something more complete, more adequate, more total than himself; or they may represent some attempts at a satisfying escape from the more mundane and unpleasant realities of everyday life.

Inevitably we are driven eventually to examine such problems as that of knowledge, or epistemology, and the different ways of knowing. We have to scrutinize carefully what we mean by Truth and Reality. Even if one were to accept Christianity, for example, as the final expression of Truth, one has to admit that it is quite unlikely that Man was without Truth until Jesus came and pronounced himself as 'the Way, the Truth and the Life'. We have to accept, insofar as we know Truth at all, that all religions possess a mixture of truth and error, and that they all retain certain mythological elements behind which we have to get in order to find Reality itself. We might be inclined to accept, with the Hindu, that 'God has a million faces', that he is to be found in every expression of life and of living; and that really it is quite impossible – in any bland sort of way – to compare one religion with another so as to elicit which is 'the best', or so as to put them into some arbitrary rank-order.

We may find religions which represent the Lowest Common

Multiple of all religions; we may discover others which seek to distil their Highest Common Factor. We may seek desperately to go beyond all the 'Isms' to discover something which we feel has engendered Truth-in-Itself and which is the Ground of all Reality. In the end, the most important question for us may be (as so many have pointed out) not '*where* am I going?', but '*who* is going where?'. In other words, our solution to our problem of Truth and Reality may well be discovered in a much deeper understanding of who and what we ourselves really are.

This work is not an attempt to solve any of those problems. At best it is a statement of such enigmas and a description of the ways in which Man has from the beginning of recorded time sought to answer or just to explicate his own questionings. It is left to the reader to examine more closely the wonderful wealth of material in our religious and philosophical inheritance, in order to see whether it is possible to find the solution to his personal problems, in a deeper, as well as broader, study of religion.

End Notes

CHAPTER ONE

1. Walker, K. *Diagnosis of Man*. Penguin Books, 1962, 178
2. John 10.16
3. St Matthew 25.31-46
4. *Vide* Morrish, Ivor. *Disciplines of Education*. Allen & Unwin, 1967
5. Marwick, A. *The Nature of History*. Macmillan & Co, 1970, 132
6. *Vide* Bottomore, T B, *Sociology*. Allen & Unwin, 2nd edn 1971, 13-84; Cotgrove S. *The Science of Society*. Allen & Unwin, 1976
7. *Vide* Durkheim E. *The Elementary Forms of Religious Life*. Allen & Unwin, 1960
8. Hobhouse L T. *Morals in Evolution*. London, 7th edn 1951
9. *Vide* Weber, M. *The Protestant Ethic and the Spirit of Capitalism*. Allen & Unwin, 1930
10. *Vide* Berger,P L & T Luckmann. *The Social Construction of Reality*. Penguin, 1967
11. Cf Berger, P L. *A Rumour of Angels*. Penguin, 1971
12. Thouless, R H. *General and Social Psychology*. University Tutorial Press, 4th edn 1963, 1of
13. Freud, S. *The Future of an Illusion*. Hogarth Press, 1928
14. Lee, R S. *Freud and Christianity*. Penguin, 1967, 11
15. Jung, C G. *Psychology and Religion: West and East*. Routledge & Kegan Paul, 1958, 42
16. Jung, C G. *Psychology and Alchemy*. Routledge & Kegan Paul, 1953, 12ff

17. Thouless, R H, op cit, 437

18. Starbuck, E D. *The Psychology of Religion.* New York, 1903

19. *Vide* Goldman, R. *Religious Thinking from Childhood to Adolescence.* Routledge & Kegan Paul, 1964; and Goldman, R. *Readiness for Religion.* Routledge & Kegan Paul, 1965

20. Cf Huxley, Aldous. 'The Minimum Working Hypothesis' in Isherwood, C (ed). *Vedanta for the Western World.* Allen & Unwin, 1948, 33-35

21. Galloway, C. *The Philosophy of Religion.* T & T Clark, 1945, 52

22. *Vide* Robinson , J A T. *Honest to God.* SCM Press, 1963

23. James, E O. *Comparative Religion.* Methuen, rev edn 1961, 33

24. Ibid, 33

25. Berger, P L. *A Rumour of Angels.* op cit, 80

26. Yeats, W B. 'He wishes for the Cloths of Heaven', 1899

CHAPTER TWO

1. Stephens Spinks, G. *Psychology and Religion.* Methuen, 1963, 73

2. Eliade, Mircea. *Myths, Dreams and Mysteries.* Harvill Press, 1960, 32

3. Eliot, T S. *Murder in the Cathedral* Faber, 1935, 69

4. Eliade, Mircea. *Patterns in Comparative Religion.* Sheed & Ward, 1958, 432-433

5. *Vide* McConnell, Ursula. *Myths of the Munkan.* Melbourne University Press, 1957, Chapter 30, 128-130

6. *Vide* ibid, 119-124

7. *Vide* Rattray, R S. *Akan-Ashanti Folk-Tales.* Clarendon Press, Oxford, 1930

8. *Vide* Morrish, Ivor. *Obeah, Christ and Rastaman: Jamaica and Its Religion.* James Clarke & Co, 1982, 21-22 & 44-45

9. Goethe, J W. *Faust: Part Two.* Penguin Books, 1959, Act I, 75-80

10. *Vide* Jung C G. *Symbols of Transformation.* Routledge & Kegan Paul, 1956, 291

11. Adapted from Bellows, H A (tr). *The Poetic Edda.* New York, 1923

12. *Vide* Morrish, Ivor. *The Dark Twin.* L N Fowler & Co, 1980

13. Eliot, T S. *Selected Poems.* Faber, 1954, 109

14. *Vide* Cohn, N. *The Pursuit of the Millennium.* Paladin, 1970, *passim*

15. *Vide* Morrish, Ivor. *Obeah, Christ and Rastaman*, Chapter 11

16. *Vide* Worsley, P. *The Trumpet Shall Sound*. Shocken Books, 1968, *passim*

17. *Vide* Radin, P. *Hero Cycles of the Winnebago*. Indiana Pub, 1948, *passim*

18. *Vide* Lessa, W A. '*Discoverer-of-the-Sun*: Mythology as a Reflection of Culture', *Journal of American Folklore*, Special Issue, 1966, 3-51

19. *Vide* Rattray, R S, op cit, 76-81

20. Ibid, 5-6

21. *Vide* Bartsch, H W (ed). *Kerygma and Myth*. SPCK, 1953, Vol I, 1ff, 'New Testament and Mythology'

22. Tillich, P. *The Protestant Era*. Univ of Chicago Press, 1948, 18ff

23. *Vide* Calder, N. *The Key to the Universe*. BBC, 1977

24. Vaihinger, H. *The Philosophy of 'As If '*. Routledge, 1968, *passim*

25. Quoted by Hazel E Barnes in *An Existentialist Ethics*. Vintage Books/Random House, 1967, 105

26. From 'Dry Salvages' in T S Eliot. *Four Quartets*, Faber, 1942

27. Eliot T S. *Murder in the Cathedral*, op cit, 24

28. For some account of the 'myths' of tomorrow, *vide* Zamyatin, T, *We*, Penguin,1972; A Huxley, A. *Brave New World*. Penguin, 1955; and Orwell, G. *Nineteen Eighty-Four*. Penguin, 1954

29. *Vide* Plato. *The Republic*. Oxford Univ Press, 3rd edn 1928, *passim*

30. *Vide* Jung C G, op cit, *passim*

31. Jung identified an archaic figure within himself, called Philemon, corresponding to the Wise Old Man. *Vide* his *Memories, Dreams, Reflections*. Collins & Routledge, 1963, 175-176

32. *Vide* Mannheim, Karl. *Diagnosis of Our Time*. Routledge & Kegan Paul, 1943, Chapter VII, 100-165

33. *Vide* Eliade, Mircea. *Patterns in Comparative Religion*, op cit, 431

34. *Vide* Barthes, R. *Mythologies*. Paladin, 1973, 'The World of Wrestling', 15-25

35. For a discussion of such social construction *vide* Berger, P L & T Luckmann. *The Social Construction of Reality*, Penguin, 1967, 122-134

36. *Vide* Calder, N, op cit, *passim*

37. Ibid, 93

38. Ibid, 94

39. Ibid, 193 with reference to Professor Fred Hoyle

40. *Vide* Brunton, P. *The Wisdom of the Overself.* Rider & Co

41. *Vide* Radhakrishnan , S. *The Hindu View of Life.* Allen & Unwin, 1927. Cf also Marlow, A N (ed). *Radhakrishnan: An Anthology.* Allen & Unwin, 1952, *passim*

42. Galatians 2.20

43. *Vide* for example, Williamson, G H. *Road in the Sky.* Neville Spearman, 1959; Brother Philip. *Secret of the Andes.* Neville Spearman, 1961; Kraspedon, D. *My Contact with Flying Saucers.* Neville Spearman, 1959

44. *Vide* Jung, C G. *Civilization in Transition.* Routledge & Kegan Paul, 1964, 'Flying Saucers: A Modern Myth'

45. Cf the psychological symbolism and religious mythology implied in Auden, W H & C Isherwood. *The Ascent of F6*, Faber 1936

46. Donnelly, I. *Atlantis: The Antediluvian World.* Sidgwick & Jackson, 1950; Spence, L. *The Problem of Atlantis.* Rider & Co, 1924; Saurat, D. *Atlantis and the Giants*, Faber, 1957

47. *Vide* Lewis, I M. *Ecstatic Religion.* Penguin, 1971, *passim*

48. *Vide* Guillaume, A. *Prophecy and Divination among the Hebrews and other Semites.* London, 1938

49. *Vide* Sargant, W. *Battle for the Mind.* Pan Books, 1959, 79-127. Cf also Deren, Maya. *Divine Horsemen; The Living Gods of Haiti.* Thames & Hudson, 1953

50. *Vide* Tolkien, J R R. *The Hobbit. Allen* & Unwin, 1937; and *The Lord of the Rings.* Allen & Unwin, 1954-56

51. Wittgenstein, L. *Tractatus Logico-Philosophicus.* Routledge & Kegan Paul, 2nd edn 1971, para 5.6

52. Maranda, P (ed). *Mythology.* Penguin, 1972, 12f (author's own italics)

53. *Vide* Malinowski, B. *Myth in Primitive Psychology* London, 1926, 21, where he suggests that the role of myth is to consolidate and stabilize society, and to fulfil its purposes as a cultural force and sociological charter.

54. McConnell, Ursula, op cit, 163

CHAPTER THREE

1. *Vide* Jung, C G. *The Structure & Dynamics of the Psyche.* Routledge & Kegan Paul, 1960, 'Synchronicity: An Acausal Connecting Principle'

2. *Vide* Gennep, A Van. *The Rites of Passage.* Routledge & Kegan Paul, 1960

3. Ibid

4. Deren, Maya. *Divine Horsemen: The Living Gods of Haiti.* Thames & Hudson, 1953, 220-224

5. Ibid, 221

6. Layard, J. *Stone Men of Malekula: Vao.* Chatto & Windus, 1942, 12

7. St Matthew 18.3

8. James, E O. *Comparative Religion.* Methuen, rev edn 1961, 86-87

9. Ibid, 88

10. *Vide* James, E O. *History of Religions.* Hodder & Stoughton, 1956, 32ff

11. *Vide* Rattray, R S. *Ashanti.* Oxford, Clarendon Press, 1923 & *Akan-Ashanti Folk-Tales.* Oxford, Clarendon Press, 1932

12. Morrish, Ivor. *Obeah, Christ & Rastaman.* James Clarke & Co, 1982, Chapter Ten

13. Henriques, F M. *Family & Colour in Jamaica.* MacGibbon & Kee, 1968, 145

14. Deren, Maya, op cit, 197-198

15. *Vide* Forrest, E R. *The Snake Dance of the Hopi Indians.* Tower Pub Inc, NY, 1961, *passim*

16. James, E O. *Comparative Religion*, op cit, 79

17. *Vide* Robinson, R. *The Feathered Serpent.* Edwards & Shaw, Sydney, 1956

18. Eliade, Mircea. *Patterns of Comparative Religion.* Sheed & Ward, 1958, Chapters VIII & IX

19. *Vide* Ezekiel 8.14

20. *Vide* Genesis 1.2 (*tehom* means 'the deep')

21. Deren, Maya, op cit, 209ff

22. Ibid, 20

23. *Vide* Frazer, J G. *The Golden Bough.* Macmillan, abridged edn, 1922, Chapter 50, 'Eating the God'

24. *Vide* Genesis 4.3ff

25. *Vide* Vaillant, G C. *The Aztecs of Mexico*. Penguin, 1950, Chapter X & Chapter XI on Religion & Ritual

26. Deren, Maya, op cit, 196

27. Homans, G C. 'Anxiety & Ritual: The Theories of Malinowski and Radcliffe-Brown', *American Anthropologist*, Vol 43, April-June, 1941, 164-172

28. Ibid, 172

29. Eliade, Mircea. *Birth and Rebirth*. Harvill Press, 1961, 59

30. Deren, Maya, op cit, 188

31. *Vide* Bocock, R. *Ritual in Industrial Society*. Allen & Unwin, 1973, 21 & 37

CHAPTER FOUR

1. *Vide* James, E O. *History of Religions*. Hodder & Stoughton, 1964, 26

2. Marett, R R. *The Threshold of Religion*. Methuen, 1914, Introduction, xxxi

3. *Vide* Layard, J. *Stone Men of Malekula: Vao*. Chatto & Windus, 1942

4. Vide Tylor, E B. *Primitive Culture*. Harpers, 1958

5. *Vide* Lang, A. *The Making of Religion*. London, 1898

6. *Vide* Schmidt, W. *Origin and Growth of Religion*. Methuen, 1931

7. Marett, R R, op cit

8. Ibid, 39

9. *Vide* Codrington, R H. *The Melanesians*. Oxford, Clarendon Press, 1891

10. *Vide* Durkheim, E. *The Elementary Forms of Religious Life*. Allen & Unwin, 1926

11. Rex, J. 'Emile Durkheim' in Raison, T (ed). *The Founding Fathers of Social Science*. Penguin, 1969, 132

12. Wach, J. *Sociology of Religion*. Univ of Chicago Press, 1962, 5

13. *Vide* Radcliffe-Brown, A R. *Structure & Function in Primitive Society*. Cohen & West, 1952

14. *Vide* Lévy-Bruhl, L. *Primitive Mentality*. Macmillan, 1923; and *How Natives Think*. Allen & Unwin, 1926

15. James, E O. *Comparative Religion*. Methuen, rev edn 1961, 511

16. *Vide* Lévi-Strauss, C. *Totemism*. Beacon Press, 1963; and *The Savage Mind*. Weidenfeld & Nicolson, 1965

17. Otto, R. *The Idea of the Holy*. Oxford Univ Press, 1925, xvi, 7, 15ff, 31ff, 228ff

18. Ibid

19. *Vide* James, W. *Varieties of Religious Experience*. Longmans, Green & Co, 1929

20. Genesis 28.17

21. James, E O. *Comparative Religion*, op cit, 55

22. *Vide* Lévy-Bruhl, L. *Primitive Mentality*, op cit.

23. Douglas, Mary. *Purity and Danger*. Routledge & Kegan Paul, 1966, 88

24. *Vide* Lévy-Bruhl, L. *Primitive Mentality*, op cit

25. *Vide* Rivers, W H R. *Medicine, Magic and Religion*. London, 1929

26. *Vide* Malinowski, B. 'Magic, Science and Religion', in Needham, J (ed). *Science, Religion and Reality*. Macmillan, 1925, 1984

27. *Vide* Evans-Pritchard, E E. *Witchcraft, Oracles and Magic among the Azande*. Oxford, Clarendon Press, 1956

28. *Vide* Evans-Pritchard, E E. *Nuer Religion*. Oxford, Clarendon Press, 1956

29. *Vide* Spencer, B & F J Gillen. *Native Tribes of Central Australia*. London, 1938

30. James, E O. *Comparative Religion*, op cit, 63

31. *Vide* Spencer, B & F J Gillen. *The Arunta*. Macmillan, 1927

32. *Vide* Evans-Pritchard, E E. *Nuer Religion*, op cit

33. Ibid, Chapter 5, 124-125

CHAPTER FIVE

1. *Yasna* 30

2. *Vide* Zaehner, R C. *Zurvan, A Zoroastrian Dilemma*. Oxford, Clarendon Press, 1955

CHAPTER SIX

1. *Vide* Spate, O H K. *India and Pakistan: A General & Regional Geography*. Methuen, 1957, 145

2. James, E O. *The Ancient Gods.* Weidenfeld & Nicolson, 1960, 26

3. Piggott, S. *Prehistoric India.* Penguin, 1950, 169

4. *Vide* Zinkin, Taya. *Caste Today.* Oxford Univ Press, 1962, *passim*

5. Wint, G. *The British in India.* Faber, 1947, 41

6. Zinkin, Taya, op cit, 1

7. Sen, K M. *Hinduism.* Penguin, 1961, 28, n 1

8. *Rig-Veda* x.90

9. *Bhavishya Purana, Brahma Parva,* 41,45

10. Prabhavananda, Swami & C Isherwood (trs). *Bhagavad-Gita.* Phoenix House Ltd, 1947, 36

11. *Vide* Sen, K M, op cit, 53; and Prabhavanada, Swami & F Manchester (trs). *The Upanishads.* New American Library, 1957, x

12. *Chandogya Upanishad,* VI Prapathaka, 2nd Khanda; *vide* Sen, K M, op cit, 134

13. *Brihadaranyaka Upanishad,* 1, 3, 27. *Vide* Prabhananda, Swami & F Manchester (trs), op cit, 80

14. Sen, K M, op cit, 122, from *Svetasvatara Upanishad*

15. *Vide* Prabhavananda, Swami & F Manchester, op cit, 80-112

16. *Vide* Dutt, R C (tr). *The Ramayana and the Mahabharata.* J M Dent, 1910

17. Tomlin, E W F. *The Eastern Philosophers: An Introduction.* Hutchinson, 1968, 232

18. Coster G. *Yoga and Western Psychology.* Oxford Univ Press, 1934, 107, Sutra 40

19. Prabhavananda, Swami & C Isherwood (trs), op cit, 83

20. to 27. Ibid, 52, 64, 104, 104, 130, 60, 171, 73

28. *Vide* Isherwood, C. *Vedanta for the Western World.* Allen & Unwin, 1948, 150-151.

29. *Vide* Parrinder, G. *The World's Living Religions.* Pan Books Ltd, 1964, 42

30. *Vide* Oakley, R (ed). *New Backgrounds.* Oxford Univ Press, 1968, Chapter III, 'The Indian Background' by Roger T Bell, 55

31. James, E O. *Comparative Religion.* Methuen, 1961, 151

32. Sen, K M, op cit, 57

33. Eliade, Mircea. *Patterns in Comparative Religion.* Sheed & Ward,

1958, 459-460

34. *Vide* Grant R M & D N Freedman. *The Secret Sayings of Jesus.* Collins, 1960, 167

35. *Vide* Jung, C G. *Psychology and Religion: West & East.* Routledge & Kegan Paul, 1958, 107-200

36. *Vide* Prabhavananda Swami & F Manchester (trs), op cit, 63-78

37. Ibid, 70

38. Ibid, 68

39. Prabhavananda, Swami & C Isherwood (trs), op cit, 145

40. *Chandogya Upanishad*, 5. 3f

41. Jeremiah 31. 29 (Moffatt's translation)

42. Ezekiel 18. 1-20 (Moffatt)

43. Galatians 6.8 (Moffatt)

CHAPTER SEVEN

1. James E O. *Comparative Religion.* Methuen, 1961, 167

2. *Akaranga Sutra*, Book VI

CHAPTER NINE

1. Storr, A. *The Integrity of the Personality.* Penguin, 1963, 36

2. *Vide* Mascaro, J (tr). *The Dhammapada: The Path of Perfection*, Penguin, 1975, 50, Chapter 8, verses 100-101

3. Ibid, 52-53, Chapter 9, verses 116 & 127

4. Ibid, 29-30

5. Ibid, 31

6. Ibid, 38-39, Chapter 2, verses 21, 28 & 32

7. Ibid, 48, Chapter 7, verse 90

8. Ibid, 48-49, Chapter 7, verses 90, 95 (in part), 97

9. James, E O. *History of Religions.* Hodder & Stoughton, 1961, 83

10. Bhikku, Ven Kapilavaddho. *An Introduction to Buddhist Philosophy.* English Sangha Trust Ltd, 1957, 34-35

11. The formula still repeated by millions of Buddhists.

12. Thapar, Romila. *A History of India: Vol I.* Penguin, 1966, 85

13. Parrinder, G. *The World's Living Religions.* Pan Books Ltd, 1964, 86

14. Humphreys, C. *Buddhism.* Penguin, rev edn 1955, 203

15. *Vide* Radhakrishnan, S. *Indian Philosophy, Vol I*. Allen & Unwin, 1931, 589-590

16. *Vide* Burtt, E A (ed). *The Teachings of the Compassionate Buddha*. New American Library, 1955, Book Two, 123-241

17. Cf St Matthew 10.39: 'He that findeth his life shall lose it: and he that loseth his life for my sake shall find it.'

CHAPTER TEN

1. Vide Ware, J R (tr). *The Sayings of Confucius*. Mentor, New American Library, 1955, 11.16

2. Ibid, 5.27

3. Ibid, 5.12

4. Ibid, 4.15

5. Ibid, 15.24

6. to 13 Ibid, 2.14, 4.16, 6.22, 9.29, 12.1, 13.23, 13.26, 14.23

14. *Vide* Ibid, 17.5

15. Ibid, 4.14

16. Ibid, 2.15

17. Ibid, 2.17

18. Ibid, 12.22

19. Ibid, 12.1

20. Ibid, 14.28

21. Ibid, 7.21

22. Ibid, 11.12

23. *Vide* Lau, D C (tr). *Lau Tzu: Tao Te Ching*. Penguin, 1963; and Blakney, R B (tr). *The Way of Life: Tao Te-Ching*. Mentor, New American Library, 1960

24. Blakney's translation, Chapter 25

25. Ibid, Chapter 56

26. Ibid, Chapters 8 & 78

27. Lau, D C (tr), op cit, 42

28. *Vide* Van Over, R. *Taoist Tales*. Mentor, New American Library, 1973, 8

29. Blakney's translation, Chapter 17

30. Ibid, Chapter 11

31. Ibid, Chapter 29

32. *Vide* Calder, N. *The Key to the Universe*. BBC, 1977, 93

33. *Vide* Blakney's translation, Chapter 30

34. *Vide* Monlin, Chiang. *Tides from the West*. Yale Univ Press, 1947

35. *Vide* Tomlin, E W F. *The Eastern Philosophers: An Introduction*. Hutchinson, rev edn 1968, 277

36. Yang, C K. 'The Functional Relationship Between Confucian Thought and Chinese Religion' in Fairbank, J K (ed). *Chinese Thought and Institutions*. Univ of Chicago Press, 1967, 282

CHAPTER ELEVEN

1. Reps, P (ed). *Zen Flesh, Zen Bones*. Penguin, 1971, 94

2. Thomas, Dylan. *Collected Poems: 1934-52*. J M Dent, 1952, 21, 'Light Breaks Where No Sun Shines'

3. Humphreys, C. *Zen: A Way of Life*. English Univ Press, 1962, 99

4. Watts, A W. *The Way of Zen*. Penguin, 1962, 153, quoted from the Zen poet, P'ang-yun

5. Ibid, 154, quoted from *Zenrin Kushu*, an anthology of some five thousand two-line poems compiled during the fifteenth century AD

6. *Vide* Beveridge W I B. *The Art of Scientific Investigation*. Heinemann, 1950, Chapter on 'Intuition'

7. Quoted by Watts, A W, op cit, 146

8. Eliot, T S. *Selected Poems*. Faber, 1961, 12, 'The Love Song of J Alfred Prufrock':

> Time for you and time for me,
> And time yet for a hundred indecisions,
> And for a hundred visions and revisions,
> Before the taking of a toast and tea.

9. Brooke, R. *The Poetical Works* (Keynes G ed). Faber, 1970, 110-11, 'Dining- Room Tea'

10. *Vide* Vaughan, H. 'The World':

> I saw Eternity the other night,
> Like a Ring of pure and endless light,
> All calm as it was bright;
> And round beneath it, Time, in hours, days, years,

Driv'n by the spheres,
Like a vast shadow mov'd; in which the world
And all her train were hurl'd.

11. *Vide* Herrigel, E. *Zen in the Art of Archery*. NY, Pantheon, 1953

12. Cf Reps, P, op cit, 23, No 9 'The Moon Cannot Be Stolen'

13. Thomsen, H. *The New Religions of Japan*. C E Tuttle, Tokyo, 1963, 28

14. *Vide* Makiguchi, T. *The Theory of Value*. Tokyo, Soka Gakkai, 1953, 'Introduction'

15. This teaching is recorded in the book by Yoshihei Kohira, *Shakufuku Kyoten*, Tokyo, 1951, or 'The Book of Purgation', which all Soka Gakkai believers have to study before they can become full members.

CHAPTER TWELVE

1. *Vide* Ezekiel 8.13f, 'Then he added, 'You shall see still worse'; and he took me to the outer door of the north gateway into the Eternal's temple, where I saw women wailing for Tammuz'.

2. *Vide* Genesis 12.6-8; 14.7; 35.8-14; Exodus 3.2-5; Joshua 15.7

3. *Vide* Genesis 1.1 where even the name for God, *Elohim*, is plural in form.

4. *Vide* Leviticus 16.7-10 which describes the sacrifice of one goat as a sin-offering to Yahweh, and another goat which was sent off alive, into the wilderness for the desert-demon Azazel.

5. *Vide* Leviticus 6.27-30; Leviticus 11

6. *Vide* I Samuel 12.16-18; I Kings 17

7. *Vide* Genesis 31.19-20; 35.8-14

8. *Vide* Exodus 3.14

9. Exodus 3.15. The tetragrammaton YHWH was considered too sacred to utter; this was certainly so from AD 70, although it was seldom uttered after 300 BC. Instead, when reading the scriptures, the Hebrew word *Adonai* or Lord was used. This explains the Septuagint *ho kurios* and the Vulgate *Dominus*, and hence LORD of the English versions. The word *Elohim* (God) was also substituted. The vowels of these substitutes (ie the Massoretic points) were inserted into the consonants YHWH, and the mediaeval (Christian) misformation 'Jehovah' was the conflation

of the consonants of one word with the vowels of another. This form was popularized during the Renaissance.

10. *Vide* II Kings 5.18

11. *Vide* Jeremiah 7.30-34; 8.lf; 9.13-16; 19.5 & 13; 32.35

12. *Vide* II Chronicles 36.23 & Ezra 6.3-5

13. *Vide* Isaiah 45.1 & 47.1

14. James E O. *History of Religions.* Hodder & Stoughton, 1964, 125

15. Eg the Book of Daniel; I Enoch, Chapters 1-36, 83-104; and the Testament of the Twelve Patriarchs.

16. I Maccabees 1.44

17. *Vide Talmud: Niddah* 31b

18. Cf Gaster, T H. *The Scriptures of the Dead Sea Sect.* Secker & Warburg, 1957, 'The Manual of Discipline', iii.13-iv.26, pages 53-56

19. Deuteronomy 6.4-9

20. Leviticus 19.18

21. Exodus 11.2

22. Matthew 5.43

23. Proverbs 25.21

24. Proverbs 24.17

25. *Vide* Gaster, T H, op cit, 'The Zadokite Document', vi.11-vii.6a, pages 78-79

26. *Vide* Numbers 16.20ff; Amos 9.2; Isaiah 7.11; Genesis 37.25; Isaiah 38.10; Psalm 6.5; Psalm 31.17; Psalm 115.17; Psalm 49.19

27. Psalm 88.10; Isaiah 14.9-10; Isaiah 26.14; Ezekiel 32.17-32

28. *Vide* Job 26.6; Proverbs 15.11; Psalm 139.8

29. Isaiah 26.19 (Moffatt's translation)

30. Wisdom of Solomon 3.1-5. Cf also Daniel 12.2-3

31. *Vide* Schonfield, H J (tr). *The Authentic New Testament.* Panther Book, 1962

32. *Vide* Isaiah, Chapters 42, 49, 50, 52-53

33. Rayner, J D. *Towards Mutual Understanding Between Jews and Christians.* Clarke & Co, 1960, 30-31

34. *Vide* Genesis 1.5,8, 13, 19, 23, 31; and 2.2-3

35. *Vide* Deuteronomy 16.1-8; Exodus 12.13

36. *Vide* Deuteronomy 16. 10-12

37. *Vide* Numbers 29.1

38. Deuteronomy 16.13-20

39. Leviticus 16.29-34

40. *Vide* I Enoch, Chapters 1-36

41. Ibid, Chapters 91-104

42. *Vide* II. Enoch (The Secrets of Enoch)

43. *Vide* The Sibylline Oracles

44. *Vide* The Testament of the Twelve Patriarchs

45. *Vide* II Baruch (The Apocalypse of Baruch):
   'They shall be made like angels and changed into every
   form they desire, from beauty into loveliness and from
   light into the splendour of glory.'

46. *Vide* Allegro, J M. *The Dead Sea Scrolls*. Penguin, 1956; Vermes,
G. *The Dead Sea Scrolls in English*. Penguin, 1990; Burrows, Millar. *The
Dead Sea Scrolls*. Viking Press, 1956; Silberman, N A. *The Hidden Scrolls*.
Putnam, 1994

47. Rayner, J D, op cit, 19

CHAPTER THIRTEEN

1. *Psalms of Solomon*, circa 70-40 BC; a pseudonymous work

2. *I Enoch*, second to first century BC; another work from the
Pseudepigrapha

3. *Testament of the Twelve Patriarchs*, circa 109-106 BC

4. *Vide* Gwatkin, H M. *Selections from Early Christian Writers*.
Macmillan & Co, 1929, section IX, 26-31

5. Ibid, section I, 2-3

6. These include the *Protevangelium of James, the Gospel of the Pseudo-
Matthew*, the *Gospel of the Nativity of Mary*, and the *History of Joseph the
Carpenter*

7. St Luke 2.47 (Moffatt's translation)

8. Ibid, 2.49 (Moffatt)

9. *Vide* ibid 2.52

10. St Mark 6.3

11. St Matthew 3.16 (Moffatt)

12. St Luke 4.13 (Moffatt)

13. *Vide* Huck, A. *A Synopsis of the First Three Gospels.* J C B Mohr (Paul Siebeck)/ Tubingen, 9th edn, 1936

14. For example, *Gospel According to St Peter, Gospel of the Ebionites, Gospel According to the Egyptians, Protevangelium of James, Gospel of the Pseudo- Matthew, Gospel of the Nativity of Mary, History of Joseph the Carpenter, Assumption of Mary, Gospel of Thomas, Gospel of Nicodemus*

15. St Luke 15.1-4

16. St John 20.31

17. *Vide* St John 20.20

18. *Vide* St John 21.25

19. *Vide* St Matthew, chapters 5-, 'Sermon on the Mount'

20. St Matthew 5.48

21. *Vide* St Matthew 5.43-45

22. St Luke 6.36-37

23. *Vide* St Matthew 18.21-22

24. *Vide* St Luke 7.47-48

25. *Vide* Acts 6.14

26. *Vide* Galatians 3.28

27. Gwatkin, HM, op cit, section IX, 30-31

28. *Vide* de Burgh, W G. *The Legacy of the Ancient World.* Penguin, 1961, 324-325

29. Marcus Aurelius, *Meditations*, xi.3

30. *Vide* Gwatkin, H M, op cit, section LXVI, 162-163

31. Romans 1.17; 5.20f; 6.5; 11.15

32 *Vide* St Matthew 16.18f

33. The Bodily Assumption of Mary into heaven was defined as a dogma of the Catholic Faith by Pope Pius XII in November 1950 by the Apostolic Constitution *Munificentissimus Deus* (*Acta Apostolicae Sedis*, Rome, XLII, 753ff); and in an Encyclical Letter, *Ad Caeli Reginam*, of October 11, 1954, Pope Pius instituted a feast to be observed yearly in honour of Mary's 'regalis dignitas' as Queen of Heaven and Earth (*Acta Apostolicae Sedis, Rome*, XLVI, 625ff.)

CHAPTER FOURTEEN

1. Guillaume, A. *Islam.* Penguin, 2nd edn, 1956, 2

2. *Vide* ibid 12

3. *Vide* Dawood, N J (tr). *The Koran.* Penguin, 3rd edn, 1968, 'The Elephant'

4. Guillaume, A, op cit, 23

5. *Vide* Isaiah 40.6-8 (AV)

6. *The Koran* , sura 96

7. *Vide* Guillaume, A, op cit, 40

8. *The Koran*, sura 9. The passage reads:

'Fight those who do not believe in Allah, and do not forbid what God and his apostle have forbidden, and do not follow the true religion of those to whom scriptures were given, until they pay tribute out of hand, and are utterly subdued. The Jews say that Ezra is the son of Allah, while the Christians say that the Christ is the son of Allah... May Allah confound them; how perverse they are!'

9. Morgan, K W (ed). *Islam – The Straight Path; Islam Interpreted by Muslims*, article by Mohammaed Abd Allah. Ronald Press, 1958, 40

10. *The Koran*, sura 6

11. Ibid, sura 4

12. Ibid, sura 76: 'Let him that will, take the right path to his Lord. Yet you cannot will, except by the will of Allah.'

13. Ibid, sura 74: 'Let him who will, take heed. But none takes heed except by the will of Allah.'

14. Ibid, sura 10

15. *Vide* Numbers 22.22; Judges 9.23; I Samuel 16.14,15,23; II Samuel 24.1ff; I Kings 22.19ff; Isaiah 45.7 ('I form light and I make darkness; I make peace and I create evil.' – Moffatt's translation)

16. *Vide* Romans 3.28-30

17. *Vide* Genesis 3.15, St John 14.16

18. *Vide* II Corinthians 12.2

19. *Vide* Isaiah 1.2

20. *Vide The Koran*, sura 19, 'Mary'; and suras 3 & 4

21. Ibid, sura 5

22. Ibid, sura 81

23. Ibid, sura 86

24. Ibid, sura 62

25. Ibid, sura 76

26. Ibid, sura 42

27. Ibid, sura 23

28. Ibid, sura 30

29. Ibid, sura 4

30. Ibid, sura 109

31. Ibid, sura 112

32. Ibid, sura 29

33. Ibid, sura 2

34. *Vide* ibid, sura 4

35. *Vide* ibid, sura 33

36. Ibid, sura 2

37. Ibid, sura 2 ('there shall be no compulsion in religion').

38. Ibid, sura 109 ('Unto you your religion, and unto me my religion') Objections to Judaism and Christianity were based almost entirely upon their *alleged* 'polytheism'.

39. Ibid, sura 9 ('Will you not fight against those who have broken their oaths and conspired to banish the apostle?')

40. Ibid, sura 75

41. Ibid, sura 21 ('We breathed into her who was chaste Our Spirit, and we made both her and her son a sign to all men')

42. Ibid, sura 15 ('And when I have made him a complete man and breathed into him my spirit, fall down prostrating yourselves before him')

43. Guillaume, A, op cit, 199

44. *The Koran*, sura 30

45. Guillaume, A, op cit, 125

46. Abu Bakr al-Kalabadhi. *The Doctrine of the Sufis* (tr by A J Arberry), Cambridge Univ Press, 1935, 6 (The writer lived in the 10th century AD)

47. *The Koran*, sura 50

48. Happold, F C. *Mysticism*. Penguin, 1963, 232

CHAPTER FIFTEEN

1. Cohn, N. *The Pursuit of the Millennium*. Paladin, 1970

2. Ibid, 13

3. *Vide* Wilson, B R, 'A typology of sect in a dynamic and comparative

perspective', in *Archives de Sociologie de Religion*, Vol 16, 1963, 49-63; Thrupp, Sylvia (ed). *Millennial Dreams in Action: Essays in Comparative Study*. NY, Humanities Press, 1962; Wilson, B R, 'Millennialism in comparative perspective' in *Comp St Soc Hist*, Vol 6, 1963, 93-114

4. St John 14.16 & 26

5. Lanternari, V. *The Religion of the Oppressed*. New American Library, 1965, 97

6. *Vide* Morrish, Ivor. *Obeah, Christ and Rastaman*. James Clarke & Co, 1982, Chapter 11

7. *Vide* Bastide, R. *Les Religions Africaines au Brésil*. Paris, Presses Universitaires de France, 1960; Herskovits, M J, 'African Gods and Catholic Saints in New World Religious Beliefs', *American Anthropologist*, 39: 635-643, 1937

8. Williams, E, 'Religious Pluralism and Class Structure: Brazil and Chile', in Robertson, R (ed). *Sociology of Religion: Selected Readings*. Penguin, 1969, 210-211

9. *Vide* Morrish, Ivor, op cit, Chapter 8

10. Lanternari, V, op cit, 160

11. *Vide* Fernandez, J W, 'African Religious Movements – Types & Dynamics', *Journal of Modern African Studies*, Vol 2, 1964, 531-549

12. *Vide* Williams, F E. *The Valaila Madness and the Destruction of Native Ceremonies in the Gulf Division*. Papuan Anthropology Reports, No 4, Port Moresby, 1923

13. Worsley, P. *The Trumpet Shall Sound: A Study of Cargo Cults in Melanesia*. Shocken Books, 2nd edn, 1968, 153

14. Ibid, 255

15. *Vide* Lanternari, V, op cit, 191-210

16 Ibid, 209

17. Fall, B B, 'The Political-Religious Sects of Viet-Nam', *Pacific Affairs*, New York, XXVIII, 3, 1955, 243-253

CHAPTER SIXTEEN

1. *Vide* Evans C. *Cults of Unreason*. Harrap & Co, 1973, *passim*

2. Joanna Southcott (1750-1814), when over fifty, announced that she was about to give birth to a divine being called Siloh. She had all the

symptoms of pregnancy and, in 1814, was examined by a Royal physician who said she was undoubtedly 'with child'. She went into labour, but produced nothing, and she died soon after. Her condition was what today would be called a 'hysterical pregnancy'.

3. *Vide* Eddy, Mary Baker. *Science and Health with Key to the Scriptures*. The First Church of Christ Scientist, Boston, Mass, 1875, rev edn 1906, 311, lines 7-8

4. Peel R. *Christian Science: Its Encounter with American Culture*. H Holt, 1958, 123

5. *Vide* Eddy, Mary Baker, op cit, 411

6. Ibid, 169

7. *Vide* Weatherhead, L D. *Psychology, Religion and Healing*. London, 1951

8. Eddy, Mary Baker, op cit, 591, lines 21-22

9. Ibid, 591, lines 16-20

10. *Vide Aid to Bible Understanding*. NY, Watch Tower Bible & Tract Society, 1971, article 'Abel', 13

11. *Vide Then is Finished the Mystery of God*. NY, Watch Tower Bible & Tract Society, 1969, *passim*

12. Revelation 16.14

13. *Vide Aid to Bible Understanding*, op cit, 714-715, article 'Har-Magedon'

14. Ibid, 1400b, article 'Resurrection'

15. *Vide* ibid, 7

16. Ibid, 885. *Vide* article 'Jehovah', 882-894

17. *Vide* Preface to Smith, Joseph (tr). *The Book of Mormon*. Deseret Enterprises Ltd, Manchester, 1971

18. Ibid

19. Ibid, 3 Nephi, Chapters 11-26

20. Ibid, 3 Nephi 15.21. Cf St John 10.16

21. *Vide* I Kings 11.3

22. 3 Nephi 28.7

23. *Vide* The Words of Mormon, 132-133

24. *Vide* Mormon, 6.6;

25. *Vide* Mormon, Chapters 8 & 9

26. Mormon 9.32-34

27. Cf 3 Nephi 12 with St Matthew 5 ('Sermon on the Mount')

28. *Vide* Ether 5, passim

29. *Vide* Besant, Annie. *The Ancient Wisdom*. Theosophical Pub House, 1897, *passim*

30. Ibid, Chapter 1

31. *Vide* Isherwood, C (ed). *Vedanta for the Western World*. Allen & Unwin, 1948

32. Ibid, 1-28

33. Ibid, 16

34. Ibid, 33-35

35. *Vide* Altizer, T J J & Hamilton W. *The Death of God*. Penguin, 1968

36. *Vide* Macquarrie, J. *Existentialism*. Penguin, 1973

37. Ibid, 199

38. *Vide* Evans, C, op cit

39. Huxley, A. *The Doors of Perception*. Chatto & Windus, 1954

40. Huxley, A. *Heaven & Hell*. Chatto & Windus, 1956

41. Huxley, A. *Island*. Penguin, 1964

42. Ibid, 178-179

43. *Vide* 'Psychotherapists or the Clergy', Chapter XI in Jung, C G, *Modern Man in Search of a Soul*. Kegan Paul, Trench, Trubner & Co, 1933

44. Ibid, 282

45. Evans, C, op cit, 'Part One: The Science Fiction Religion', 15-134

46. Ibid, 127-128

47. Pelz, Werner & Lotte Pelz. *God Is No More*. Penguin, 1968, 116

CHAPTER SEVENTEEN

1. Pelz, Werner & Lotte. *God Is No More*. Penguin, 1968, 36

2. Ibid, 36

3. *Vide* Jung, C G. *Psychology & Religion: West and East*. Routledge & Kegan Paul, 1958, 58-59

4. Ibid, 334

5. Ibid, 58-59

6. Shinn, R L. *Man: The New Humanism*. Lutterworth Press, 1968

7. Ibid, 27

8. It has been suggested that this statement is open to question, and that (for example) during the period of 'The Warring States' (circa 400-250 BC) under the Chou Dynasty, there were mass executions over a period of two hundred years. It is reported that these executions numbered some 60,000, 80,000, and 400,000. How accurate such statistics are we cannot say. We do know, however, that when the atom bomb was dropped on Hiroshima on 6th August 1945, 60,000 Japanese were killed and another 100,000 were terribly injured or mutilated. We also know that over a period of about a decade more than six million Jews were 'liquidated' in Nazi Germany, and that during the reign of the tyrant, Stalin, 20 million of his own people were murdered.

9. *Vide* Tertullian's treatise *De Testimonio animae naturaliter Christianae*, in which he derived the proof of Christianity from its correspondence with the nature of man.

10. *Vide* St Augustine's essay *De Vera Religione*, Chapter 10

11. *Vide* Bonhoeffer, D. *Prisoner for God*. Macmillan & Co, 1954, 166-168

12. *Vide*, for example, Keniston, K. *The Uncommitted: Alienated Youth in American Society*. Dell Pub Co Ltd, 1967

13. Tillich, P. *The Courage To Be*. Collins, 1962

14. Ibid, 180-183

15. *Vide* Teilhard de Chardin, P. *Letters from a Traveller: 1923-1955*. Collins, 1967, 224-225

16. Ibid, 225

17. *Vide* Teilhard de Chardin, P. *The Phenomenon of Man*. Collins, 1965, *passim*

18. Sartre, J-P. *Existentialism and Humanism*. Eyre Methuen Ltd, 1973, 28

19. Sartre, J-P. *Huis Clos*. Methuen Educational Ltd, 1964, 46 – 'L'enfer, c'est les autres'

20. Teilhard de Chardin, P. *The Phenomenon of Man*, op cit, 281-282

21. Altizer, T J J. *The Gospel of Christian Atheism*. Westminster Press, 1966

22. *Vide* Shinn, R L, op cit

23. *Vide* Teilhard de Chardin, P. *Letters from a Traveller: 1923-1955*, op cit, 176

24. Ibid, 176

25. Pelz, Werner & Lotte, op cit, 116

CHAPTER EIGHTEEN

1. Zaehner, R C. *Mysticism, Sacred and Profane*. Oxford Univ Press, 1957, 2

2. Browning, R. *Poetical Works*. Oxford Univ Press, 1970, 'Paracelsus', 57, line 726

3. St Augustine, *The Confessions* (tr E B Pusey). Dent, 1907, VII.10

4. *Vide* Huxley, A. *The Perennial Philosophy.Chatto* & Windus, 1946

5. Prabhavananda, Swami & Isherwood, C (trs). *Bhagavad-Gita*. Phoenix House, 1947, 171

6. *Vide* Berger, P L & Luckmann, T. *The Social Construction of Reality*. Penguin, 1971; Douglas, J D (ed). *Understanding Everyday Life*. Routledge & Kegan Paul, 1971

7. *Vide* Custance, J. *Wisdom, Madness and Folly: The Philosophy of a Lunatic*. V. Gollancz Ltd, 1951.

8. Ibid, 20ff

9. Ibid, 20

10. Thompson, Francis, 'The Mistress of Vision'

11. Attar of Nishapur, 'The Conference of the Birds' (tr Edward Fitzgerald)

12. Alfred Lord Tennyson, 'Flower in the crannied wall', 1869

13. *Vide* Custance, J, op cit, *passim*

14. *Vide* in particular Shah, Idries. *The Way of the Sufi*. Penguin, 1974

15. Ibid, 13 & 38.n3

16. Ibid, 16

17. Ibid, 9

18. Ibid, 113, 'He was in No Other Place'

19. Grant R M & Freedman, D N (eds). *The Secret Sayings of Jesus*. Collins, 1960, 167, para 77

20. Shah, I, op cit, 109

21. Teilhard de Chardin, P. *The Phenomenon of Man*. Collins, 1965, 287

22. *Vide* Calder, N. *The Key to the Universe*. BBC, 1977, *passim*

23. Shah, I, op cit, 91, 'The Pearl'

BIBLIOGRAPHIES

I GENERAL

Allen, E L. *Christianity Among the Religions.* Allen & Unwin, 1960

Ashby, P A. *The Conflict of Religions.* Scribner's, 1955

Banton, M (ed). *Anthropological Approaches to the Study of Religion.* Tavistock, 1966

Berger, P. *The Sacred Canopy.* Doubleday, 1967

Berger, P. *Rumour of Angels.* Penguin, 1971

Bishop, P & Darton, M (eds). *The Encyclopaedia of World Faiths.* Macdonald & Co Ltd, 1978

Broad, C D. *Religion, Philosophy & Psychical Research.* Routledge & Kegan Paul, 1953

Eliade, M. *Patterns in Comparative Religion.* Sheed & Ward, 1951

Fromm, E. *Psycho-Analysis and Religion.* Gollancz, 1951

Hick, J & Hebblewhite, B (eds). *Christianity and Other Religions.* London, 1980

Hilliard, F H. *The Buddha, the Prophet and the Christ.* Allen & Unwin, 1956

Hinnells, J R (ed). *A Handbook of Living Religions.* Penguin, 1985

James, E O. *Comparative Religion.* Methuen, rev edn, 1961

Jenkins, D. *Beyond Religion.* SCM Press, 1962

Kraemer, H. *World Cultures and World Religions.* Lutterworth Press, 1963

Macquarrie, J. *Twentieth-Century Religious Thought.* SCM Press, 1968

Neill, S. *Christian Faith & Other Faiths.* Oxford Univ Press, 1961

Noss, J B. *Man's Religions.* London, 1974

Otto, R. *The Idea of the Holy.* London. 1969

Parrinder, G. *Comparative Religion.* Allen & Unwin, 1962; Parrinder, G (ed). *Man and His Gods.* London, 1973

Ramsey, I T. *Religion and Science.* SPCK, 1964

Robertson, R. *The Sociological Interpretation of Religion.* Blackwell, 1969

Smart, N. *The Religious Experience of Mankind.* London, 1971

Smart, N. *The Phenomenon of Religion.* Macmillan, 1973

Spalding, H N. *The Divine Universe.* B Blackwell, 1958

Spiegelburg, F. *Living Religions of the World.* Thames & Hudson, 1957

Stephens Spinks, G. *Fundamentals of Religious Belief.* Hodder & Stoughton, 1961

Toynbee, A. *An Historian Looks at Religion.* Oxford Univ Press, 1956

Zaehner, R C. *At Sundry Times.* Faber, 1958

2 BUDDHISM

Conze, E. *Buddhist Texts.* Oxford Univ Press, 1954

Conze, E (tr). *Buddhist Scriptures.* Penguin, 1973

Conze, E. *A Short History of Buddhism.* London, 1980

Ch'en, K. *Buddhism in China.* Princeton, 1964

Evans-Wentz, W Y. *The Tibetan Book of the Dead.* Oxford Univ Press, 1969

Humphreys, C. *Buddhism.* Penguin, rev edn, 1955

Jones J G. *Tales & Teachings of the Buddha.* London, 1979

Mascaro, J. *The Dhammapada.* Penguin, 1973

Thomas, E J. *The History of Buddhist Thought.* Routledge, 1951

3 CHINESE RELIGION

Blakney, R B (tr). *The Way of Life: Tao Te-Ching.* New American Library, 1961

Dawson, P. *Confucius.* Oxford, 1981

Hughes, E R & K. *Religion in China.* Hutchinson, 1956

Smith, D M. *Chinese Religion.* London, 1968

Van Over R (ed). *I Ching.* New American Library, 1971

Waley, A. *The Analects of Confucius.* London, 1938

Waltham, C (ed). *Chuang-Tzu: Genius of the Absurd.* Ace Books, 1971

Ware, J R (tr). *The Sayings of Confucius.* New American Lib, 1964

Welch A. *Taoism: The Parting of the Way.* Boston, 1966

4 CHRISTIANITY

Brandon, S G F. *The Trial of Jesus of Nazareth.* Paladin, 1971

Davies, H. *Christian Deviations.* SCM Press, 1954

Déchanet, J M. *Christian Yoga.* Burns & Oates, 1960

Frend, W H C. *The Rise of Christianity.* London, 1984

Grant, R M & Freedman, D W. *The Secret Sayings of Jesus.* Collins, 1960

Holmes, J D & Bickers, B W. *A Short History of the Catholic Church.*

Tunbridge Wells, 1983

James, M R. *The Apocryphal New Testament.* Oxford Univ Press, 1926

Meyendorff, J. *Byzantine Theology.* New York, 1974

McCabe, H. *The Teaching of the Catholic Church.* Oxford, 1986

Neill, S. *Christian Faith and Other Faiths.* Oxford Univ Press, 1961

Neill, S. *A History of Christian Missions.* Harmondsworth, 1977

Payne, E A. *The Baptist Union. A Short History.* London, 1958

Pelz, W & L. *God Is No More.* Penguin, 1968

Reardon, B. *Religious Thought in the Reformation.* London, 1981

Robinson, J A T. *Honest to God.* SCM Press, 1968

Scarisbrick, J J. *The Reformation and the English People.* Oxford, 1984

Slack, K. *The United Reformed Church.* London, 1978

Smith, E D. *The Teaching of the Catholic Church.* Burns & Oates, 1952

Strobel, Lee. *The Case for Christ.* Zondervan Pub House, 1998

Teilhard de Chardin, P. *The Future of Man.* Collins, 1964

Teilhard de Chardin, P. *The Phenomenon of Man.* Collins, 1965

Toynbee, A J. *Christianity Among the Religions of the World.* Oxford Univ Press, 1958

Visser't Hooft, W A. *The Genesis and Formation of the World Council of Churches.* Geneva, 1982

4 HINDUISM

Basham, A L. *The Wonder That Was India.* London, 1971

Daniélou, A. *Hindu Polytheism.* Routledge & Kegan Paul, 1964

Dutt, R C (tr). *The Ramayana & the Mahabharata.* J M Dent, 1910

Piggott, S. *Prehistoric India.* Penguin, 1950

Prabhavananda, Swami & Isherwood, C (trs). *Bhagavad-Gita.* Phoenix House Ltd, 1956

Radhakrishnan, S. *The Hindu View of Life.* Allen & Unwin, 1927

Sen K M. *Hinduism.* Penguin, 1961

Smart, N. *Doctrine & Argument in Indian Philosophy.* London, 1964

Srinivas, M N. *Caste in Modern India.* Asia Pub House, 1962

Wood, E. *Yoga.* Penguin, 1959

Zaehner, R C. *Hinduism.* Oxford Univ Press, 1962

5 HUMANISM

Altizer, T J J. *The Gospel of Christian Atheism.* Westminster Press, 1966

Blackman, H J. *Humanism.* Penguin, 1968

Fromm, E. *Man For Himself.* Routledge & Kegan Paul, 1949

Gibson, A. *The Faith of the Atheist.* Harper & Row, 1968

Macquarrie, J. *Existentialism.* Penguin, 1973

Maritain, J. *True Humanism.* E Scribner's Sons, 1938

Sartre, J-P. *Existentialism & Humanism.* Eyre Methuen, 1973

Shinn, R L. *Man: The New Humanism.* Lutterworth Press, 1968

Tillich, P. *The Courage To Be.* Collins, 1962

6 ISLAM

Anderson, J N D. *Islamic Law in the Modern World.* London, 1959

Arberry, A J. *Islam Today.* Faber, 1943

Dawood, N J (tr). *The Koran.* Penguin, rev edn, 1968

Guillaume, A. *The Life of Muhammad.* Oxford Univ Press, 1955

Guillaume, A. *Islam.* Penguin, 2nd edn, 1956

Haleen, M A S Abdeel. *The Qu'ran.* Oxford Univ Press, 2004

7 JAINISM

Jain, J P. *Religion & the Culture of the Jains.* New Delhi, 1975

Jaini, P S. *The Jaina Path of Purification.* Berkeley, 1929

Stevenson, M A. *The Heart of Jainism.* New Delhi, 1970

8 JAPANESE RELIGION

Bunce W K. *Religions in Japan.* Tuttle, Tokyo, 1955

Hanser, R. *Japan's Religious Ferment.* London, 1962

Herbert, J. *Shinto.* London, 1967

Ikeka, D. *Soka Gakkai.* Tuttle, Tokyo, 1961

Underwood, A C. *Shintoism.* Epworth Press

9 JUDAISM

Baeck, L. *The Essence of Judaism.* 1961

Blau, J L. *(ed). Reform Judaism: A Historical Perspective.* 1973

Jacobs, I. *Principles of the Jewish Faith.* Vallentine, Mitchell, 1964

Jacobs, L. *A Jewish Theology.* 1973
Schechter, S. *Studies in Judaism.* Meridian, 1962
Scholem, G G. *On the Kabbalah & Its Symbolism.* Schocken, 1965
Sharot, S. *Judaism: A Sociology.* Holmes & Meier, 1976
Unterman, A. *Jews: Their Religious Beliefs & Practices.* Routledge, 1991
Unterman, A. *Judaism.* 1981

10 MILLENARIAN SECTS

Cohn, N. *The Pursuit of the Millennium.* Paladin, 1970
Daniels, W M. *American Indians.* New York, 1957
Elkin, A P. *Social Anthropology in Melanesia.* London, 1953
Lanternari, V. *The Religions of the Oppressed.* New American Lib, 1965
Morrish, Ivor. *Obeah, Christ & Rastaman: Jamaica & Its Religion.* James
    Clarke & Co, 1982
Slotkin, J S. *The Peyote Religion: A Study in Indian-White Relations.* Free
    Press, 1956
Thrupp, Sylvia L (ed). *Millennial Dreams in Action: Essay in Comparative
    Study.* New York, Humanities Press, 1962
Turner, H W. *Religious Innovation in Africa.* Boston, 1979
Wallis, W D. *Messiahs: Their Role in Civilization.* Washington, 1943
Wilson, B R. *Magic and the Millennium.* London, 1973

11 MODERN RELIGIOUS MOVEMENTS

Altizer, T J J & Hamilton, W. *The Death of God.* Penguin, 1968
Besant, Annie. *The Ancient Wisdom.* Theosophical Pub House, 1897
Blavatsky, H P. *The Key to Theosophy.* Theosphical Pub House, 1880
Churchward, J. *The Children of Mu.* N Spearman, 1959
Eddy, Mary Baker. *Science & Health With Key to the Scriptures.* First
    Church of Christ Scientist, Mass, 1906
Evans, C. *Cults of Unreason.* Harrap, 1973
Farquhar, J N. *Modern Religious Movements in India.* London, 1976
Glock C Y & Bellah, R N (eds). *The New Religious Consciousness.* London,
    1976
Isherwood, C (ed). *Vedanta for the Western World.* Allen & Unwin, 1948
Macquarrie, J. *Existentialism.* Penguin, 1978

Miller, W M. *Bahaism, its Origin, History & Teachings.* New York, Revell
Richards, J. *The Religion of the Bahais.* SPCK
Story, R. *The Space-Gods Revealed.* Book Club Assoc, 1977
Wallis, R. *The Elementary Forms of the New Religious Life.* London, 1954
Wilson, B R (ed). *The Social Impact of New Religious Movements.* New
    York, 1991

12 MYSTICISM

Arberry, A J. *Sufism.* Allen & Unwin, 1950
Butler, C. *Western Mysticism.* Grey Arrow, 1960
Happold, F C. *Mysticism: A Study & An Anthology.* Penguin, 1970
Heywood, Rosemary. *The Sixth Sense.* Chatto & Windus, 1959
Huxley, A. *The Perennial Philosophy.* Chatto & Windus, 1946
James, W. *The Varieties of Religious Experience.* Longmans Green, 1902
Johnson, R C. *A Religious Outlook for Modern Man.* Hodder & Stoughton,
    1963
Nicolson, R A. *The Mystics of Islam.* Routledge & Kegan Paul, 1963
Otto, R. *Mysticism, East & West.* Macmillan, 1932
Scholem, G G. *Major Trends in Jewish Mysticism.* Thames & Hudson, 1955
Shah, I. *The Sufis.* London, 1969
Shah, I. *The Way of the Sufi.* Penguin, 1970
Spencer, S. *Mysticism in the World Religions.* Penguin, 1963
Teilhard de Chardin, P. *Le Milieu Divin.* Collins, 1964
Underhill, Evelyn. *Mysticism.* Methuen, 1930
Van Over, R (ed). *The Chinese Mystics.* Harper & Row, 1973
Watts, A W. *The Supreme Identity.* Faber, 1950
Zaehner, R C. *Mysticism, Sacred & Profane.* Oxford Univ Press, 1957
Zaehner, R C. *Hindu & Muslim Mysticism.* Univ of London Press, 1960

13 MYTHOLOGY

Barthes, R. *Mythologies.* Paladin, 1973
Bultmann, R. *Jesus Christ & Mythology.* SCM Press, 1960
Cairns, D. *A Gospel Without Myth.* SCM Press, 1960
Campbell, J. *The Masks of God: Primitive Mythology.* Viking Press, 1959
Eliade, M. *Myths, Dreams & Mysteries.* Collins, 1968

Henderson, I. *Myth in the New Testament.* SCM Press, 1952

Hick, J (ed). *The Myth of God Incarnate.* SCM Press, 1977

Jensen, A E. *Myth & Cult Among Primitive People.* Univ of Chicago Press, 1963

Leach, E R. *The Structural Study of Myth & Totemism.* Tavistock Press, 1970

Macquarrie, J. *The Scope of Demythologizing.* SCM Press, 1960

Maranda, P (ed). *Mythology.* Penguin, 1972

Ruthven, K K. *Myth.* Methuen, 1976

Watts, A. *Myth & Ritual in Christianity.* Beacon Press, 1968

14 PRIMAL RELIGION

Berger, P. *The Social Reality of Religion.* Faber, 1969

Douglas, Mary. *Ritual & Danger.* Routledge & Kegan Paul, 1966

Douglas, Mary. *Natural Symbols.* Cresset Press, 1970

Durkheim, E. *The Elementary Forms of Religious Life.* Collier, 1961

Evans-Pritchard, E E. *Theories of Primitive Religion.* Oxford Univ Press, 1965

Gennep, A van. *The Rites of Passage.* Routledge & Kegan Paul, 1960

James, E O. *The Beginnings of Religion.* Grey Arrow, 1958

Lévi-Strauss, C. *The Savage Mind.* Weidenfeld & Nicolson, 1965

Malinowski, B. *Magic, Science & Religion.* Free Press, 1948

Marett, R. *The Threshold of Religion.* Methuen, 1914

Parrinder, G. *Religion in Africa.* Penguin, 1969

Radcliffe-Brown, A R. *Structure & Function in Primitive Society.* Cohen & West, 1952

Radin, P. *Monotheism among Primitive Peoples.* London, 1924

Turner, V. *The Ritual Process.* Routledge & Kegan Paul, 1969

Tylor, E B. *Primitive Culture.* Harpers, 1958

Wilson, B. *Religion in Secular Society.* C A Watts, 1966

15 SIKHISM

Cole, W O. *Sikhism & Its Indian Context.* London, 1974

Cole W O. & Sambhi, P S. *The Sikhs.* London, 1986

Singh, K A. *History of the Sikhs.* Oxford Univ Press, 1963

Singh, K (ed). *Selections from the Sacred Writings of the Sikhs.* Allen &

Unwin, 1960

Singh, T. *Sikhism.* Longmans, 1938

16 ZEN

Blyth, R H. *Zen in English Literature & Oriental Classics.* Tokyo, 1942

Graham, Dom A. *Zen Catholicism.* Collins, 1964

Herrigel, E. *Zen in the Art of Archery.* Pantheon, 1958

Pirsig, R M. *Zen in the Art of Motorcycle Maintenance.*

Reps, P. *Zen Flesh, Zen Bones.* Penguin, 1971,   Bantam, 1977

Suzuki, D T. *Living by Zen.* Rider, rev edn, 1972

Watts, A W. *The Way of Zen.* Penguin, 1962

17 ZOROASTRIANISM

Boyce, M. *Textual Sources for the Study of Zoroastrianism.* Manchester, 1984

Hinnells, J R. *Zoroastrianism & the Parsis.* 1981

Insler, S. *The Gathas of Zarathustra.* Leiden, 1975

Zaehner, R C. *The Teachings of the Magi.* London, 1975

Index

O

is a symbol of the world,
of oneness and unity. O Books
explores the many paths of wholeness and spiritual understanding which
different traditions have developed down
the ages. It aims to bring this knowledge in
accessible form, to a general readership, providing practical spirituality to today's seekers.

For the full list of over 200 titles covering:
ACADEMIC/THEOLOGY • ANGELS • ASTROLOGY/
NUMEROLOGY • BIOGRAPHY/AUTOBIOGRAPHY
• BUDDHISM/ENLIGHTENMENT • BUSINESS/LEADERSHIP/
WISDOM • CELTIC/DRUID/PAGAN • CHANNELLING
• CHRISTIANITY; EARLY • CHRISTIANITY; TRADITIONAL
• CHRISTIANITY; PROGRESSIVE • CHRISTIANITY;
DEVOTIONAL • CHILDREN'S SPIRITUALITY • CHILDREN'S
BIBLE STORIES • CHILDREN'S BOARD/NOVELTY • CREATIVE
SPIRITUALITY • CURRENT AFFAIRS/RELIGIOUS • ECONOMY/
POLITICS/SUSTAINABILITY • ENVIRONMENT/EARTH
• FICTION • GODDESS/FEMININE • HEALTH/FITNESS
• HEALING/REIKI • HINDUISM/ADVAITA/VEDANTA
• HISTORY/ARCHAEOLOGY • HOLISTIC SPIRITUALITY
• INTERFAITH/ECUMENICAL • ISLAM/SUFISM
• JUDAISM/CHRISTIANITY • MEDITATION/PRAYER
• MYSTERY/PARANORMAL • MYSTICISM • MYTHS
• POETRY • RELATIONSHIPS/LOVE • RELIGION/
PHILOSOPHY • SCHOOL TITLES • SCIENCE/
RELIGION • SELF-HELP/PSYCHOLOGY
• SPIRITUAL SEARCH • WORLD
RELIGIONS/SCRIPTURES • YOGA

Please visit our website,
www.O-books.net